Lectures on
Esther

By Alexander Dyce Davidson, D.D.

Lectures on Esther

Copyright ©2020 by Waymark Books.

All rights reserved. No part of this publication may be reproduced, distributed or transmitted in any form or by any means, including photocopying, recording, or other electronic or mechanical methods, without the prior written permission of the publisher, except in the case of brief quotations embodied in critical reviews and certain other noncommercial uses permitted by copyright law.

Waymark Books
P. O. Box 7
Cedar Lake, MI 48812-0007

www.waymarkbooks.com

ISBN # 978-1611047868

Table of Contents

Preface 4

Lecture 1: Esther 1:1-12 7
Lecture 2: Esther 1:13-22 24
Lecture 3: Esther 2:1-4 39
Lecture 4: Esther 2:5-20 54
Lecture 5: Esther 2:21-23, 3:1-5 70
Lecture 6: Esther 3:6-11 85
Lecture 7: Esther 3:12-15 and 4:1-9 100
Lecture 8: Esther 4:10-17 116
Lecture 9: Esther 5:1-8 132
Lecture 10: Esther 5:9-14 147
Lecture 11: Esther 6:1-14 163
Lecture 12: Esther 7:1-10 180
Lecture 13: Esther 8:1-14 195
Lecture 14: Esther 8:16-17 and 9:1-19 211
Lecture 15: Chapter 9:20-32 and 10:1-3 227

Appendix: Historical Context 244

Preface

THE dedication prefixed to these lectures accounts for their being published. I believe it is because there is less of what is purely devotional in the Book of Esther than in any other book of Scripture, that the attention of my people was attracted to an exposition of it in which points bearing upon the leading doctrines of grace are here and there illustrated. As to the form in which the Lectures are presented, it may be mentioned, that they are printed just as they were delivered, with the exception of a few verbal corrections.

The Book of Esther might have been more graphically commented on. There are four pictures which might have been selected from it, and sketched, viz. that of Mordecai and Esther, and of the king and Haman, which, if well drawn, with the lessons which the history of each teaches, might have formed an interesting study. But as the understood and usual plan of lecturing in Scotland, is to examine and expound chapter after chapter of the Divine word in order, so that plan was adhered to in the delivery of the following series of discourses. The charge may be brought against the adoption of this method, that it leads to a repetition of the same truths in different words: but when we have in the Bible "line upon line, and precept upon precept," it does not seem that there can be great error in pursuing a similar course in the exposition of it.

But leaving the method which has been followed to be approved or censured as it may deserve, I would here take leave to offer a remark or two upon the general subject of the exposition of

Scripture. There are three things, I apprehend, which must be kept in view by a conscientious and judicious expounder of the Old Testament.

First, he must endeavor to ascertain the precise meaning of the Divine word, and its application to the people to whom it was originally addressed. This is indispensable; because, whatever other purpose the Old Testament Scriptures were designed to answer, they were certainly intended to instruct and guide the Jewish nation.

Secondly, in what relates to types and to prophecy, care must be taken to bring out the true spiritual signification of the type, and to demonstrate the fulfilment of the prophecy. There must be no wresting of the words of inspiration at the bidding of fancy!

Thirdly, there is a *practical* use to be made of Scripture, for "doctrine, and reproof, and correction, and instruction in righteousness." Here a wide field is opened up to the expositor, although in traversing it he must be careful to be guided by the analogy of faith. Thus guided, he can bring one part of the word to throw light upon another; and can enforce doctrine and duty from passages which seem at first sight to contain in them little that is worthy of notice. Now it is this kind of exposition, which may be termed the *suggestive,* as contrasted with the other two kinds, which may be called respectively the *literal* and the *explanatory,* that is especially applicable to such a book as that of Esther.

If we were to restrict our remarks to the mere incidents recorded in it, and to endeavor to depict only the manners and customs represented in it, a very small space would contain everything that required to be stated. But no portion of Scripture must be isolated from the rest. And when we look at what is presented to us in this Book and compare it with other portions of the sacred record, we find that it is suggestive of important principles, which refer both to doctrine and to duty. It is on this plan that these lectures have been composed.

Before concluding this preface, I would take the opportunity to say, that in the matter of suggestive exposition good old Matthew Henry stands pre-eminent. His intimate acquaintance with the whole word of God, his singular power of comparing spiritual things with spiritual, his sound views of evangelical doctrine, and his deep personal piety, render his "Commentary," with all its quaintness and homeliness, in my humble estimation, the best which we yet possess in the English language. Anyone who reads Dr. M'Crie's *Lectures on the Book of Esther*, or those here given, will perceive that Henry's Commentary must have been freely consulted.

In one sentence more, I would say that for the illustration of Eastern manners Kitto's *Illustrated Commentary* upon the Bible has been of great use to me, and that I have not scrupled to draw from it whatever might serve to illustrate the particular passage under review.

ALEXANDER DAVIDSON
ABERDEEN, *29th April* 1859

Lecture 1: Esther 1:1-12

It is not without some misgivings that I enter upon a brief review of the Book of Esther—not so much because there are some difficulties in the interpretation of it, as because, not very many years ago, there was published a volume of lectures on this book by the late venerable Dr. M'Crie, which must be known to many of you. There is an ancient fable of a king who was gifted with the power of turning everything he touched into gold; and this eminent divine and historian possessed remarkably the gift of rendering every subject he handled so precious, as at least to discourage any one from attempting to follow in his track.

In his lectures upon the Book of Esther, he has certainly left little for any to say who may come after him; and thus it happens, that it is scarcely possible to comment upon this book now, without exciting in the minds of some the suspicion that something has been borrowed from him. And as nothing could be more discreditable than the unscrupulous appropriation of the fruits of other men's labors, so it is not easy to avoid, as indeed it would be foolish to endeavor to avoid, making some use of what the wise and good have left behind them in illustration of the sacred volume. Yet sufficient allowance is not always made for this circumstance, and it is therefore with a kind of reluctance that I proceed to turn your attention to the Book of Esther.

I shall endeavor to embrace the narrative in a very few lectures.

But, in the outset, it is necessary that we offer some preliminary remarks of a general kind upon the book itself. And first, as to the subject of it—the whole scene, if we may so speak, is laid, and the whole action takes place, in the palace of the King of Persia, who was at that time the greatest potentate in the world. The prophetic words of Daniel had so far been fulfilled, that the kingdom of Babylon had given way to the Medo-Persian empire; and the Jews, humanly speaking, were wholly dependent upon the caprices of the Persian ruler. To this circumstance we must attribute the prominence that is given to a heathen king and the measures of his government, in this part of the sacred record. To some this characteristic of the book has appeared strange, but without reason, inasmuch as many parts of the prophetic Scriptures, for instance, bear upon the destinies of heathen kingdoms, and have their place in the Scripture, because the interests of the people of God were most closely interwoven with the fortunes of these kingdoms. Then next, with respect to the authorship of the book we have no certain information.

There have been various conjectures; but of course, when there is need of conjecture, there can be no certainty. Some have ascribed it to Mordecai, and others to Ezra. Neither supposition is altogether improbable, because the events recorded in the book certainly took place about the time when Ezra nourished; and Mordecai occupies a very important place in connection with them. And besides, to Ezra is attributed, by universal consent, the great work of arranging the sacred books of the Old Testament in the order in which they now stand. Still, the matter must remain undecided. The uncertain authorship, however, does not invalidate either the genuineness or authenticity of the book.

But it requires to be specially noticed, that objections have been raised to the receiving of the Book of Esther as a portion of the inspired record. Some of these objections are very weak, and unworthy of notice; but there is one which must be acknowledged

Lecture 1: Esther 1:1-12

to have some weight—viz. this, that from the beginning to the end of it there is not a single reference made to the name of God.

This, unquestionably, is strange. There is only one other book to which the same remark is applicable—the Song of Solomon; and on account of this apparently inexplicable omission, some would have both these books excluded from the sacred canon. Now we think it is not a circumstance to be regretted, that such objections should have been felt and stated, but something rather to be rejoiced in. That we should be sure that the books which professedly contain the revelation of God's will to us possess divine authority, is a matter so momentous that it should be most fully investigated, and settled upon unquestionable evidence; and where there is doubt, the doubt should be expressed, and the reasons given. But after all that has been written in opposition to the canonical authority of the Book of Esther—and I may add also of the Song of Solomon— the whole weight of conclusive argument lies in favor of both the books as divinely inspired.

Whatever sins the Jewish Church was chargeable with, this is not one of them, that it corrupted the sacred record. On the contrary, there was rather an extremely minute and devout care exhibited that there should be no admixture of the divine and human in the canon of Scripture. The sacred books we have, and that of Esther among the rest, were among the oracles of God when the Savior was on earth, as has been fully proved by many writers. He appeals to them as such. Many transgressions He lays to the charge of the people of that generation, but He never accuses them of interpolating, or vitiating in any respect, the divine Word.

He blames them for making it void by their traditions, but he never even hints that they received as Scripture what should not be regarded as such. And the same remark is applicable to His apostles. They bow with reverence to the Old Testament Scriptures, and these were just as we have them. The Jewish Church was a jealous keeper of the Scripture. Thus, for example, there is a large apocryphal addition to the Book of Esther, extending it to sixteen chapters, which never was allowed a place in the Old Testament canon, and which is not contained in our version. Some later writer, perhaps with good enough intention, had added it; but it was rejected by the Jews as an unauthorized addition.

In their faithful guardianship of the Scriptures, they would not admit a sentence about which there was any doubt. I may mention here in passing, that in the apocryphal addition to the Book of Esther the name of God is often introduced, and always in suitable connection with the context. But this only strengthens the argument for the genuineness of that portion which the Jews admitted into the canon, because truth needs no particular coloring to commend it to the acceptance of men. But while on this consideration alone, that our Lord gave His sanction to the Old Testament Scriptures as we have them, and among the rest to this book, we feel warranted to regard it as of equal authority with the books of Moses, with the evangelical histories, or with the epistles of Paul, there is another very important argument in favor of it to be derived from the subject matter of the book itself There is reference made in it to the institution of a festival which was designed to commemorate the deliverance of the Jews from a plot against them by their cruel enemies, which plot is also recorded in it. Now, the festival has been celebrated in every age from that time downward, and the Book of Esther has been read from that time, and is still read every year, in the Jewish synagogues, on the

Lecture 1: Esther 1:1-12

festival day. This, it must be allowed, furnishes no slight proof of its title to hold a place in the sacred canon.

Yet, after all, the remarkable circumstance does deserve to be noticed, that the name of God is not mentioned in this book, and that only in one place there is particular allusion made to a superintending providence. I would say, then, in connection with this circumstance, that it does not affect in the slightest degree the divine authority of the book, nor weaken its title to be regarded as a part of the inspired record. It has been well observed, that although it does not make formal reference to the providence of God, it contains in itself the history of a most remarkable interposition of providence in favor of the seed of Abraham—indeed, of an interposition as striking as any that we read of. It is true, that it introduces us into the palace of the King of Persia, and detains us there, looking at the movements of a heathen prince, and at the corruptions and abuses which accompany despotic power. It is true, that when we read the Book of Esther, we must remember that the delineation of character and of sentiment which it places before us is not to be viewed as in itself praiseworthy, but must be measured by the law and the testimony. But this does not in any respect give warrant to the notion that the book was not written by the inspiration of the Spirit. In fact, there is an erroneous idea cherished by many on the whole subject of inspiration.

Our belief is, that the Bible is an inspired book; not merely that the writers of it were under the special teaching and guidance of the Holy Spirit, but that what they wrote is the mind of the Spirit, in the words which He deemed most suitable for the instruction of the Church. Yet who would take the language in which Pharaoh, for example, is represented to have expressed his hardened unbelief, as a pattern for imitation? Who would appropriate the words of the Israelites when they murmured in the wilderness? And in like manner, in the New Testament, who among us, while we read, would join in the blasphemies which were uttered by the enemies of the Savior? Yet all these form part of the Word of God, written by the inspiration of the Holy Ghost, and are a truthful record of events and circumstances which He has judged it good for the Church to know. And even so in the case before us; we have in the Book of Esther, *practically,* although not in so many words, an illustration of the overruling providence of God, whereby the enemies of His ancient people were defeated and put to shame, and the greatest heathen potentate at the time was unconsciously rendered instrumental in advancing their interests.

It is no argument against the divine authority of this book, that there is not direct reference made in it to Jehovah, but rather we think an argument for its truthfulness, inasmuch as it does not profess to carry us to Jerusalem and Mount Zion, where Jehovah was worshipped, but to the court of the king of Persia, where he was not known except by the dispersed children of Judah* With these preliminary remarks, then, let us now proceed to consider the verses which form the subject of the present lecture.

* *The whole subject is satisfactorily treated in Stuart's work on the Old Testament Canon.*

Verses 1-9

"Now it came to pass in the days of Ahasuerus, (this is Ahasuerus which reigned, from India even unto Ethiopia, over an hundred and seven and twenty provinces) that in those days, when the king Ahasuerus sat on the throne of his kingdom, which was in

Lecture 1: Esther 1:1-12

Shushan the palace, in the third year of his reign, he made a feast unto all his princes and his servants; the power of Persia and Media; the nobles and princes of the provinces, being before him," etc.

By almost universal acknowledgment now, the sovereign here referred to is Artaxerxes, surnamed Longimanus, or the long handled; the term Ahasuerus being like that of Pharaoh, expressive of the kingly dignity, and not the name of an individual. In his time the Persian empire was of vast extent, comprehending all the countries from the river Indus on the east to the Mediterranean on the west; and from the Black Sea and the Caspian in the north, to the extreme south of Arabia, then called Ethiopia. This gigantic dominion was divided, as we are informed in the text, into one hundred and twenty-seven provinces, or governments, each of which was placed under a Satrap, or in modern language, a Pasha, who managed its affairs, and annually transmitted a certain sum as revenue to the king. The seat of government was variable, according to the season of the year, the summer months being spent by the court at Ecbatana, or as it is called in the Book of Ezra, Achmatha; and the winter months at Susa, or as it is called in the text, Shushan the palace.

In the days of the great Cyrus, the Persians were a manly and warlike race; but their conquests had made them degenerate; so that, from all we read of their intercourse with ancient Greece, we are led to associate with their very name luxury and effeminacy. These were evidently their characteristics in the age of Artaxerxes, as the sacred history plainly teaches.

The form of government in the East has from the earliest times been despotic, one man swaying the destinies of millions, and having under him a crowd of smaller despots, each in his more limited sphere oppressing the people subjected to his rule. Despotism, however, while it has its caprices of cruelty, has also its occasional fits of generosity and kindness. And it is as a kind-hearted and not a cruel despot that Artaxerxes is brought before us in the text. He was spending the winter months at Susa, where he had a palace, it is said, of unrivalled splendor.

Those eastern palaces, for their immense extent, were rather cities than mere separate buildings. The retinue of the monarch was vast, and the fountains and gardens, and other arrangements which ministered to a luxurious taste, were on a scale of grandeur which we cannot well conceive. There then the king, but little concerned about the welfare of his subjects, was spending his time, chiefly in selfish ease and unbounded revelry. To him it was of no moment how his people were oppressed by those whom he set over them: his sole concern was to enjoy his pleasures.

It has been started as an objection by some, to the credibility of the Book of Esther, that the period of feasting should be represented as extending to a hundred and eighty days, and that all the governors of the provinces should have been for the whole of that time assembled at Shushan the palace. But this objection is very frivolous. It does not follow from the narrative here given that the feasting was without any intermission, nor that all the rulers of the empire were withdrawn at once and for half a year from their respective provinces. All that is recorded is, that the festivities lasted for about half a year; and during this time the governors, as they came in succession to Susa, may have been required to give some account of their procedure, and may have received orders as to the course they were to pursue for the future. This at least is certain, according to the usages of the country, that each one would bring some rich present to the sovereign, extorted in some way or

Lecture 1: Esther 1:1-12

other from his province, and adding to the magnificence of the imperial city. So that, as it is said in verse 4, there would be "a display of the riches of the glorious kingdom of Artaxerxes, and of the honor of his excellent majesty."

Then after this long-continued reveling, in which the satraps of the most distant parts of the empire were permitted to share, it is said in verse 5, "that the king made a feast unto all the people that were present in Shushan the palace, both unto great and small, seven days, in the court of the garden of the king's palace." The decorations were exceedingly magnificent. The whole space was converted into a festal hall, screened from the weather by curtains of various colors, fastened with cords of fine linen and purple to silver rings and pillars of marble. The couches on which the guests might recline were covered with cloth embroidered with gold and silver, and the pavement was of Mosaic work of marble, red, blue, and white.

The whole scene reminds us of the fanciful pictures with which childhood is delighted in eastern tales of fiction. One thing, however, is noticeable, that with all the luxury and temptation to self-indulgence that was exhibited, there was no compulsion employed to draw any one beyond the bounds of temperance. "The drinking was according to the law; none did compel; for so the king had appointed to all the officers of his house, that they should do according to every man's pleasure." And while there was this feasting in the court of the garden, presided over by the king himself and the principal lords of the kingdom, it is added that Vashti the queen made a feast for the women in the royal house which belonged to king Artaxerxes.

In the East, at that time as now, there was kept up an entire separation between the two sexes in all the ordinary intercourse of life. This is one of the unhappy arrangements which, by contributing to the degradation of the female sex, has prevented the advancement of civilization and real refinement in eastern countries. In all these, woman has been treated rather as a slave and an inferior being, than as the partner of man's joys and hopes. She has been degraded to be the object of his passing caprices, rather than regarded as the help meet for him which God designed her to be. The spread of Christian truth will in time remedy this evil, one of the greatest under which society labors throughout a large portion of the world; but no other influence can teach man to know how far, in this one respect at least, he has been governed by maxims opposed to his real happiness and well-being.

Now let us endeavor to make some application of these verses which have been considered. And the lesson which most obviously presents itself to us is the sufficiently common place, but at the same time very important one, of *the inadequacy of all earthly good to make man truly happy.* There is what may be called a pensive or sentimental kind of morality, in which true religion has not necessarily any share; but which can dilate upon, the transitory nature of all merely animal enjoyment rightly enough, and turn it to good enough account. Here is a specimen of it from one of the apocryphal books; which, to say the least, is equal to much that poets have written upon the same subject.

"Come, therefore," they say, "and let us enjoy the pleasures that are present; let us fill ourselves with costly wine and ointments; let us crown ourselves with rose-buds before they be withered: such things do they imagine and go astray; for their own wickedness hath blinded them." These words might form an appropriate commentary upon the procedure of Artaxerxes as it is described in the word of God. But with the light of His word we can look farther into the subject than such reflections as these carry us. Surveying then the whole scene which is portrayed in these verses, we might imagine, first of all, that the sovereign who ruled over this vast empire; upon whose nod the interests of so many millions depended; and for whose pleasure the products of so many various climes could be gathered together, had surely all the elements of enjoyment at his command, in the ordinary sense of that term. And in his willingness to exhibit the splendor of his kingdom to others, and to admit them to share with him in the pleasures which his power could collect, we see one evidence at least of a desire to make others happy, whatever the ruling principle in his own heart may have been.

But then, further, we perceive, from the social arrangements of the age and nation, that this great king, while exhibiting all the glory of his kingdom to others, had no one near him in whose face he could read a real response to any kindly feeling that he cherished, and from whose smile he could learn that there was one who truly loved him in the midst of all his regal greatness.

And therefore, looking at this great festival even from this point of view, we must say that the mightiest sovereign of his time, with one hundred and twenty-seven provinces subject to him, with princes serving him, and slaves kissing the dust at his feet, was not half so happy as the humblest individual here, who knows what is meant by the comforts of home, where he is in the midst of those who love him.

There have been many treatises written to prove that happiness does not consist in external show and grandeur. And a believing reader of the "Word of God will acquiesce in the general principle which they enforce; because Christ has said, with reference to this very subject, "a man's life consisteth not in the abundance of the things which he possesseth." But then it must be confessed, that the parties who do truly feel that wealth and luxury are not handmaids to happiness, are those who do not require the argument, because they have found out a more excellent way. Dr. Paley, for example, has a short treatise upon the subject, in which he shews most convincingly that the *rich* is not the *happy* man; but his conclusions will never come home to any save those who have discovered where the true riches are to be found. We would therefore dismiss all the reasonings which would go to make a man satisfied with his more limited enjoyments, on the plea that wealth has its counterbalancing cares, and troubles, and diseases, and would take up higher ground, and speak from thence of *spiritual* privilege, as that which constitutes true enjoyment.

There is a want in the soul of man, which all the wealth of one hundred and twenty-seven provinces cannot supply. There is a want which the best social arrangements cannot supply. There is a craving in the heart of man beyond all creature power to satisfy. Guilty man needs to be placed in a right relation toward God. Money cannot purchase for him peace and pardon. Artaxerxes was as poor as the humblest serf in his dominions in this respect; and far poorer than the poorest of the children of Judah, dispersed through his empire as exiles, but knowing Jehovah. When the soul can repose itself on God, as the God of redemption, when it can claim Jesus Christ as its portion, then all outward inequalities of rank and fortune become subordinate. The rich and powerful man, believing in Christ and loving Him and all who are His, has learnt to make his riches subservient to their proper use.

The poor man, believing in Christ and loving Him, feels that he has in Him an all-satisfying portion. Thus the extremes of wealth and poverty, of power and weakness, may meet without pride on

Lecture 1: Esther 1:1-12

the one part, or envy and murmuring upon the other. The Christian possessor of a large inheritance feels that his chief good is in Christ. The poor believer feels that he has a share of the same exhaustless fullness. Their outward lot is different, but all their hopes and real enjoyments are substantially the same. And therefore we would say to believers in Christ, envy not the present portion of the great, who, like Artaxerxes, enjoy all the good the world can give, and have nothing better. But rejoice that God has called you to a portion which no shifting of the affairs of kingdoms and principalities on earth can either change or destroy. "Delight thyself in the Lord, and He will give thee the desire of thine heart."

But we proceed now to consider verses 10-12, "On the seventh day, when the heart of the king was merry with wine, he commanded Mehuman, Biztha, Harbona, Bigtha, and Abagtha, Zethar, and Carcas, the seven chamberlains that served in the presence of Ahasuerus the king, to bring Vashti the queen before the king with the crown royal, to shew the people and the princes her beauty: for she was fair to look on. But the queen Vashti refused to come at the king's commandment by his chamberlains: therefore was the king very wroth, and his anger burned in him."

In these verses we have the turning point of the whole narrative, so far as the interests of the Jewish people were concerned. It is apparently a slight event which forms the hinge, but the results were momentous. "On the seventh day of the feast, when the heart of the king was merry with wine, he would have the queen brought into the banquet."

Now it is rather a singular circumstance, that some modern critics have objected to the genuineness of the book upon this single point, the argument being, that it could never have suggested itself to the mind of the king to propose what he is here represented to have done. His proposal was certainly an outrage upon all the established customs of the age; and they say it could not have been made, and therefore the book cannot give a truthful representation of events which took place. But the passage contains its own vindication. The king had given way to the influence of wine, and to the flatteries which were poured into his ear, and therefore, although such a thing was unheard of in all history, he would have the queen brought in with unveiled face, that the beauty of her countenance might excite the applause of the revelers who were gathered around him.

The royal message was set at nought by Vashti; and it could not well have been otherwise. Some have blamed her conduct; but we think that she knew her place and kept it. According to the custom and feelings of the time, she would not have been regarded as a virtuous matron, had she complied with the king's commandment. And in his sober moments, he would have been the first to condemn her had she done so.

But the spirit of the despot was aroused at the moment; "the king was very wroth, and his anger burned in him." When he was heated with wine, he was enraged at what should have pleased and gratified him. He devised evil against the queen for refusing to do what the madness of intemperance could only have made him think she should do.

The lesson which these verses teach us, respects the extravagances and follies into which men may be betrayed by intemperance, and the necessity therefore of guarding against the evil. The law was good by which the banquet of Artaxerxes was regulated, that every man should be left to his own freedom. But the king himself had too largely used the liberty, and hence his loss of all self-control, and all sense of propriety.

We can *account* for what he did on the supposition that he had indulged beyond measure in the wine which was liberally circulated around him. But this forms no justification of his conduct. In the state in which Artaxerxes was, men may perform acts which no future repentance will rectify, so far as temporal interests are concerned; and any apology for such unbecoming acts is wholly untenable. That a man should for a time lose his reason by what he himself voluntarily does, will not excuse him even in the sight of his fellow men, and far less in the sight of God. That which dethrones reason and destroys intellect should surely be avoided. And if it is not, all the consequences which affect the man individually, and others also, rest upon the head of the transgressor.

Intemperance blots out the distinction between right and wrong in many respects: it foments all the evil passions of the natural heart. It destroys the proper exercise of the power of the will, and thus makes man no better than the lower animals. And it often inflicts grievous wounds upon the innocent, as the case of Queen Vashti here too clearly demonstrates. She fell a sacrifice to the intemperance of her lord. Whatever we may think of the overruling providence, which in this case brought good out of evil, we must acknowledge that Vashti was unrighteously dealt with by the king.

And if among the great we can trace disorder and misery to intemperance, assuredly we can do so too easily in the homes of the humbler members of society. There is not a more fruitful source of domestic misery than that which was exemplified in the palace of the king of Persia.

I could draw many pictures here; let me just take two. First, the picture of a family where the husband forgets his obligations; and leaves his wife and his children to misery, because he will be intemperate. What a wreck we have here! That which might be profitably expended in domestic comfort, and in the education of the children, is squandered every week in self-indulgence. And when the brutalized man comes to his house, how can he expect a smile or a welcome? Who is to welcome him? He has driven himself as far from all the real endearments of life as the eastern king did, who was a stranger to all real family affection. How can there be comfort in the house which the victim of intemperance will not make a home? There is the mother and the children, but what can they do? Is she to yield to the temptations which are spread before her, and to become like her husband? She may not. But what else has he to expect? How is the wife to keep her place, and to bring up her family, and to maintain her respectability, when all the means are cast away by him in the gratification of his sinful appetite. Ah! it is because of derangements of this kind that society groans under so many pressing evils. Men destitute of the fear of God will expend their earnings in intemperance. Thus they have no home, or at least they have a home so miserable, of their own making, that they care not to enter it; and their wives and children come to be reckoned among the destitute.

But secondly, there is a darker picture still, which, although not drawn directly from the text, is yet suggested by it. Vashti the queen acted rightly, although she had to suffer. But it is not always so. The unfaithfulness of the husband corrupts the wife. She struggles for a time, but she falls a victim at length to his neglect, and seeks a consolation for her miseries in intemperance also. Then the family, if there is a family, is lost; and we have a generation growing up to corrupt the generation which is to follow. The very lowest point of misery is reached when the wife follows the husband in his career of intemperance. There may be a home for the children when he forgets his duty, but there is none when the mother fails in hers.

Therefore, I would say, let the well-ordered families among us be thankful for their privileges, and let them not shut their ear to the call from time to time addressed to them, to aid in lifting up the outcast to the enjoyment of the happiness with which God has blessed themselves.

Now, in conclusion, I would leave with you two practical lessons, suggested by the whole subject we have reviewed.

In the first place, you will perceive how the most exalted station does not give real happiness. As has been said, there was more true enjoyment among the Jewish exiles, who were dispersed through the dominions of Artaxerxes, than he himself had. He wanted what they had, the knowledge of the true God. He sought for happiness in mere excitement; and he did not find it, as no man has ever yet derived it from that source.

In the second place, I am commissioned to offer to all here something better than the whole hundred and twenty-seven provinces over which Artaxerxes reigned. His revenues could not purchase real comfort, far less could they procure life for him; but he that hath the Son of God hath life eternal. His animal pleasures could not make him happy; but in Christ is the fountain of blessedness. When death came, this great prince had to leave all good behind him; but if you are Christ's, when the end comes, you enter upon an inheritance incorruptible and undented, kept for you by Him who hath given you His own Son, and thus made you joint-heirs with Christ, who is the Lord of glory. Amen.

Lecture 2: Esther 1:13-22

In the last lecture we saw the unhappy consequences of intemperance. Artaxerxes, excited by wine, issued his command that the Queen Vashti should be brought into the hall where he feasted with his lords, and a vast assemblage besides, that his guests might see her beautiful countenance, "for she was fair to look upon." This command the king in sober mood would never have given forth. It was an outrage upon all the customs of the age and country, and the queen, receiving the order even from the mouth of the king's chamberlains, might well doubt whether they spake with due authority. We cannot, indeed, fully sympathize with her feelings, so different are our manners; but she only acted in accordance with all standing law, and with all the ceremonial of the time, when she refused to obey the king, and would not appear unveiled in the presence of the multitude which was then assembled around him. Then the king, it is said in verse 12, "was very wroth, and his anger burned in him." He was not properly his own master at the time, and his despotic will being crossed, and that publicly, he fumed and raged like a beast of prey.

The issue comes to be considered in the present lecture. Verses 13-18: "Then the king said to the wise men which knew the times, (for so was the king's manner toward all that knew law and judgment: and the next unto him was Carshena, Shethar, Admatha, Tarshish, Meres, Marsena, and Memucan, the seven princes of Persia and Media, which saw the king's face, and which sat first in the kingdom) 'What shall we do unto the Queen Vashti according to law, because she hath not performed the commandment of the king Ahasuerus by the chamberlains?'"

With all his excitement and disregard of established maxims, Artaxerxes did not venture upon a personal exercise of arbitrary power, which might have appeared too great, even in the eyes of the submissive multitude, to whom usually his will was law. He turned to his counselors and asked of them what should be done in consequence of the queen's

Lecture 2: Esther 1:13-22

contempt of his authority. In Persia there were seven great men, who saw the king's face (*i.e.,* had free access to him) and were first in the kingdom. History informs us that about half a century before the occurrences related in this book took place, the succession to the throne of Persia was interrupted by a conspiracy, in which seven of the principal men in the kingdom were engaged; and from that time, for many years under the new dynasty, these seven, and their descendants after them, enjoyed peculiar privileges. They wore a dress different from that of all other subjects and were permitted to deliver their opinion before all others with regard to matters of state.

These were the men who knew the times, and saw the king's face, as it is expressed in the text; and to their judgment, as sitting next to him, Artaxerxes at present appeals. It is very seldom that the counselors of despotic princes give their opinion honestly. They speak to flatter. They usually echo the sentiments of the sovereign, or say, at least, what they think will gratify him at the time. And so it was on the occasion here referred to. The seven counselors, by the mouth of one of them—Memucan—instead of interposing between the king and the innocent object of his wrath, encouraged him in his unreasonable violence. We have already said, that, according to the maxims of the age, the queen acted rightly. She could not, indeed, have acted otherwise, without doing what was at once inconsistent with her station and with her character as a virtuous woman. And it may be safely affirmed, that not one of those who united together in condemning her, would have dared even so much as to hint that the king should issue a command to bring her into the midst of that company, or would have been prepared for her acceding to it. It would have been regarded by them as a crime equivalent to treason to have suggested such a thing.

Yet Memucan, falling in with the present temper of his imperious master, declared that the queen had not only slighted her royal husband, but had set an example, which, if followed throughout the empire, would tend to the breaking up of all domestic order. We may take occasion to observe here, that there were two evils which arose from the peculiar family arrangements in eastern countries, and which, as the customs of these countries have been but little altered, they still produce. In the first place, the condition of the female sex was that of degradation. The married woman was not really, what the divine institution intended her to be, the true companion and friend of her husband. She was kept in a state of seclusion. Real freedom she knew not. She was, in truth, only a slave, having power to command some other slaves. She was without education, and generally unintelligent, frivolous, and heartless. She was guarded with jealous care, as if she had been very precious, but at the same time she was wholly dependent upon the caprices of her lord.

Yet, strangely enough, in the second place, it is to be noticed that, as if to afford evidence that the law of nature cannot be trampled upon with impunity, it very frequently happened that the female influence was felt by the despotic husband, so as to make him in reality the slave. Not conscious of it but imagining that he held the place of absolute authority, he was himself governed; yet not through the power of true affection, but through the imbecile doting which constituted all that he knew of affection. Common history abounds with illustrations of this fact, and in the sacred history we have examples of the same kind. Thus, it is obvious that David was ruled by Bathsheba, and Solomon by some of the strange women whom he gathered about him, and Ahab by Jezebel.

There is never a violation of God's righteous appointments, but it is followed by some penalty. From the Book of Esther, now under our review, it appears very obviously that Artaxerxes, with all his caprices, and his stern, imperious self-will, was at first completely under the influence of Vashti, as he afterwards came to be under that of Esther. The whole domestic system being unnaturally constructed, there were of necessity derangements in the conducting of it. The despot might be one day all tenderness and submission, and the next day he might, to gratify his humor, exact from his slaves what, a short time afterwards, he would have counted it absolutely wrong in himself to command, and punishable

Lecture 2: Esther 1:13-22

in them to do. These general considerations would require to be kept in view, because otherwise it is not easy for us to account for the apparent contradiction which we have to notice in this book and elsewhere, between regal power arbitrarily put forth, and something like puerile weakness, almost at the same time in the same person. But to return from this digression. We have to look to the circumstances which are brought before us in the narrative.

At a season when sound counsel could scarcely have been expected, and when he who sought it was not in a condition to profit by it, the serious question was proposed by the king, "What shall we do unto the Queen Vashti according to law, because she hath not performed the commandment of the king Ahasuerus, by the chamberlains?" To defer the consideration of so grave a subject to a more fitting season would have been so clearly the path which a wise counselor would have recommended, that we feel astonished that it was not at once suggested. But the wrath of the king was so strongly exhibited, that his compliant advisers did not venture to contradict him.

Memucan answered, before the king and the princes, "Vashti the queen hath not done wrong to the king only, but also to all the princes, and to the people. For this deed of the queen shall come abroad unto all women, so that they shall despise their husbands in their eyes. Thus shall there arise too much contempt and wrath."

Now, with respect to this opinion of the chief counselor, it may be observed that it was based upon a principle which in itself is unquestionably right, although there was a wrong application made of it. The right principle lies here—that the example of the great carries vast weight in it. Rank and station, while they command a certain measure of respect, involve very deep responsibility. Every act of the Queen Vashti, so far as it was known and could be imitated, would no doubt be taken as a warrant by the ladies of Persia and Media for the regulating of their conduct. If what she did was palpably wrong, and was suffered to pass unchecked, they would count themselves authorized to do the same, fortified by her authority. Fashions and maxims usually go downward from one class of society to another. Customs, adopted by the higher orders as their rule, gradually make their way until at length they pervade all ranks. Thus far Memucan spoke wisely, when he pointed to the example of the queen as that which would certainly have an influence, wherever it came to be known throughout the empire.

But as we have said, the principle in the present instance was wrongly applied, when it was made the ground of condemning the conduct of Vashti. The design was to make her appear guilty of an act of insubordination, which it was necessary for the king to punish, if he would promote the good of his subjects. Whereas, in reality, she had upon her side all the authority of law and custom: and was to be made the victim both of the ungovernable wrath of the king, who was beside himself with wine, and also of flatterers, who to gratify him, would do wrong to the innocent.

I have remarked above that we cannot easily sympathize with the peremptory refusal of the queen to appear unveiled at the royal banquet. Our customs are so different, and happily all the arrangements of domestic life with us are so different, and so much more fitted to promote the real happiness of husband and wife, that it requires something like reasoning to satisfy us that the king after all was in the wrong. But take this as an illustration, that if any husband among us were to require peremptorily that his wife should abjure her religion, and adopt sentiments and engage in a form of worship which in her conscience she abhorred: he would not make a greater exaction, all things considered, than was made of Vashti, when she was commanded to appear publicly at the king's banquet, that the guests might behold and admire her beauty. But because such was the monarch's will, his counselors acquiesced in it, and condemned the procedure of the queen.

Now before proceeding further, let us make some practical improvement of the passage which has been reviewed.

Lecture 2: Esther 1:13-22

Lesson #1: The Dangers of Flattery

In the first place there is a general lesson suggested by what passed between the king his counselors, as to the danger of flattery. It is natural to all men to desire to have their opinions confirmed and approved by others. The feeling of self-approbation, which forms one element of happiness, is gratified and strengthened, when several persons give their verdict in favor of a choice which we have made, or a course of action which we have judged it right to pursue. But then, when men occupy exalted stations, and have it in their power to reward richly those who are in any way instrumental to the advancement of their comfort and happiness, they are exposed to the very serious calamity of having counsels and opinions poured into their ear for the purpose of pleasing them, and not of presenting truth to them or guiding them rightly through difficulties. Thus it fared with the great king in the case before us! And a similar penalty all have to pay in greater or smaller measure according to the number of those who are dependent on them, and the means they have at their disposal to purchase favor.

There is hardly anyone, indeed, who is exempted from the influence of flattery. It is less and less exercised as wealth and power diminish; but when a man is possessed of anything that can afford gratification to others, he will find some to fall in with his wishes and approve of his opinions, until all he has is expended. Perhaps it is in the condition of absolute poverty alone that the voice of flattery is not heard.

But under the present head, I would not restrict my remarks to the subject of flattery in the popular sense of the word, and with reference merely to temporal things. There is a still more important aspect in which it is to be viewed. Whether we have or have not wherewithal to bribe others to our way of thinking and feeling, and to secure their approval of our conduct, certain it is that we have a flatterer in our own hearts, whose insidious attempts to mislead us we should guard against most anxiously.

In every man there is a conflict between inclination and the power of conscience. This conflict arises and is carried on without reference to a man's religious knowledge or belief. The heathen were as conscious of it as those are who possess the oracles of God. When unlawful desire prompts in one direction, there is another influence, the natural conscience, which points in a different way, and has its strong arguments to repress the cravings of desire. But in answer to these arguments, there are numberless subtle reasonings, all pleading upon the side of desire, and drawing the will to give verdict in its behalf: so that the heart is like a little fortress beleaguered on all hands, and sorely put to it to decide what course to take. Now all the reasonings against the conviction of what is right are just so many self-flatteries by which we are seduced into sin. And their strength is too great. They put a false coloring upon the objects of human pursuit, they make what is wrong appear right, and what is hurtful seem innocent, and thus the maxim is verified, "there is a way which seemeth right unto a man, but the end thereof are the ways of death."

But it is not only in the natural man that there is a conflict between good and evil. Even where grace reigns, "the flesh lusteth against the spirit, and the spirit against the flesh," as two antagonists that cannot be reconciled. And, although there is a heavenly power in this instance brought in to aid the believer in the conflict, yet there are specious and beguiling flatteries which too often, even in his case, gain for the fleshly nature the advantage over the spiritual!

It is one of the proofs of Bunyan's deep acquaintance with the human heart, and with the realities of Christian experience also, that he represents his pilgrims, after they had gone through the greatest hardships of their journey, and when they were beginning to enjoy their sweet foretastes of the heavenly rest, as caught within the net of the flatterer, and subjected to sore discipline on that account.

We may wonder at the folly of Artaxerxes, in allowing himself to be guided by the judgment of men who only spoke what they supposed

Lecture 2: Esther 1:13-22

would please him! But all men have as good reason—yea Christ's own people have as good reason to wonder—at the strange flatteries by which at one time their progress heavenward is interrupted, and at other times their will is enlisted on the side of what is positively evil. We might speak at great length here in illustration of this part of our subject. But we must be contented with one or two examples.

First, take one which has reference to active exercises in the way of well-doing and of glorifying Christ, in which all His followers ought to be engaged. There is no doubt that the tendencies of the renewed heart lie in the same direction to which the word of God points, when it says—" ye are not your own, but bought with a price, therefore glorify God in your body and in your spirit which are God's." At the same time, it is unquestionable that what the believer feels he should do, and what he often sees he might do, he is opposed in doing by considerations which address themselves to his selfishness, his worldliness, and his natural love of ease.

Your health is precious, why should you expend it in efforts which, after all, will not repay the trouble you bestow? Better care for yourself, and let others attend to those departments of the work of Christ which require activity. Or, would it not be better that you should commit to others the conducting of affairs which require more strength and energy than you can command? This is the flatterer within, endeavoring to make the believer feel that he is doing more than he ought to do, and that he should contract his efforts, and let the world lie in its wickedness so long as it does not immediately disturb him. And verily this flattery is often too powerful. When such arguments as these are employed to a Christian: you are safe yourself; be satisfied with your own interest in Christ, and let the godless world pursue its own course; you are too weak to set yourself against its ways and maxims; and when the Christian yields to these arguments, and draws away his hand from the work of Christ, he is as truly led by the seducing voice which causeth to err, as if he were surrounded by thousands of pretended friends who echo his wishes.

But again, Christ's people are liable to the advances of flattery, when it comes to them saying, "ye are strong and powerful, and require not the aid of divine grace to help you, as some others do." It was this aspect of the subject that Bunyan had chiefly before his mind, when he pictured his pilgrims as caught within the net of the flatterer.

We smile at the foolish weakness of the great king, when he would make his own will a law; and we despise the men who submitted to him and brought him to the belief that his opinion was sufficient to bear away before it every difficulty. But herein we are as weak as he was, when, self-pleased and self-confident, we suppose that we *ourselves* can overcome the obstacles which lie across our path. This is one of the snares into which Christians are very ready to fall. And it is a most dangerous snare. It amounts actually to an exalting of the creature above the power of God. Or if this language is too strong, it amounts at least to the denial of the necessity of special grace at all times to keep Christ's disciples in the right path. It cannot be questioned, that it is a pleasing doctrine which is propounded to us when our own hearts suggest that we have power ourselves to do what is right, and to keep us from the way of backsliding into which so many fall. But it is a doctrine most pernicious, suggested by the wicked one.

As we would have never been brought from sin to God, without the special aid of His Spirit, so we cannot take one step of advancement in the way of life, or do anything pleasing to God, without the same aid. If we forget our dependence upon sovereign grace and think that at any time we can dispense with its assistance, we are assuredly incurring the condemnation pronounced by the wise man when he says, "he that trusteth to his own heart is a fool."

Once more under this head, there is a flattery which would draw Christ's people into conformity to the world, and into many of the world's sins, while at the same time they appear to themselves to be pursuing the path of duty with all consistency. Every man has his weakness and his besetting sin. Get him persuaded that, such as he is, he is as really a follower of Christ as many others, whose religious sincerity no one questions, and then you have him supposing that he is in the way to heaven—perhaps with a weight of covetousness about him which tells that he is of earthly mind, or with an immoderate selfishness, which proclaims that his heart is not warmed by the love of Christ. He may be sadly fallen from the position which he once occupied; but still he thinks he is a Christian, and he has some argument to produce in defense of his conduct, while he falls away from the spirit of Christianity. In such circumstances, he is under the leading of the most dangerous kind of flattery; and he will find, when he awakes from the delusion into which he has been drawn, that there have been dark influences leading him astray, more powerful than the counselors of the great king, when they suggested to him that he should do what his own ungovernable spirit had disposed him to do.

To sum up our remarks here: of all the kinds of flattery by which men are drawn aside from the way of truth, there is none half so dangerous as the prompting of the heart itself. It is not easy to resist inducements to evil from without, when they are clothed in the garb of friendliness; but when the conflict comes to be between what we desire and what we are doubtful of, then, if we are not on our guard, we shall be led to put light for darkness and darkness for light—sweet for bitter and bitter for sweet. Thus it is with many, to their present and everlasting ruin.

Lesson #2: The Power of Example

But now, in the second place, there is another lesson suggested by the text, which is not unworthy of our notice, although it comes to us, as it were, from the mouth of a heathen. We must not forget that the great principles of right and wrong are to some extent known to all; and although the maxim drops from the lips of Memucan the Persian counselor, it is not to be overlooked that high rank and station, while they have their honors, have also their responsibilities.

"What the queen doth will be done by all," was his statement, and we must feel the truthfulness of it. It embodies a maxim peculiarly applicable to the followers of Christ. They are supposed to be separate from the sinful world by the very circumstance of their being Christ's. Their whole life is described in the Scripture as involving separation from the world's sins. Then, if they become worldly—if they act inconsistently—their acts do not terminate in and with themselves. What they say and do produces effects far beyond their own calculation and their own sphere.

A word spoken for Christ may bear fruit where they would not have been prepared to look for such a result. A determined endeavor to honor Christ on their part may be the instrument of arresting the attention of the ungodly, and leading some to life; but on the other hand, an inconsistency in speech or action on their part may produce incalculable evil, leading others to sin, or hardening them in guilt. These considerations it would be well for us always to keep in view. While there are many inducements, or, as we may well call them, flatteries, put forth to seduce us from the path of rectitude, it may help to render us superior to them, if we remember that by the grace of God we are entrusted with a solemn charge—even to make the power of His truth known to all with whom we come in contact—by our life as well as by our speech—and if, looking to the aid of the same grace, we resolve to live so that Christ in all things shall be magnified by us in our life.

But we proceed now to consider the remaining part of Memucan's counsel to the king, as contained in verses 19-22: "If it please the king, let there go a royal commandment from him, and let it be written among the laws of the Persians and Medes, that it be not altered, that Vashti come no more before king Ahasuerus; and let the king give her royal estate unto another that is better than she. And when the king's decree which he shall make shall be published throughout all his empire, (for it

Lecture 2: Esther 1:13-22

is great,) all the wives shall give to their husbands honor, both to great and small. And the saying pleased the king and the princes; and the king did according to the word of Memucan: for he sent letters into all the king's provinces, into every province according to the writing thereof, and to every people after their language, that every man should bear rule in his own house, and that it should be published according to the language of every people."

It is not necessary that much should be said in the way of comment upon this passage. We must keep this in mind, however, that the verses which have been read do not contain the expression of the mind of the divine Spirit, but only a literal and true account of what was proposed as good counsel to the king of Persia, and approved by him. Then, so far as the document really goes, the only point contained in it which enacts anything new, is that which refers to the degradation of Vashti the queen from her dignity. She was no longer to be first among the king's wives and concubines, as she had been hitherto. She was to live as it were in a state of widowhood.

All this might have fallen out by the mere arbitrary will of the king; but it is solemnly decreed, and word is to be sent into all the provinces, in order that it might be known that every man should bear rule in his own house. Now, if this law had extended to the breaking down of that barbarous usage which prevented females in the East from occupying the place which rightly belongs to them, it would have been worthy of all praise; but as we read it in the text, it only gave greater sanction to the established custom, that the wife should be in all respects subjected to the will of the husband. It afforded the tyrant power to be, if he chose, more tyrannical still. If the purport of the enactment had been that there should be such a change made upon the law, that the wife was no longer to be kept in seclusion as a slave, but should appear publicly as the sharer of her husband's titles, and honors, and joys, the new arrangement would have been for the manifest advantage of the whole community; but as it stands, it was plainly designed for no good purpose, but to punish Vashti, and to rivet the chains of servitude upon the female sex.

One point deserves some attention before we proceed to make application of the subject, e.g. the request that the law to be enforced with regard to domestic government, "should be written among the laws of the Persians and Medes, that it might not be altered." The first time that we meet with this form of expression is in the Book of Daniel, and that is just at the commencement of the Medo-Persian rule—or, at least, more than a century before the period to which the Book of Esther brings us down. The law of the Medes and Persians was then held to be immutable—that is to say, the appointment of the king, sanctioned by his counselors, could not be changed by him or them. It was one of the absurdities of despotism, that its enactments should have the character of immutability.

The idea was, that the judgment of the king was so perfect, that to suppose it changeable was to suppose it wrong, and therefore it must stand. There are some curious historical notices, which tend to show, that down to a period not far from our own time, the notion has descended among the Persians, of the will of the sovereign being unchangeable. But without alluding to these at present, most certainly at the period referred to in the text, the law of the Medes and Persians—of the sovereign and his counselors—was regarded as above change; and so in these terms it was enacted that Vashti should be degraded, and that "every man should bear rule in his own house."

Now let us extract some practical lessons from this part of our subject.

Lesson #1: Every Man Should Bear Rule in His Own House

In the first place, a few remarks may be offered upon the great domestic question, which is here so authoritatively settled by the king of Persia and his wise men, as to the supremacy of the man in his own house. So far as the mere letter of common law goes—and we may also say so far as the spirit of divine law goes—the enactment which is here recorded was right. Every man should bear rule in his own house. But when we come to examine all that is written in the Scripture upon this topic, we are led at once to dismiss the wise men of Persia from the position they assume of giving forth any law upon the subject at all. How could they pronounce a sound judgment upon a question which their customs prevented them from rightly knowing? Taught by the gospel of Christ, we are able to give forth practically what is the true law upon this point, so interesting and so important to mankind. ""Wives, submit yourselves unto your own husbands, as it is fit in the Lord. Husbands, love your wives, and be not bitter against them." Thus runs the law of Christ. And how does it operate practically? In a way which the king of Persia and his counselors could have no conception of.

The husband is the head, and yet he has a counselor, from whom he is willing to take the counsels which love and prudence give. The wife is subject, but she has as her lord one whom she loves as her very self—on whose arm she leans, and on whose arm she feels that she needs to lean, while she speaks her mind and gives her counsels freely. And thus there is the supremacy and the submission—yea, and the submission quietly and gently making the supremacy itself subject, so that God's blessed object is wrought out—these two are one.

Such, practically, is the law of husband and wife in the Christian family, and the establishment of it is one of the highest temporal blessings which the Gospel has conferred on man.

Lesson #2: Like the Medes and the Persians, Christians Honor a Law that "Changes Not"

In the second place, we have in the text a law spoken of which changeth not. And, my friends, there is such a law; but it is not the law of the Medes and Persians: it is the law of the Eternal Jehovah's law changeth not. And what does it say? "This do and live." "Cursed is every one that continueth not in all things written in the book of the law to do them." That seals us all up under wrath. But we turn the page, and we read and see that "Christ is the end of the law for righteousness." And is not this our conclusion, then "I will flee from the curse of the immutable law, and shelter myself under the righteousness of Christ, which is also perfect and immutable, that through Him and from Him I may have mercy and life eternal?" Amen.

Lecture 3: Esther 2:1-4

The last lecture comprehended the latter portion of the preceding chapter, which records the results of those festivities in which the king of Persia, his counselors, his princes, and his people, had been engaged. It very seldom is found that great assemblages for feasting, or for dissipation of any kind, pass by without some untoward and miserable consequences. We verily believe, that an honest acknowledgment of the experience of all who frequent public festivals and ballrooms, and such other places of amusement, would consist rather in a detail of disappointments and vexations than of real satisfaction. It is not with any feeling of morbid disrelish of those things, which appear for a time to make some people happy; but as bearing testimony to an unquestionable fact, that we would say, that the inscription which Solomon long ago wrote over the festivities and gaieties of life—"all is vanity and vexation of spirit,"—gives the true account of them. Yea, and we would add, this is the real estimate formed of them by most of the very parties who have joined in them, imagining that they would make them happy.

At all events, whatever may have been the experience of those who were invited to partake of the festivities of the Persian court, it is manifest, that when they were concluded, the king himself had nothing to look back upon with comfort. In a fit of wrath, when he was excited by wine, he had decreed the degradation of his queen Vashti. His counselors, who should have given him better advice, had encouraged him in the perpetration of this unrighteous act. The sentence was passed upon the queen without a voice raised in her defense, or opportunity afforded to her to justify herself. And according to the foolish notion, that the laws of the Medes and Persians were unchangeable—that sentence must take effect, however irrational it might afterwards be found and felt to be.

These remarks bring us down to the second chapter, in which we are permitted to see the consequences which resulted from the banquet. The present lecture, however, will consist rather in the statement and enforcing of one or two general principles, than in what may properly be called exposition. Verses 1-4: "After these things, when the wrath of King Ahasuerus was appeased, he remembered Vashti, and what she had done, and what had been decreed against her. Then said the king's servants that ministered unto him, Let there be fair young virgins sought for the king: and let the king appoint officers in all the provinces of his kingdom, that they may gather together all the fair young virgins unto Shushan the palace, to the house of the women, unto the custody of Hege the king's chamberlain, keeper of the women; and let their things for purification be given them: and let the maiden which pleaseth the king be queen instead of Vashti. And the thing pleased the king; and he did so."

We have here first to notice the regret of the king for his rash and unwarrantable act. It is very obvious from the narrative, that when he came to himself, and had time to reflect upon all that had taken place, he was sensible that he had committed injury; and that he had not only wronged Vashti, but also made himself a sufferer. At the same time, he could not devise a remedy. There are wishes which even the most powerful despots cannot get gratified, and limits to their will which even they cannot overpass. It seemed to be by a simple exercise of supreme authority that Artaxerxes triumphed over the helpless, and had his desire carried into effect. But when he would have retraced his steps, he could not. The law of the Medes and Persians must stand, although the enactment which did wrong to the innocent queen, at the same time recoiled upon the head of the king himself.

But again, secondly, we have to notice the expedient which his counselors suggested to free him from his difficulty. Very probably he would be moody and harsh toward them, when he saw to what issue their advice had brought him. But despotism is like spoilt childhood, it must be soothed and flattered; and in this way the wise men of Persia dealt

Lecture 3: Esther 2:1-4

with their sovereign. He had degraded his queen, but another might be found at least as worthy as she to occupy the place from which she had been removed. It is a description of Eastern manners altogether that we have presented to us in the suggestion of the Persian counselors contained in verse 3-4, that the monarch should have all the beauty of the empire placed at his disposal, and that the maiden who pleased him should be chosen queen instead of Vashti.

As was mentioned in the first lecture, we are not to regard these arrangements as referred to by way of approval in the divine records. It is, indeed, the opinion of some commentators, that all the allusions made in this book to public affairs, are to be considered as actual extracts from the chronicles of the kingdom of Persia. And this opinion may be correct. But whether it be so or not, what we are principally concerned with is the fact, that we have here a true account of what took place at the time—inserted in the Scripture by the Spirit, for the purpose of showing how the Divine Providence makes even the sins, and follies, and passions, of men subservient to the accomplishment of its own high purposes. And the point in the history which bears upon this is, that the humor of the king on the present occasion fell in with the suggestion of his counselors, and he consented to the arrangement proposed by them, which ultimately led to the promotion of Esther, a Jewess, to the high dignity of being queen of Persia.

Nothing further requires to be stated in the way of comment upon the verses which have been read. But they are well worthy of our attention in the way of practical application. They suggest several lessons which may be profitable to us.

Lesson #1: Rash Actions Often Lead to Irreversible Consequences

In the first place we may draw from them this lesson, that when men suffer themselves to be carried away by the excitement of intemperance, or by the impulse of any violent passions, they may commit acts which cannot afterwards be remedied, and which they themselves may have especially to lament. We think it is plain from the words, "the king remembered Vashti, what she had done, and what had been decreed against her;" that when he was able to reflect calmly upon the decree which had been issued for the degradation of Vashti, he was conscious that she had been faithful to her place and character, while he himself had forgotten what was due to both. All the past he would have gladly cancelled, but it was beyond his power. His will could work evil, but it could not undo the evil which had been wrought.

Now, very frequently it happens that intoxication, and the force of headlong passion, lead to the perpetration of crimes, the remembrance of which in their sober and cool moments makes those who have committed them shudder. In these circumstances, what would they not give to be able to efface the reality as well as the memory of the past? But this may not be. What has been said or done remains indelible.

And the point I would chiefly desire to impress upon you in connection with all this is, that it does not form an excuse for sin committed, that the transgressor had reduced himself to a condition in which he ceased to retain his full consciousness of the distinction between right and wrong. He is responsible for being in that condition. It is with his own consent that he passes the boundary line between reason and folly; and although, in one aspect of the case, he may not be precisely answerable for all his acts when the power of self-government is gone, yet obviously he is to be called to account for reducing himself to that state.

Let us take an illustration from the history of Saul, king of Israel. At the commencement of his reign, the happiest anticipations might have been formed of the career which he was to pursue. Largely furnished with the common gifts of the Spirit and having the prophet Samuel for his friend and counselor, he might have been, both as a man and as king, a model to the sovereigns who were to come after him. But he failed to improve his privileges. By his disobedience he drew down upon him the

Lecture 3: Esther 2:1-4

divine displeasure. The Spirit of the Lord departed from him, his heart was darkened, and his great endowments were withdrawn. An evil spirit took possession of him, and under this malign influence he was hurried into the commission of crimes which now and then he himself bewailed.

Now, although we can account for the evil which he did by the fact that he was instigated by an evil spirit, we must not forget that the evil spirit only got the ascendancy over him, because he would not be guided by the counsels which were sent to him from heaven. He acted as he did because he was prompted by that spirit of wickedness; but he was morally responsible all the while, because he had himself forsaken the better guidance which he might have enjoyed and had thus subjected himself to the malignant power.

It was Saul that slew fourscore and five of the Lord's priests; it was Saul that again and again attempted to take the life of David. *He* was held responsible although the evil spirit prompted him, because he had laid his heart open for the reception of the evil spirit. And just so it is in all cases, we say, when men allow their reason to be clouded by intemperance, or any other vice or passion. There may be nice questions in human law founded upon responsibility, when reason has been driven from her place. There may be visitations of providence so palpably accounting for mental aberration, that everyone must feel that in certain cases the very idea of responsibility is destroyed. But when a man has perpetrated a criminal act, having *willfully* deprived himself of the power that would have restrained him from it, he has no right to claim immunity from the consequences of his miserable self-will; or to complain that he is unrighteously dealt with, when he is visited with punishment. These remarks we ground upon the regret which the king of Persia felt for the wrong which he had done to his queen Vashti.

Lesson #2: Repentance May Come Too Late

But now, in the second place, there is a more general application which may be legitimately made of this part of our subject; e.g., that repentance may come too late. Artaxerxes, as we have said, would have willingly retraced his steps, and freed Vashti from the sentence which had gone forth against her; but an unalterable law prevented him. And even so it is with respect to matters unspeakably more important. There is a regret for evil done, which may be awakened in the heart of the sinner, when there is no time allowed for its being, if we may so speak, carried out into true repentance.

A man may pause in his career of wickedness, and be constrained to feel that he has treated the divine law with contempt, dishonored Christ, trampled on the gospel, and done despite to the Spirit of grace; but he may only feel all this when it is too late for him to repent. Remorse is not repentance; with whatever anguish of mind it may be accompanied. There is many a cry for mercy raised, when the time for the exercise of mercy has passed away; and this, not because the mercy of Jehovah is not infinite, but because the sinner has resolutely rejected it. We are reminded here of the incident in the history of Esau, which the apostle Paul so forcibly applies in his epistle to the Hebrews.

"Look diligently," he says, "lest there be any fornicator or profane person, as Esau, who for one morsel of meal sold his birthright. For ye know how that afterward, when he would have inherited the blessing, he was rejected; for he found no place of repentance, though he sought it carefully with tears." Now it is true that the rejection of Esau alluded to in this passage, has reference to his father Isaac, who having previously conferred the blessing upon Jacob, could not be moved to change his mind by all the vehement pleading and piteous cries of Esau. But the incident is put on record, to warn us against procrastinating in our dealings with Jehovah, until we provoke Him to leave us to ourselves. For certainly, such a result is possible. It may seem a strange thing, that a

Lecture 3: Esther 2:1-4

sinner should plead for mercy, and that his prayer should not reach the mercy-seat. But consider this, how often the invitation of the Lord may have been addressed to that sinner, when he only either neglected it, or treated it with contempt. Surely it is no impeachment of the mercy of God, that when men will not listen to its voice, while it invites them to come and walk in the broad sunshine of the divine favor, they should be made feel, when remorse is kindled in them, as by a lightning flash, how terrible and inevitable their doom now is. Is there any good reason to be assigned, I would ask, wherefore a man who has often been warned, and called to repent, but who recklessly has not listened to the call, should not be left to reap as he has sown? Is there room for bringing the charge either of unkindness or injustice against the principle embodied in the following awful passage of God's word: "Because I have called, and ye refused; I have stretched out my hand, and no man regarded: but ye have set at nought all my counsel, and would none of my reproof: I also will laugh at your calamity; I will mock when your fear cometh?" Assuredly there is not. Indeed, the only wonderful thing connected with God's procedure toward sinners is, that His forbearance should be so long continued. After the scornful rejection of His first gracious offer, He might justly leave the sinner to the choice which he has made. But instead of this, there is pleading and remonstrance, threatening and promise held out to him, to allure or terrify him from his course of self-destruction, in many cases for a long series of years. Most of us here can bear testimony to this fact. But then, when all the divine long-suffering is without effect, can it be made subject of complaint that it should terminate, and that the sinner should be given over to pursue his own way hopelessly?

My friends, the text teaches us that, by the law of the Medes and Persians, which could not be changed, the king of Persia found himself in a condition from which he would gladly have been extricated but could not devise the means. Now, by the unalterable law of heaven, it is ordained that except we repent we must perish. And by the same law it is required that the repentance be immediate. The mere circumstance, that many who have long neglected to obey the divine requirement, have nevertheless been accepted in the end, does not make the demand upon any of you the less imperative, to seek the Lord now, while He may be found. We cannot tell but that for each individual case where there has been room for repentance, even at the eleventh hour, there may be a thousand to the opposite effect, showing that the eleventh hour was too late. At all events, God's time to us is the present time. The interests of eternity may to you be hinged upon this day—this hour—this moment. "Wherefore, my brethren, take heed lest there be in any of you an evil heart of unbelief, in departing from the living God. But exhort one another daily, while it is called today, lest any of you be hardened through the deceitfulness of sin."

But now there is altogether another line of remark opened up to us by the advice which the counselors of King Artaxerxes gave him to relieve him from his difficulty. I have said already that we are not to regard their procedure in any other light than an attempt to pander to the feelings of a weak minded and despotic voluptuary; but at the same time, the whole train of events which we have afterwards to consider furnishes such evidence of the power of an overruling Providence, that I would take this opportunity of referring with some minuteness to the subject.

Lesson #3: Even Amid Confusion and Evil, God Still Guides Events

The lesson which the text teaches is, in one sentence, this—that amid all the workings of human passion and folly, there is a power exercised which brings order out of confusion, and good out of evil. It will be best for us first to present the case briefly as the text brings it before us, although we may seem to state only what has been referred to already. Revelry had produced disorder in the court of Persia. It had led to most unjust measures toward the queen. Those who were the advisers of these measures, finding it necessary to soothe the feelings of their despotic sovereign, recommended to him a certain mode of procedure. That mode was in opposition to all our notions of propriety, but it was adopted; and the result of it, as we shall see, was Esther's advancement to the queenly dignity, and great favor and enlargement thenceforth to the Jewish people. Now, in all this we say we have an illustration of the working of a special providence, bringing good out of evil, and overruling the sins of men for the promotion of the interests of the people of God. It may be remarked, that in the observations which are to be offered, we to some extent anticipate what follows in the story; but the general bearing of the narrative is sufficiently known to all to admit of our doing so without inconvenience, and without involving the subject in any obscurity.

Firstly

In the first place, then, we see—and it is the only thing prominently brought before us in the text—a specimen of the absolute and unrestrained will of man put forth to accomplish ends which had no apparent connection whatever with the will of God, or with what would be pleasing to Him. Jehovah was no more thought of at this banquet than He was at that one in Babylon, described in the Book of Daniel, when "Belshazzar the king, with his princes, drank wine out of the vessels which were taken from the temple at Jerusalem, and praised the gods of gold and of silver, of brass, of iron, of wood, and of stone."

No one, looking upon the wild riot of Artaxerxes and his lords, could have imagined that there was the slightest thread of union between what they did and heaven's purposes. They were heathens, professing no allegiance to Jehovah, and, as such, governed by impulses altogether different from the teachings of His word. A calm spectator of the scene would have acknowledged at once, that not only were all these left to act as they chose, without any external influence being put forth to bias them, but that they were even permitted to exercise their freedom *licentiously*.

A pious mind, on the perusal of the narrative, would draw the conclusion, that so far from there being any harmony between heaven and earth at this festival, there was, on the contrary, a complete antagonism. "What could there be productive of good result," one might well have asked, "in the excesses of a heathen king, and in the flattery of his counselors, who cared as little as he did himself for the interests of truth, and justice, and pure religion?" And verily the answer might have been returned, that if there ever was an occasion when all thought of a divine providence was cast aside, and when men might have been regarded as left to themselves, to work out the counsels of their own will, without reference to any controlling power above, it was that occasion referred to in the text.

Secondly

But then, secondly, turning away from the king of Persia and his counselors, who were reveling in the gratification of their animal propensities, and were full of the conceit that their will was above every ordinary law, we have to notice that there was a people scattered through the provinces of the Persian empire, separate from all the other nations that were comprehended under the government of the great king, and known to him and his princes only as captives and tributaries, whose religion made them a laughingstock to the votaries of idolatry. This strange people had attracted the favorable regard of the great Cyrus, the founder of the Persian monarchy, and had received liberty from him to return to their own city, Jerusalem. And many of those who had not chosen to avail themselves of his permission, had, by their industry and intelligence, acquired considerable wealth. This tended, however, to excite against them the envy and hatred of not a few of the chief men of Persia, and of the governors of the provinces more especially.

In this way it had been brought about, that those of the Jews who had gone to Jerusalem, or we should now rather say their descendants, had never been able to take due advantage of the benevolent designs of Cyrus toward them. And such of them as were dispersed through the provinces of the empire were in constant danger of being assailed by their heathen enemies, and exterminated, that their wealth might be a spoil to their destroyers. Such was the condition of the Jews at the period referred to in the text. But it was written in the infallible word, that though they should be scattered among the nations, yet the eye of the Lord would be upon them, and none would be permitted to injure them with impunity. This word, however, was unknown to Artaxerxes and those who were about him. And the destinies of the Jewish people were no further a subject of interest to them than as they formed a portion of the inhabitants of the vast empire of Persia.

Now, there does not seem any bond of connection between these two points in our discourse, the banquet of Artaxerxes and the fortunes of the Jews; between a heathen carousal and the building of the wall of Jerusalem, together with the deliverance of the great body of the descendants of Abraham from imminent destruction. The two events seem to be separated by the widest possible chasm. But it is precisely here that we would have you look at and mark the operation of the Divine Sovereignty in Providence. The earthly scene which you contemplate as you look upon the festival of the heathen monarch, the luxury and folly that prevailed at it, and the evil passions that were excited at it, would lead you to anticipate any result from it rather than one which would secure the repairing of the waste places of Jerusalem, and the advancement of the interests of all her children. But when the curtain which conceals the movements of Providence is withdrawn—as with respect to the affairs of the Jewish people, it is withdrawn in this book—we can manifestly trace the connection between the follies and passions of men and the production of important results which they could not even have dreamt of.

We can perceive the hand of the Lord working where we would not have looked for it, and understand how the very wrath of men is made to praise Him. Take together all the leading circumstances in the case more immediately before us, and notice how the overruling power makes them conducive to the advancement of the prosperity of the Jewish people, who formed at that time the Church of God. Had the king of Persia remained devoted to his queen Vashti, it is very likely that he would have scarcely wasted a thought upon the Jews or their affairs—at all events, they would have been but secondary matters in his mind. But there is nothing to indicate that any change would have been made in his domestic arrangements, had not the season of banqueting come, which led to his quarrel with the queen, and to her removal from her place. Then was given forth the judgment of the seven great men of Persia upon the question, and their advice, that the king, without restriction, should choose whom he would to fill the dignity which Vashti had forfeited. In all probability, some of them may have had relations of their own whom they sought to have advanced, but if so, their designs were discomfited.

Upon Esther, the Jewess, the choice of the king fell; and then, to her influence over the monarch must be attributed the mission of Nehemiah to Jerusalem, to rebuild the walls of the city, as well as the defeating of Haman's design for the destruction of the Jews, of which we shall have to speak more particularly afterwards. Here then, we say, is the evidence of an overruling Providence, in that the festivities at the palace of Susa, where Jehovah was not known, were made instrumental toward the prosperity of Jerusalem and her children. And this is not to be regarded as an isolated case, to which nothing similar is to be found in the record of human affairs. On the contrary, we would look upon it as furnishing a key to the opening up of many strange passages of ordinary history, or as a light for the illustration of many historical incidents which, to some minds, are dark and inexplicable. Thus, just to take one example, the details of which are no doubt familiar to most of you. The Reformation in England had its origin certainly not in any love of truth on the part of the imperious and dissolute king who then reigned, but rather in his strong passions and licentious propensities. He did not cast off the papal

Lecture 3: Esther 2:1-4

authority, because he felt it to be unscriptural and ruinous to the souls of men, but because it was a spiritual despotism, thwarting at the time his own fierce and ungovernable will.

Now, on this ground an argument has always been constructed by the friends of popery against the Protestant cause, that it owed its triumph in England not to its being the cause of pure religion and sound morality, but to the circumstance, that the licentious monarch would not submit to the restraints which the Church of Rome imposed upon his licentiousness. And some people of weak mind have been affected by the apparent force of this argument, and have felt as if it told against Protestantism and in favor of popery. But we think that the movement of Providence in the instance brought before us in the text, places the whole matter in a light sufficiently clear and satisfactory.

It will not be said that the furtherance of God's work at Jerusalem, and in the saving of his people from destruction throughout the empire of Persia, is to be deplored; because humanly speaking, that which led to it was the self-will, luxury, and voluptuousness, of the Persian king. And so neither, we say, does it dim the glory of the truth, nor detract from the benefits which have resulted from the diffusion of it; neither does it mar the holiness of the Bible, nor make the free circulation of it less a blessing to the nation, that Heaven rendered the unruly desires of Henry VIII. subservient to those great ends.

The sin of the monarch was not one whit diminished, because it was overruled for good; but neither is the good to be regarded as evil, because it was the undesigned fruit of man's unholy passions.

We may illustrate the subject farther, by referring to a case infinitely more important. "The heathen raged, and the people imagined vain things; the kings of the earth stood up, and the rulers were gathered together, against the Lord and against his Christ, but He that sitteth in the heavens did laugh, the Lord did hold them in derision." In all that they did, acting freely according to the impulses of their own evil hearts, they only accomplished whatsoever God's hand and His counsel had determined before to be done. And so, amid all the wild tumult of human passion, the will of Providence calmly works its way, bringing order out of confusion, and converting miseries into blessings.

These remarks upon the subject of providence might have been carried much farther, and many more illustrations might have been given. But our purpose has so far been answered, if what has been said has the effect of leading you to a more devout and reverential contemplation of this department of the divine procedure. There are many things in the providence of God which must ever remain sealed up in mystery to us, while we are in this world—many dispensations with respect to which we must be contented to take home to us Jehovah's words by the Psalmist, "Be still, and know that I am God." But there are also many cases in which, if we would but look carefully, we might trace the operation of the divine hand, and have our faith and hope invigorated mightily. As we proceed in our examination of the book of Esther we shall have to advert again to this subject; but in the meantime, we must bring the present discourse to a close. And in doing so I would leave with you two practical remarks, in the way of application:

Application #1:

In the first place, I think we are evidently warranted to draw this conclusion from the subject, that if the purposes of ungodly and licentious men, have been overruled in the providence of God for good, much more may it be expected that the designs and efforts of those who seek to advance God's glory in the way which His word prescribes will be made instrumental toward that end.

If, by the help of Scripture removing the veil which hides the connection between what is done on earth and what is transacted in heaven we have been able to see that human passions and vices, in themselves unmixedly evil and hateful, are made to subserve the advancement of God's gracious purposes, then surely, when it is written in His word that the prayers of His people are heard, and that their hands are strengthened by Him, we are encouraged to expect that there will be a connection traceable between their energies, rightly put forth, and the progress of His cause in the world. Even here, indeed, there may be need for the exercise of large faith and patience. But this is written, and it will be verified, "My beloved brethren, let us be steadfast, immoveable, always abounding in the work of the Lord: forasmuch as we know that our labor is not in vain in the Lord."

Application #2:

In the second place, as we have been speaking of God's overruling providence, I would now say, in conclusion, that each of you is specially watched by Him; and more particularly, I would address the remark to those who are still strangers to the grace of God in Christ. My friends, the eye of the Lord has been upon you, and His hand too, although you have not felt it. He has pled with you, and sometimes made you feel the weight of His rod, to arrest you in your career of sin, but ye have continued to escape, and to deaden conviction by saying, There will be time enough hereafter. You have been thrown into trouble, and then fear overtook you. The trouble has been removed, and then you have become as thoughtless as before. How long is this to last? You say, "Not always." "But when," we ask, "are you to submit to the Lord, and to renounce your sins?" If not now, oh, remember the doctrine we have this day had under review—that repentance may be too late. May the Lord give us wisdom to understand His dealings, and to improve the day of merciful visitation.

Amen.

Lecture 4: Esther 2:5-20

In the last lecture, which embraced the opening verses of this chapter, the topic which chiefly engaged our attention was that of the overruling providence of God, which converts even the sins and follies of men into instruments for working out His sovereign purposes. There was nothing in the transactions referred to that could in any sense have been called miraculous; and yet the deliverance of the Jews, which, as we shall see, was effected through the instrumentality of Esther, was as really brought about by the hand of God as was their escape from Egypt by the passage which He opened up for them through the Red Sea. And so in the history of every man there are divine interpositions, which, although to us they may appear the simple results of the common laws of nature, are as illustrative of the all-controlling power of Jehovah as were those miracles by which bread was rained from heaven for the supply of Israel's wants in the wilderness, and water drawn for their refreshment from the flinty rock.

The miracles recorded in the Scripture, which consisted in works performed by superseding or setting aside the ordinary laws of nature, were necessary for the confirmation of the truths revealed in the Scripture, as truths dictated by the Spirit of God. But the more closely we inspect the whole scheme of providence, the more satisfied we shall be that even those parts of it, those events which present to our view nothing that is accounted mysterious or miraculous, are as truly regulated by divine power and wisdom as if we actually saw that wisdom and power immediately exercised in the disposal of them. And if no other lesson than this were to be derived from an examination of this book, it would be profitable for us to direct our attention to it.

In the verses which form the subject of the present lecture, there is laid before us the opening scene of the strange and eventful history of Esther. Look first to verse 5-7: "Now in Shushan the palace there was a

Lecture 4: Esther 2:5-20

certain Jew, whose name was Mordecai, the son of Jair, the son of Shimei, the son of Kish, a Benjamite; who had been carried away from Jerusalem with the captivity which had been carried away with Jeconiah king of Judah, whom Nebuchadnezzar the king of Babylon had carried away."

It is singular that it should have ever been imagined, although it has been by some, that it was Mordecai who had been carried from Jerusalem to Babylon, at the time when Jeconiah, also called Jehoiachin, was dethroned, and led into captivity by Nebuchadnezzar. In that case, he must at this time have been considerably more than a hundred years old, which is altogether inconsistent with the part he is represented as performing in this book. It is evidently Kish, his great-grandfather, who lived in Jeconiah's time, and who was carried to Babylon, on which supposition Mordecai would be a man probably in the prime of life at the period referred to in the text.

His cousin Esther, or Hadassah (which was her Jewish name), had been left an orphan. Whether Mordecai had any family of his own we are not informed; but, moved with compassion for her in her desolate and unprotected state, he took her to his house, and brought her up as his own daughter. The maiden was fair and beautiful, it is said—the expressions mean that she was of graceful form and beautiful countenance—and from what is brought out in the history, the endowments of her mind were in harmony with the graces of her person. Sad, however, might the destiny of the lovely orphan have been, but for the kind and tender-hearted Mordecai If she had been cast upon the world without friends and without a home, the very beauty and accomplishments with which she was so highly gifted might have rendered her only a prey to some of those designing and selfish wretches whose chief object it is to seduce and ruin those who are fair and beautiful as she was. But the eye of the Lord was upon the helpless maiden, to protect and guide her; and Mordecai had her brought to his house as her home. No doubt he felt that he was sufficiently rewarded for his benevolence, in watching over a creature so interesting as Esther must have been—in marking her progress and receiving the tokens of her confidence and affection. But there were other rewards in store for him, which he dreamt not of, to recompense his work of faith and labor of love. In taking her into his house, and charging himself with the expense of her education and maintenance, he may have been regarded by some of his covetous neighbors, especially if he had a family of his own, as laying himself under a burden which a prudent man would have rather endeavored to avoid. But he thought not of this. He acted according to the spirit of the divine law, and the impulses of his own generous heart; and that from which selfishness would have turned away as a burden, he found eventually to be in every respect a precious treasure. A blessing followed him because he had pity upon the orphan.

Now, there are some remarks very obviously suggested by this part of the narrative. I should say that here we have a fine example of the practical power of true religion, in leading to a benevolent regard for the comfort and well-being of the unprotected. It cannot be denied indeed, that specimens of the same kind of benevolence are to be found among the heathen. The ties of kindred have been felt and acknowledged where the light of divine truth was never enjoyed, and there are on record acts of generosity and self-denial performed by men ignorant of the Bible, which put to shame the selfishness of many who live under the teaching of the word of God. But there is this difference; that Mordecai, in what he did for Esther, acted only in accordance with the maxims and spirit of the law which came from heaven—only did what the law positively enjoined, and what, as professing to be subject to it, it became him to do. One manifest purpose of the Mosaic dispensation was, while it separated the seed of Abraham from all other nations, to unite them closely among themselves as brethren. And this purpose it effected to a wonderful extent, notwithstanding the opposition which it had to encounter from the corrupt heart and groveling propensities of the people among whom it was set up.

Lecture 4: Esther 2:5-20

It is peculiarly interesting to notice, that it was during the captivity, when the Jews were scattered hither and thither throughout the Persian dominions, and when every man might have been supposed to have enough to do in attending to his own interests, and providing for his own family, that Mordecai took charge of his uncle's orphan daughter, and gave her a refuge in his own house. Whatever care and difficulty he had to undergo in supporting himself in the land of exile, he remembered the injunction of the law, "Ye shall not afflict any widow or fatherless child; if thou afflict them in any wise, and they cry unto me, I will surely hear their cry;" and the prophet's commentary upon it, "Is not this the fast that I have chosen, that thou deal thy bread to the hungry, and that thou bring the poor that are cast out to thy house? When thou seest the naked, that thou cover him; and that thou hide not thyself from thine own flesh?"

Now, while it is impossible for us to read what Mordecai did, without feeling that his memory deserves to be had in respect, as a man who had imbibed the spirit of the law, and who, amid many temptations to set its injunctions aside, endeavored to regulate his conduct by its requirements; while we see in him an exemplification of that principle of brotherly love, which the law so earnestly inculcates, let us not forget that the gospel of Christ is designed at once to deepen the feeling of brotherly affection, and to give it a far wider range of operation.

If the poor exiled Jew had compassion on his orphan niece, and brought her up as his own daughter, how sacred should the claims of orphanage be in the view of those who profess to follow Him who said, "Blessed are the merciful, for they shall obtain mercy;" and, "By this shall all men know that ye are my disciples, if ye love one another; a new commandment give I unto you, that ye love one another; as I have loved you, that ye also love each other."

The charities of the Jews were confined almost exclusively to those of their own nation. This was indeed a natural consequence of their being isolated from the rest of the world; a result of the particular light in which they were taught to regard the heathen, and in which the heathen in turn regarded them. But "in Christ Jesus there is neither Greek nor Jew, Barbarian nor Scythian, bond nor free; but all are one in Him." Not that the ties of ordinary relationship are weakened by the gospel, and that we are to overlook the special claims of kindred in the enlarged field which it opens up for the exercise of our benevolent affections. By no means. But we are to act toward all men as if they were our neighbors, and toward all who are of the household of faith as brethren. This is the lesson which we learn from our Lord's teaching, and more emphatically still from His example. And it must be confessed, to the honor of Christianity, that one circumstance which distinguishes the countries which have been even only in name brought under its influence, is the provision that has been made in various forms for the distresses of suffering humanity.

The institutions for the relief of the diseased, of the destitute, of the fatherless and the orphan, and of the erring who would fain return into the paths of rectitude, are to be regarded as so many evidences of what the gospel has effected for the removal of the temporal evils under which society groans. Different opinions there may well be as to the wisdom of the rules by which some of these institutions are governed, and of the means by which they seek the attainment of their objects; but there can be no dispute as to their benevolent design, or as to the point, that their origin is to be traced up to the diffusion of the knowledge of the Word of God. At the same time, my friends, I cannot help remarking, that there is something in the conduct of Mordecai, as recorded in the text, and of those who, like him, exercise their benevolence personally in assisting and protecting the helpless, and endeavoring to ameliorate their condition—something that raises it far above that of the people who contribute, however largely and willingly, toward the support of public institutions for the relief of the distressed. It is an easy matter for the wealthy to be charitable, when their gifts, administered by others, involve no sacrifice of time or labor, and no care and anxiety to themselves. But the noblest exercise of charity is exhibited when we take

Lecture 4: Esther 2:5-20

an interest personally in the well-being of the unprotected, and when they can look to us as their friends and counselors, to whom they can have recourse in their sorrows, and troubles, and difficulties.

It may not be that we have opportunity to act literally as Mordecai did, and to give shelter to the orphan in our own homes; but we only act in the spirit of the gospel of Christ, when, according to our means, we make some of the helpless the objects of our special care, and regard them as a trust committed to us by our heavenly Father. The exercise of the kindly affections toward any such carries in it its own reward, and with these labors of love on the part of His people God is well pleased.

But we pass now from this topic to consider verse 8-14: "So it came to pass, when the king's commandment and his decree was heard, and when many maidens were gathered together unto Shushan the palace, to the custody of Hegai, that Esther was brought also unto the king's house, to the custody of Hegai, keeper of the women. And the maiden pleased him, and she obtained kindness of him; and he speedily gave her her things for purification, with such things as belonged to her, and seven maidens, which were meet to be given her, out of the king's house: and he preferred her and her maids unto the best place of the house of the women. Esther had not showed her people nor her kindred; for Mordecai had charged her that she should not show it. And Mordecai walked every day before the court of the women's house, to know how Esther did, and what should become of her. Now when every maid's turn was come to go in to king Ahasuerus, after that she had been twelve months, according to the manner of the women, (for so were the days of their purifications accomplished, to wit, six months with oil of myrrh, and six months with sweet odors, and with other things for the purifying of the women:) Then thus came every maiden unto the king; whatsoever she desired was given her to go with her out of the house of the women unto the king's house. In the evening she went, and on the morrow she returned into the second house of the women, to the custody of Shaashgaz, the king's chamberlain, which kept the concubines: she came in unto the king no more, except the king delighted in her, and that she were called by name."

There is unquestionably a difficulty connected with the interpretation of verse 8. If Mordecai of his own accord presented Esther as a candidate for the royal favor, then he acted in opposition to the enactment of the law of Moses, which forbade that the daughters of Israel should be given to the heathen; and it would not be an apology for his conduct that he designed by what he did to advance the interests of his nation. What is forbidden by the law must not be done that good may come of it. Many interpreters, therefore, suppose that those who were commissioned to select the virgins for the king's seraglio executed their office without respect to the feelings of the parties interested, and that Esther was taken without there being any choice left, either to her or to Mordecai, in the matter. Others, indeed, would have it, that as the whole transaction was so manifestly providential, Mordecai may have received special intimation from heaven to bring his orphan cousin under the notice of the king's officers—in which case, certainly, he would have been free from blame. But there is nothing said in the history to warrant this opinion, and therefore we rather embrace the first supposition, as the most probable account that can be given of the affair. And it may be observed, that if it was regarded as a degradation by Mordecai that a child of Abraham should be united even to a heathen prince, still, according to the custom of the age, whether Esther was to be raised to the queenly dignity or not, like the others who were taken into the palace, she would ever afterwards rank as one of the king's wives or concubines.

Miserable and revolting to our minds as were the usages which then prevailed, and which still prevail in the East, and of which in this book we have a specimen, there was no abandoning of the female who had once been numbered among the royal favorites. She might not enjoy the smile of her lord, or exercise any influence over him, but she was not afterwards turned out into the world as a lost creature, to lead a life of infamy. She ended her days in the palace, if not in honor, at least not in

Lecture 4: Esther 2:5-20

disgrace. But whatever may have been the feelings of Mordecai and Esther, we see the special working of providence in her behalf. She obtained favor of the chief of the eunuchs above all the other maidens who had been committed to his care; so that, without solicitation on her part, not only was there more than ordinary indulgence shown toward her, but she was even treated with a degree of respect that seemed as it were the prelude to yet higher advancement.

The chief of the eunuchs was an officer of high rank, who enjoyed the full confidence of the king, and who had it in his power materially to forward the interests of any of the females who especially attracted his regard; and thus the commencement of Esther's life in the palace gave promise of a prosperous issue.

We cannot read this passage without remembering the resemblance between her history thus far and that of Joseph when he was sold into Egypt. When he was in the house of Potiphar, "his master saw that the Lord was with him, and that the Lord made all that he did to prosper in his hand. And Joseph found grace in his sight, and he served him: and he made him overseer over his house, and all that he had he put into his hand." And then again, when Joseph was imprisoned, "the Lord was with him, and showed him mercy, and gave him favor in the sight of the keeper of the prison. And the keeper of the prison committed to Joseph's hand all the prisoners that were in the prison; and whatsoever they did there, he was the doer of it." Similar, also, was the commencement of Daniel's history in the palace of Nebuchadnezzar. "God," it is said, "brought Daniel into favor and tender love with the prince of the eunuchs."

Now there can be no doubt that in all these cases there was something in the appearance and demeanor of these youthful Israelites that made a favorable impression upon the minds of those who had it in their power to contribute to their advancement, as we all feel that there are persons whose look and deportment attract us, and make us disposed to aid and oblige them, while we cannot well give any reason for it; but yet we learn from the sacred history that there was something more in these instances than the operation of natural sympathy—that there was a divine influence exerted, to gain for Daniel, and Joseph, and Esther, favor in the eyes of those who, humanly speaking, had so much power either to hinder or to forward their prosperity in the world. And if any of us have received favor at the hand of others, by which, in a strange and unaccountable way, we have obtained singular advantages, let us, while we are grateful to the instruments, look beyond them to Him by whose hand our lot is ordered, and who maketh all things work together for good to them that love Him.

But to go on with the narrative. It is said that "Esther had not showed her people nor her kindred: for Mordecai had charged her that she should not show it." We are not to suppose that she was instructed to practice duplicity, or to give a false statement if any question should be directly put to her; but merely that she was not unnecessarily to make known her origin. It could not have been that Mordecai was ashamed himself or would have her be ashamed to be known as a descendant of Abraham. On the contrary, the Jews have always, and with good reason, counted this a high honor. But at present Mordecai was not sure how far the fact of Esther's being a Jewess might stand in the way of her preferment, should it be known. Many Jews, indeed, from the time of Daniel, had been advanced to places of dignity under both the Babylonian and the Persian kings; but no female had risen to such honor as he had a presentiment was reserved for Esther, and as a matter of prudence, therefore, he counselled her to say nothing of her people or her kindred. Speaking. generally, as captives and exiles, the Jews were no doubt looked upon with contempt by the people among whom they were scattered, and it might be expedient for them sometimes to conceal their origin, although it would have been unmanly and unlawful expressly to deny it, and much more so to do violence to their religious convictions by denying it.

Lecture 4: Esther 2:5-20

In times of persecution, it was not necessary for the followers of Christ to come publicly forward with a profession of their faith in Him, thus courting destruction; but it would have been to make shipwreck of faith, if, when they were challenged, they had acted like Peter, disclaiming all connection with the Savior. And in ordinary cases, while the followers of Christ must always strive to act in a manner consistent with their profession, and so that He may not be dishonored by them, yet it is not necessary that they have their profession constantly in their mouth. There are occasions and circumstances which demand an avowal of their discipleship, as when by their silence they would compromise the truth, and give it to be thought that they approved of words and deeds which in their heart they disclaim; but often there is expediency, and wisdom also, in letting our Christianity be known rather by our conduct than by our words.

But next in the narrative we have an account of Mordecai's anxiety for the welfare of his former charge. Verse 11: "And Mordecai walked every day before the court of the women's house, to know how Esther did, and what should become of her." This renders it probable that he had some occupation about the palace, although he did not yet sit in the king's gate; for otherwise it would have been dangerous for him to walk every day before the court of the women's house, a place which was guarded with the most jealous care. At all events, however, whether he incurred hazard or not, he was so deeply interested in the fate of Esther, that day after day he was found watching any opportunity that might occur, to learn from some eunuchs passing in or out how Esther fared, and what her prospects were. Perhaps there may have been others in similar circumstances with himself, solicitous about their daughters or friends; and if so, his conduct would attract the less notice. But what we have principally to remark, is the paternal interest which all along he took in the orphan whom he had reared. She was evidently his chief earthly care; and now, when she was as it were taken out of his hand, and no longer dependent upon his bounty and his kindness, he was as much concerned about her, as when in her childhood she had sat upon his knee and returned his affectionate embrace. And so parental love is always exhibited. Although the grown-up youth is treated differently from the mere child, and there may be fewer of the words and outward tokens of endearment than there were, the heart of the parent has not become colder; but there are now deep anxieties connected with the progress of the youth, with his settlement in life, and his whole future career, which were not felt before; and though it may not outwardly appear, the most solicitous and intense affection is experienced by the parent, at the time when the objects of it are beginning to feel that they can do something for themselves in the world. Then I would say that there is a lesson here for the young.

How can they repay in any measure—for fully they can never repay—the tenderness of their godly parents to them in their youth, and the anxiety which has been felt on their account as they advanced toward maturity? In one way only—by endeavoring to pursue the path which leads to present respectability and usefulness, and which Christ in His word has marked out as that which His disciples must tread. As there could not be a greater earthly satisfaction than that which a parent derives from marking the progress of a dutiful child, who gives evidence of being influenced by the love and by the law of Christ; so there are no deeper pangs than those which are inflicted by filial waywardness and depravity. And in like manner, as there could not be a better omen of a man's well-doing in the world than when the beginning of his career is marked by reverence for his parents, and desire to make them happy, so there could not be a more gloomy presage of wreck, and ruin, and misery, than is to be found in the case of anyone who has lived only to wound his parents' hearts.

"My son, hear the instruction of thy father, and forsake not the law of thy mother; for they shall be an ornament of grace unto thy head, and chains about thy neck."

Lecture 4: Esther 2:5-20

It is not necessary that we comment upon the verses from 12th to 14th. They present to us a picture of a luxurious and voluptuous court, which is utterly inconsistent with all the usages of European nations, not to speak of its repugnance to the law of Christ. Yet, like other descriptions of what is revolting to all right feeling, it may be turned to some profitable account. There are two remarks which it suggests to us.

Firstly

In the first place, when we read here and elsewhere of the domestic manners and enjoyments of the despots and great men of the East, where polygamy with all its attendant evils has prevailed from the earliest times, we may well feel thankful that we live under the light of Christianity, by which these abominable evils have been swept away. The law which Christ proclaimed was a republication of that which was designed for man at the beginning, that there should be one husband and one wife. It is the prevalence of this law, with the other softening and purifying influences of Christian truth, which has given you your happy homes, where, with the moderate supply of all your temporal necessities, in the interchange of mutual affection and confidence, with the friend dearer than all other friends, with the counselor in difficulty, the sympathizer in sorrow, and the gladdener of your prosperity, you enjoy satisfaction and happiness to which the palace of the king of Persia, with all its luxuries, was an utter stranger.

Secondly

In the second place, while every well constituted mind shrinks from the contemplation of the picture of Eastern licentiousness; and while the gospel has exercised a mighty influence in elevating the standard of public morality; yet alas, we have great cause to be humbled when we think of the prevailing dissoluteness and profligacy of our own times.

The Eastern voluptuary did not cast off the victims of his guilty passion and leave them to die in wretchedness and infamy. But the modern man of pleasure, the seducer of the innocent, is more cruel. He degrades his poor miserable victims, and then rejects them, that they may plunge into deeper misery, and make shipwreck both of body and soul. O guard, my young friends, against the alluring voice that would lead you the first step astray; and pray for grace that you may be kept from those pollutions and lusts by which so many are dragged into perdition.

But we now come to consider verses 15-20: "Now when the turn of Esther, the daughter of Abihail, the uncle of Mordecai, who had taken her for his daughter, was come to go in unto the king, she required nothing but what Hegai the king's chamberlain, the keeper of the women, appointed. And Esther obtained favor in the sight of all them that looked upon her. So Esther was taken unto king Ahasuerus into his house royal in the tenth month, which is the month Tebeth, in the seventh year of his reign. And the king loved Esther above all the women, and she obtained grace and favor in his sight more than all the virgins; so that he set the royal crown upon her head and made her queen instead of Vashti. Then the king made a great feast unto all his princes and his servants, even Esther's feast; and he made a release to the provinces, and gave gifts, according to the state of the king. And when the virgins were gathered together the second time, then Mordecai sat in the king's gate. Esther had not yet showed her kindred nor her people; as Mordecai had charged her; for Esther did the commandment of Mordecai, like as when she was brought up with him."

It seems to be implied in the text, that while the other maidens endeavored by dress and ornament to make an impression upon the heart of the king, Esther had recourse to no such artifice. If she was to gain the royal favor, which no doubt she desired to do, she trusted to her native graces and accomplishments as the means of obtaining it, rather than to the splendor of her attire. And such will always be the procedure of true beauty and modesty. Excessive attention to the decoration of the person,

Lecture 4: Esther 2:5-20

and the lavish use of gaudy ornament, indicate the consciousness of some personal defect, and are inconsistent alike with good taste, with female delicacy, and with the law of Scripture. Esther, in her comparatively simple and plain attire, gained the affection of the king; her *real* accomplishments procured for her grace and favor in his sight; so that he set the royal crown upon her head, and the orphan Jewess became queen of Persia. It may be noticed here, that while the working of the divine providence is manifest in all this, there is nothing in the circumstance itself outwardly very remarkable. Under the most despotic governments it has often happened, that the highest honors of the state have been conferred upon individuals raised from the very lowest ranks of life. Under free governments, also, like our own, the pathway to the greatest preferment is open to all, according to the use they make of their talents and opportunities. It is only where there is a haughty aristocracy standing between the throne and the people that there is a monopoly of honors. But at all events, so little was the article of rank and birth thought of at this time in connection with the queenly dignity in Persia, that Esther's parentage had not been made a subject of inquiry, and it was not known that she was a Jewess.

Upon her elevation, we are told that the king made a great feast, performed acts of favor and mercy in the provinces, and gave gifts to his servants. By some means or other, Mordecai shared in the royal favor, for when the virgins were gathered together the second time, no doubt to pay homage to the new queen, then Mordecai sat in the king's gate. This was not a place so humble and menial as the expression would seem to imply. When Daniel was advanced by Nebuchadnezzar, we read that he sat in the gate of the king. The office is said to have been one of considerable responsibility, and filled only by those who were counted peculiarly trustworthy. He who sat at the gate of the king was ready to obey any command which the king might issue; and among the Persians it was usually men of some note who occupied this place.

Thus, then, by a special providence, Esther and her guardian were both promoted, because they had to subserve important purposes, which neither of them at the time had any conception of. It is interesting, however, to read the statement, verse 20: "Esther had not yet showed her kindred, nor her people; as Mordecai had charged her; for Esther did the commandment of Mordecai, like as when she was brought up with him."

Her elevation did not make her head giddy, or lead her to forget the lessons which she had learnt under the humble roof of Mordecai. Many people when they prosper in the world look down with contempt upon the friends of their youth, even upon some who have assisted them to gain their present elevation, yea, even sometimes upon their very parents, whose honest industry and hard labor secured for them the education which has been the means of their advancement. Nothing could more clearly indicate a bad heart and a groveling mind than such conduct. The man who is chargeable with it is truly an object of contempt. While, on the other hand, there is something noble and refreshing in conduct like Esther's, when benefits conferred are remembered and repaid, and worldly honor, instead of chilling warms the affections of those who have been raised to it towards the friends who helped them onward.

Now, in conclusion, there is an application I would make of the whole subject, which is to be regarded as rather suggested by it, than as directly deducible from it, or founded on it. Esther's advancement from low estate to share the throne of Persia, reminds us of what God does for His people, in raising them from the miry clay to sit with Christ upon His throne. The language of Ezekiel, in describing the privileges conferred upon Israel is singularly applicable here: "When thou wast born none eye pitied thee, but thou wast cast out into the open field, to the loathing of thy person, in the day that thou wast born, Now when I passed by thee, and looked upon thee, behold thy time was the time of love. Then washed I thee with water, and I anointed thee with oil; I clothed thee also with broidered work, and covered thee with silk; I decked thee also with ornaments, and put a beautiful crown upon thine head; and thy renown went forth among the heathen for thy beauty, for it was perfect, through my comeliness which I had put upon thee, saith the Lord God."

Such, in the language of poetry, is God's dealing toward His people. But the reality surpasses all that the most glowing language can describe. Through faith in Christ Jesus, sinners are delivered from guilt and wrath; received into God's family; made partakers of a divine nature; exalted to be heirs of God, and joint heirs with Jesus Christ. Is this your privilege, believers? Have you been brought nigh to God by the blood of Jesus, and made to sit in heavenly places with Christ? Oh, then, walk worthy of your dignity; and let the sense of the benefits you have received stir you up to render more and more fully the sacrifices of praise and of willing obedience, which in the sight of God are acceptable through Christ Jesus.

Amen.

Lecture 5: Esther 2:21-23, 3:1-5

In the last lecture, we entered on the consideration of the personal history of Esther, which may be truly said to be invested with all the interest of romance. At a very tender age deprived of both her parents, and in a strange land, she might have been regarded as one of those unfortunates who, by a mysterious providence, seem born only to suffer adversity. But a bright destiny awaited her. Mordecai her cousin took pity on the orphan, received her into his house, and brought her up as his daughter. Thus she never knew the bitterness of being left unprotected in the world; and as she grew up fair and graceful, and, what was better still, dutiful and modest, and intelligent and pious, Mordecai reaped the reward of his compassion, and felt that his youthful charge was not a burden to him but a blessing. We repeat again our belief, that he did not present Esther, of his own accord, as a candidate for the royal favor; but that she was taken into the palace without either his or her own consent. At the same time, as there was no appeal against such exertion of despotic power, Mordecai might soon take a favorable view of her removal from him, and cherish the hope that her beauty and accomplishments might win the favor of the king, and raise her to the place from which Vashti had been degraded. And this hope, however wild it may have seemed to be, was realized. "Artaxerxes loved Esther above all the virgins who were brought to him, so that he set the royal crown upon her head and made her queen instead of Vashti." Mordecai, also, although we are not informed for what reason, was promoted, he sat in the king's gate.

This brings us now to consider verses 21-23: "In those days, while Mordecai sat in the king's gate, two of the king's chamberlains, Bigthan and Teresh, of those which kept the door, were worth, and sought to lay hand on the king Ahasuerus. And the thing was known to Mordecai, who told it unto Esther the queen: and Esther certified the king thereof in

Lecture 5: Esther 2:21-23, 3:1-5

Mordecai's name. And when inquisition was made of the matter, it was found out; therefore, they were both hanged on a tree: and it was written in the book of the chronicles before the king."

History is full of examples of plots and assassinations in the palaces of Eastern princes. Favoritism, founded usually upon mere caprice, is one of the characteristics of a despotic government. Then envy and hatred are naturally excited in consequence of this, among such as think themselves as well entitled to preferment as those on whom it has been bestowed. And thus it comes to pass, that the life of the monarch who seems to have the persons and property of all his subjects at his disposal, is in reality the most insecure of all. On the single word of Artaxerxes depended the life and fortune of many millions, and more especially of those who were more immediately about him; but, as we learn from the text, he himself, in all the proud consciousness of irresponsible power, was, when he thought not of it, on the very point of being struck down by the dagger of the assassin.

We have no means of knowing what led the two chamberlains to conspire against the king. An angry word, or some apparent slight or insult, may have provoked them to revenge, or they may have been bribed by other parties whom the king had injured. But whatever was the cause of their treasonable design, they had the easiest possible way open to them of secretly accomplishing it, through the office they held. The narrative in the text is given so briefly that we are not told how Mordecai came to discover the plot. He may have been requested to become an accomplice, in order that by his assistance the actual perpetrators of the bloody deed might the more easily effect their escape. But whether in this way, or by overhearing the conspirators as they were speaking together of the time and manner of carrying out their purpose, he became aware of it, he immediately took measures to counteract the dark design. Another person might have been glad to secure for himself the credit of making a discovery so important to the king. But Mordecai, who thought more of Esther's interests than of his own, made her the channel of communication, that she might be raised yet higher in the esteem and love of her husband, which she could not fail to be when she appeared as the preserver of his life. At the same time, while Mordecai was careful of her interests without reference to his own, she repaid his kindness with equal generosity, giving the king to understand that she had discovered the plot against him by information conveyed to her from him who sat at the gate. Upon careful investigation the whole conspiracy was detected; the guilty parties were put to death, and the affair was noted among the other memorable incidents of the king's reign, in the public annals of the kingdom. Yet, when the danger was averted, and the event recorded, the indolent and luxurious king thought no more of the matter, and Mordecai remained unrewarded for his fidelity. But though unrequited in the meantime, his name was in the record, and his good service was singularly noticed afterwards.

Let us now make some practical improvement of the incidents related in these verses. There are three topics suggested by them, to which we may briefly advert.

Firstly

In the first place, we cannot read this narrative without drawing from it a lesson as to the uncertainty of life. It might seem as if the ordinary contingencies to which those are exposed who traverse the ocean, who have to rush into the battlefield, or who are engaged in other perilous employments, could not possibly reach the luxurious inmate of a palace, who is guarded by troops of armed men, and whose wish can command everything that pertains to safety, health, and enjoyment. But the destroying sword may be hanging as by a single hair over the head of the ruler of a vast empire, making his life as contingent as that of the mariner when the storm suddenly bursts forth upon him, or of the soldier when he is under the thick fire of the enemy.

Lecture 5: Esther 2:21-23, 3:1-5

Humanly speaking, those who occupy the middle class of society, whose wants are supplied without any danger or painful toil, and who have nothing to dread from the envy and enmity of others, live in greatest security, and have least occasion to fear what is usually called accident, as affecting their life. But even they have no better reason than others to imagine themselves secure. "The silver cord may be loosed, and the golden bowl broken" in a moment, and when there is no external violence put forth to give the decisive blow. This we learn from the experience of every day, and yet men will hardly open their ears to hear this statement pressed upon their attention: it is so often urged. It would be well, however, if you would fix your minds upon it for a moment. If many around you, without respect to age or condition, have been cut down with little warning, have had their fairest plans and prospects made void by sudden disease, followed by unexpected death, the same may be your fate. Now if the stroke descends upon you while you are unconverted, you are forever lost.

Is it then a small thing we ask of you, is it not what the forecasting sagacity which you exercise with regard to worldly things would warrant us to suppose that you would do, when we beseech you to keep in view the end and measure of your days, and to live so under the power of the world to come as if at every moment you might be summoned into it? My meaning is not, that we should go about with the fear of death upon us continually, and look upon this world as a graveyard, all gloomy and terrible. To live under the servile fear of death is not the way to prepare for it. But to have our faith resting upon Christ, the sure foundation, to have the anchor of hope cast within the veil, and to have all our temporal interests so subordinated to those which are eternal, as to shew that we look for our proper existence hereafter, this is to be prepared for the great summons when it is sent to us. And the practical use which we should make of the uncertainty of the present life, is to have a sure interest in Christ, which will render the life to come all certainty and blessedness to us. If a moment transports the victim of sin and folly, the impenitent and unbelieving, into the place of darkness; a moment, a quick knock by Christ at the door of His people, raises them to the region of light and glory, where they see Him as He is, and rejoice forever in His love.

Secondly

In the second place, the narrative before us teaches us, that whatever station in providence men are called to fill, they may be instrumental in conferring important benefits on others. Mordecai, a man of humble rank, exercising compassion and benevolence, trained up the orphan girl who became queen of Persia, and through whose instrumentality vast benefits were conferred upon the Jews. Mordecai, who sat in the king's gate, saved the life of the king. And many incidents there are, recorded both in ancient and modern history, which illustrate the truth that in human society the several classes are so dependent on one another, that the highest may be made debtor to the lowest, and that the humblest may render services to those above them, which cannot be adequately repaid. Such fidelity as Mordecai exhibited has been often exemplified.

But the remark which we have just made may be transposed to services more important than those which have reference to the present life and its concerns. What an immense power, for instance, is possessed by the nurse to whose care the children of a family are committed, and who, by the faithful execution of her trust, may implant the seeds of truth in the youthful heart so deeply that no worldly influence will afterwards efface them. There is something higher here than the mere saving of life. It is good service when the nurse interested in her charge watches over them in their infant troubles, and spends many a sleepless night when disease has fastened on them, and when the hand of affection must be continually about them; but surely it is higher service—service of the kind which it is scarcely possible to recompense—when the growth of right principle in the young, the knowledge of divine truth, and the practical exemplification of the power of the truth, can be traced back, as it can sometimes be, to the lessons and training of the nursery. And what we have remarked with respect to Christian fidelity in one particular department of service, may be applied generally.

Every follower of Christ, in whatever sphere he moves, may do incalculable good to those around him, even to those who are placed high above him. Everyone may be instrumental in bringing the knowledge of eternal life within the reach of some who are perishing for lack of it. And the very exhibition of faithfulness to Christ, in discharging the ordinary duties of life so that He may be glorified, has a power in it to arrest the attention of the thoughtless, and to commend the gospel even to some who are disposed to regard a very high profession of religion as little better than hypocrisy. Let no Christian, then, say, "I can do nothing." If you cannot do so much as you would, a consistent and faithful life, spent in all the unobtrusiveness of true humility, will be a lesson to some that may be productive of vast benefit.

Thirdly

In the third place, from the narrative under review we are led to think of a record of unrequited deeds. Mordecai's information saved the life of the king and was duly noticed in the annals of the kingdom; but it lay there for a considerable time, apparently as a dead letter. There is evidently a twofold application that may be made of this particular. The acts of wicked men are all recorded and will be brought into judgment. The hand of justice does not always follow the perpetration of the evil act. Sentence against sin is not always executed speedily; and therefore, transgressors harden themselves in their wickedness. Yet the retribution, if it be slow, is certain. Sinners forget their sins; but a book of remembrance is kept on high, and there will be a rendering to every man according to his works.

But it is not so much this aspect of the question that is presented to us in the text, as the more pleasing one, that the services of God's people are recorded, and are not suffered to pass unrewarded in the end. The reward, indeed, may not come in the present life. The faithful disciples of Christ have often been left to contend with the world's opposition, and to fall victims to the world's enmity, just on account of their steadfast attachment to the truth. Not, indeed, that they have been ever so deserted by their Lord as to be without the precious consolations of His Spirit, and that good hope which nerves the soul for any trial; but outwardly it has often happened, as it happens still, that they appear to be forgotten, and that their works of faith and love are not acknowledged *here*. But they are all recorded, and the record will be produced hereafter.

The Scripture teaches us this very plainly. "God is not unrighteous," says the apostle, writing to the Hebrews, "to forget your work and labor of love, which ye have shewed toward His name, in that ye have ministered to the saints and do minister." "The judgment will be set and the books will be opened." "Then shall the King say unto them on his right hand, Come, ye blessed of my Father, inherit the kingdom prepared for you from the foundation of the world: for I was an hungered, and ye gave me meat: I was thirsty, and ye gave me drink: I was a stranger, and ye took me in: naked, and ye clothed me: I was sick, and ye visited me: I was in prison, and ye came unto me: and inasmuch as ye have done it unto one of the least of these my brethren, ye have done it unto me." The reward, then, is sure; and although it is not the mere hope of reward that is the great stimulant of Christ's people, but love to Him who first loved them, yet the hope of reward is presented to them as an encouragement to zeal, and perseverance, and faithfulness. "Wherefore, my beloved brethren," says the apostle, "be ye steadfast, unmovable, always abounding in the work of the Lord, forasmuch as ye know that your labor is not in vain in the Lord."

But we now proceed to consider chapter 3 verses 1-6: "After these things did king Ahasuerus promote Haman the son of Hammedatha the Agagite, and advanced him, and set his seat above all the princes that were with him. And all the king's servants, that were in the king's gate,

Lecture 5: Esther 2:21-23, 3:1-5

bowed, and reverenced Haman: for the king had so commanded concerning him. But Mordecai bowed not, nor did him reverence. Then the king's servants, which were in the king's gate, said unto Mordecai, Why transgressest thou the king's commandment? Now it came to pass, when they spake daily unto him, and he hearkened not unto them, that they told Haman, to see whether Mordecai's matters would stand: for he had told them that he was a Jew. And when Haman saw that Mordecai bowed not, nor did him reverence, then was Haman full of wrath. And he thought scorn to lay hands on Mordecai alone: for they had shewed him the people of Mordecai: wherefore Haman sought to destroy all the Jews that were throughout the whole kingdom of Ahasuerus, even the people of Mordecai."

In these verses, we are introduced to the history of a personage, upon whose procedure great part of the interest of the whole narrative turns: Haman the Agagite, or Amalekite. It has been supposed from his being designated the Agagite, that he was descended from the kings of Amalek, whose royal title seems to have been Agag, as Pharaoh was for a long time that of the kings of Egypt. But whether this be true or not, it is allowed by all that the term Agagite implies that Haman was of the race of Amalek, between whom and the Jews there had been, from the days of Moses, the most bitter enmity.

The country of the Amalekites at this time, no doubt, formed part of the empire of Persia, and Haman, if he was of royal descent, may, with his family, have been at the court of Artaxerxes, as a kind of hostage for the submission and good conduct of his countrymen. By some means he had contrived to attract the favorable regard of the king, who, guided in this case as in others by mere caprice, took him into his intimate confidence, and "set his seat above all the princes that were with him;" *i.e.,* made him his chief minister of state. Such sudden advancement, as we had occasion to remark before, has always been so common in despotic governments as to excite no surprise. Daniel, a captive, was raised to high honor at Babylon, and, as we shall soon see, Mordecai's turn came, all unexpectedly, to bask in the sunshine of the royal favor. Haman, of course, would possess certain talents and qualities that recommended him to the king; but his real character, as it is developed in this book, was that of a haughty, vain, revengeful and cruel man, who, like all sycophants, was overbearing and oppressive to those beneath him, in proportion to the servility with which he himself cringed to his master.

The homage that is paid to rank and dignity, even in free countries like our own, is sometimes excessive, and we might say humiliating to witness; but among the Orientals it almost amounts to worship. The king is approached as if he were a heavenly being, and his favorites share in the adulation. So we read in verse 2, that "all the king's servants, that were in the king's gate, bowed and reverenced Haman: for the king had so commanded concerning him. But Mordecai bowed not, nor did him reverence."

The conduct of Mordecai has been differently accounted for by different writers, as there is nothing said from which we can gather the real motive by which he was influenced. Some suppose that he refused to pay the prescribed homage, because it exceeded that which it was proper to pay to a mere mortal. But it seems much more likely, that his refusal was grounded on the circumstance of Haman's being an Amalekite—a nation which lay under the malediction of Jehovah, and whose very name was hateful to the Jews. That he should do reverence to one of that accursed race, which would have been extirpated ages before if Israel had been careful to comply with the divine commandment—was what Mordecai could not bring his mind to, although it was required by royal edict. And so, while all others fell down before the favorite, kissing the dust beneath his feet, Mordecai sat immoveable, and no doubt eyed with disdain, both him who received and those who paid the reverence. Now it becomes a question how far he was justified in acting thus, and it is to be regretted that he was not so pressed upon the point as to be constrained to give a formal reason for his conduct.

Lecture 5: Esther 2:21-23, 3:1-5

The commandment of the king was very express, and Mordecai manifestly exposed himself to imminent danger by disregarding it. If, indeed, his objection to pay homage to Haman was founded upon a conviction that such homage amounted to something like idolatry, then we might regard his refusal as ranking him with the three illustrious youths who braved the wrath of Nebuchadnezzar, rather than they would submit to worship the image which he had set up. But we can scarcely take this view of the matter, as it is not likely that Mordecai would have withheld from the king himself the outward reverence which the law and usage of the country required. But if it was because Haman was of the seed of Amalek, that the Jew would not bow to him nor do him reverence, then intense must have been the detestation of that race, when he would rather run the risk of incurring the displeasure of the king than pay respect to one of them who stood so high in the royal favor. Yet we conceive that he might feel himself fully vindicated in his own conscience for acting as he did. It was after all, a high religious scruple by which he was influenced.

By the law of Moses, the Amalekites were condemned to perpetual infamy. No earthly rank or station could blot out or modify that sentence. In this view of the subject, Mordecai would have supposed himself an apostate from his religion, had he done reverence to Haman, and therefore he refused to do it, whatever might be the consequence to himself. We cannot but respect such a feeling as this, generated as it was by regard for the divine law. It could not be appreciated by the other servants of the king, who may have attributed Mordecai's conduct to a sullen and haughty temper: but, although the matter in itself was apparently unimportant, it was an evidence of real heroism of character in this man to obey the dictate of conscience at the hazard of personal suffering.

True religion does not interfere with the discharge of the ordinary courtesies of life, nor does it forbid our rendering that honor to rank and station which is their due. But when vice and real infamy are shrouded under high rank, the Christian must beware of acting, so as to make it supposed that the rank forms an apology for the vice and infamy or renders them less hateful than they really are.

But to prosecute the narrative, we find that Mordecai's fellow-servants, noticing the disrespect with which he treated Haman, were not disposed to let his conduct pass without comment. Verses 2-4: They said unto him, "why transgressest thou the king's commandment? Now, it came to pass, when they spoke daily unto him, and he hearkened not unto them, that they told Haman, to see whether Mordecai's matters would stand; for he had told them that he was a Jew." They naturally wondered that anyone should venture to disobey the king's order, because such procedure was punishable with death, whoever might be the offender. Mere personal dislike was not sufficient to account for Mordecai's exposing himself to such hazard; and therefore, they continued to expostulate with him upon the subject, until they drew from him the acknowledgment, that as a Jew, he could not pay homage to Haman. Whether he explained all the circumstances, and the particular relation in which, as a Jew, he felt himself placed toward an Amalekite, we are not informed. But thus much was made plain, that it was because he was a Jew that he would not in this instance obey the edict of the king.

The best of men have their enemies; and more especially, when an opportunity can be found of gaining the favor of the great, by apparent zeal for their honor, mere flatterers will seek their own advancement at the expense of those men of high principle, who will not stoop to acts of mean servility. So it fared with Mordecai.

It would seem that Haman, dazzled with his elevation, and gratified with the sight of so many of the king's officers prostrating themselves before him, had not for a season observed the Jew sitting apart, and looking with mingled contempt and indignation from day to day upon the whole scene. But at length, some of the officious courtiers, who wished to insinuate themselves into the good graces of the haughty favorite, informed him of the circumstance, and pointed to the man who was bold

Lecture 5: Esther 2:21-23, 3:1-5

enough to set at nought the king's commandment, and to treat his prime minister with disrespect. His attention being thus excited, he marked the incident, "and when Haman saw that Mordecai bowed not, nor did him reverence, then was Haman full of wrath."

It is to be regarded as a kind of retribution, in the case of ungodly and wicked men, that the very irregularity and violence of their passions contains in itself what is sufficient to embitter the whole cup of their enjoyment. This is matter of universal experience. In the instance before us, it is very plain, that Mordecai's unbending and contemptuous attitude, rendered Haman altogether indifferent to the homage which was rendered to him by others. Formerly he had retired from his attendance upon the king, through the crowd of obsequious and prostrate slaves, with the highest desires of his heart gratified. His greatness was acknowledged. His will was law. There was no man in the kingdom next to the sovereign himself to whom such incense was offered by all.

He had reached a higher elevation than the greatest nobles of the kingdom occupied. Unbounded power and wealth were within his grasp, and what more could he wish for? But now, one incident, in itself so trifling that we wonder it could have even occasioned him pain for a moment, strips his grandeur and power of all their charms. Mordecai will not bow to him, nor do him reverence. The slavish homage of thousands ceases to gratify him, because this one man— a Jew, will not recognize his greatness, nor honor him. His feeling is brought out afterwards very graphically in the history, when, after recounting to his family and friends all the dignities and advantages which, through the favor of the king, he enjoyed, he says: "all this availeth me nothing, so long as I see Mordecai the Jew, sitting at the king's gate."

I have adverted already to the hereditary enmity of the Jews to the Amalekites: and there is no doubt that the enmity was reciprocal. It is not fanciful to suppose that it was transmitted from generation to generation, among the latter as well as among the former. And a reason can be assigned for this. So far back as the days of Moses, when Balaam was hired by the king of Moab to curse Israel, and when against his will he was constrained to bless them; the destinies of Israel and Amalek were represented by the prophet as antagonistic.

Of Israel, Balaam said: "his king shall be higher than Agag, and his kingdom shall be exalted." And again: "Amalek was the first of the nations, but his latter end shall be that he perish forever." Very probable it is that Balaam's predictions were handed down by tradition from age to age, and that the children of Amalek were taught in this way, as well as by the incursions made on some occasions upon their territories by the kings of Israel and Judah, to regard the Jews as their irreconcilable foes. This consideration, then, we may suppose aggravated the wrath of Haman, when he found that the only individual who refused to humble himself before him was Mordecai the Jew. His whole soul was fired with the insult, and nothing could give him pleasure until he had his revenge.

Now, it may be thought by some, that the case of Haman allowing himself to be so chafed and perturbed by a trifle, as to be made miserable in the midst of so many advantages, is to be regarded as altogether extreme and without parallel; but, as has been already said, we believe, that on examination, it will be found that the wicked always receive part of their punishment in the violence of some unhallowed passion which blinds them to all the real benefits of their lot.

Is there not a gnawing disease in the heart of the covetous man, for example, which prevents him from enjoying the good things which are placed within his reach, just because he has not yet acquired all that he wishes to possess. And still, as he gets more and more, is he not as far as ever from being satisfied, since he has not yet reached the point at which he aims. Or again, look to the man who is the slave of envy, and mark how miserable this base passion makes him. He has ample means of enjoyment, which he can call his own; but his neighbor has something which pleases him better, and just because that one thing is awanting to himself, he can find no satisfaction in the varied blessings which a kind Providence has showered upon him. His neighbor's good is to him what

Lecture 5: Esther 2:21-23, 3:1-5

Mordecai at the king's gate was to Haman. In like manner, I might advert to the working of the more violent passions of anger and revenge, as a cause of intense torment to those who cherish them, and as altogether preventing them from taking advantage of many sources of happiness which lie open to them on every side. I might also allude to the misery which wounded vanity and affronted pride often bring to those who have high notions of their own importance, as when a trifling word or action will discompose them for many days together, and deprive them of their relish for the things that formerly pleased them, and made them happy. But enough has been said to show how by a just retribution the ungodly, following their natural tendencies and passions, work out their own punishment.

How different is the picture presented to us, where grace reigns in the heart! Although corruption is not altogether eradicated from the spiritual man, yet its power is subdued; the fierce passions are tamed, love takes the place of envy, malignity, and wrath: and the believer, seeking and finding his chief enjoyment in God, remains comparatively unruffled by those incidents which breed so much vexation and disquietude in the breast of the ungodly. The wise man says, that "he who is of a merry heart hath a continual feast;" and emphatically it may be said, that the heart in which the Spirit of God dwells, is a peaceful sanctuary, the seat of pure enjoyment.

I would now conclude the present lecture with one remark—that Christ's people must endeavor to exhibit the difference which grace effects between them and the unbelieving world, in the power which they have been enabled to gain over the violent impulses and passions of their nature. My friends, if we are as much at the mercy of anger, and envy, and covetousness, and pride, as those are who make no profession of religion, it is too manifest that we do not know Christ and have not been baptized with His Spirit. The great work of the Spirit in sanctification, is to raise us to the likeness of Christ. Let it be our aim, therefore, to be fellow workers with Him in this, that we may be known as the followers

of Jesus, who was meek and lowly in heart, and who, amid all the world's opposition and cruel persecution, still possessed His soul in patience.
   Amen.

Lecture 6: Esther 3:6-11

The last lecture introduced to our notice Haman the Agagite, or Amalekite, from whose history the remaining part of the book derives much of its interest. Having by some means or other insinuated himself into the favor of King Artaxerxes, he was promoted by that prince to the highest honor in the kingdom, and by royal edict was declared worthy to receive such marks of reverence as were shown to the king himself.

There was one man, however, who would not pay him homage, Mordecai the Jew. Even at the hazard of incurring the displeasure of the king, and being visited with capital punishment, he refused to prostrate himself before Haman, although in this matter he stood alone.

At first the haughty favorite did not observe the disrespect which the Jew manifested toward him, being elated by the profound reverence which was paid him by so many others. But in a short time some of Mordecai's fellow-servants, who were desirous to raise themselves in the favor of the great man, drew his attention to the contemptuous attitude which Mordecai maintained: and when Haman saw that this one individual took no notice of him, he was filled with wrath. The servile adulation of the multitude ceased to gratify his vanity and to give him pleasure: he could think of nothing but the studied insult which, from day to day, was put upon him by this man. This brings us to verse 6: "Now *he* thought scorn to lay hands on Mordecai alone: for they had shewed him the people of Mordecai: wherefore Haman sought to destroy all the Jews that were throughout the whole kingdom of Ahasuerus: even the people of Mordecai."

We can easily conceive how a haughty, vain, and wicked man, ignorant of the law of God, might have been stirred up to inflict the direst vengeance upon the individual who publicly treated him with contempt. For very often more trifling insults are fearfully resented by those who have been better taught, and who have been brought up under the influence of better principles than Haman was. Few passions are more fierce than those which are excited by wounded pride or vanity. And while it is what may properly be called *vindictive* in its nature, yet it is not like violent anger, which bursts forth and flies at once upon its object. The malignant feeling engendered by the insult real or supposed which humbles pride and vanity, can postpone vengeance. It can brood over the wrong which has excited it, and can lay its dark plans deliberately, in order that the vengeance may be complete. It was thus that Haman was exercised under the intense desire he felt to have satisfaction for the contempt and scorn with which Mordecai treated him. A single word from his mouth could have been the death warrant of his adversary, but that would have been poor revenge. He must strike a heavier blow.

Satan is always ready to take advantage of the season when the mind is perturbed by any strong passion, in order to hurry his victims onward to some act of violence, from which in other circumstances they would have shrunk. Haman at this time was precisely in such a mood as made him an easy prey to the enemy. His self-importance, his worldly grandeur, the king's favor, all set at nought by Mordecai, aggravated his deadly resentment. Then he was ready to receive the suggestion, "Will it be enough to crush the presumptuous slave who has dishonored me? Nay, he is but *one* of a race who are the irreconcilable enemies of Amalek—let the whole race, then, perish, that the insult may be wiped out which has been put upon the man whom the king delighteth to honor."

It could not have been but by Satanic influence, that a scheme of such vast and daring atrocity was devised. There is nothing said in the history to show that the disposition of Haman was habitually cruel; that he was one who would have taken pleasure in inflicting pain, for no reason but to gratify a propensity of his nature. From the brief glances we obtain of his domestic life, he seems to have enjoyed the confidence and affection

Lecture 6: Esther 3:6-11

of his family, as far as was compatible with the usages of the age and country; a circumstance which certainly seems to warrant the conclusion, that he was not of a temper unmixedly cruel and tyrannical. But when the master passion of revenge took possession of him, then by working upon it Satan transformed him into a very fiend. And it has always been one of the devices of the enemy, to drive men into criminal excesses to their own ruin, through the instrumentality of some favorite lust or appetite.

It was the covetous spirit of Judas that opened a way to the tempter to hurry him on to betray the Savior. It was an unmanly fear on the part of Pilate, lest he should be misrepresented to the Roman emperor, that the tempter took occasion of to lead him, in opposition to all his convictions, to deliver up Jesus to be crucified. All need to be upon their guard, then, against the wiles of the crafty adversary, and to strive to have their desires and feelings so kept under the control of the divine law, that he may not through their own sinful inadvertence obtain the mastery over them, and lead them captive at his will.

But we proceed now to consider verse 7: "In the first month, that is the month Nisan, in the twelfth year of king Ahasuerus, they cast Pur, that is, the lot, before Haman from day to day, and from month to month, to the twelfth month, that is the month Adar."

There is a little obscurity in the language here, which may be easily removed. As soon as Haman had formed the design of cutting off all the Jews who were scattered throughout the Persian empire, he had recourse to one of the superstitious devices which were commonly practiced at the time, to ascertain what particular day would be most suitable to his purpose. What precise form of divination was employed in order to decide this important question, we are not told, for there were many ways of it. All that is said is that they cast Pur, that is, the lot. But the method of procedure seems to have been this, that at the beginning of the first month, Haman caused the diviners whom he kept about him to cast the lot to determine what day of the month and what month of the year would bring his design to a successful termination. In this manner he learnt that the thirteenth day of the twelfth month would be the propitious day.

The interval was long, nearly a whole year, but this was brought about by a special providence, in order that the scheme might be defeated, and the projector of it visited with the punishment he merited. This point, however, will come to be more particularly adverted to afterwards. The chief thing to be noted in connection with the verse before us, is the superstitious practice of casting the lot, for the purpose of discovering when a favorable issue might be expected to the design which was contemplated.

Under all systems of false religion, divination, or the attempt to pry into futurity so as to get light cast upon contingent affairs, has been largely practiced. We find reference made to it in the Book of Genesis, as an Egyptian custom, when the cup which was put into Benjamin's sack is called that by which Joseph divined. The Babylonians or Chaldeans, however, seem to have been addicted to divination beyond all other nations, and were indeed proverbial for the use of it. There are several references made to this in the prophetic books. Thus Isaiah, foretelling the downfall of Babylon, says, (chapter 47): "Stand now with thine enchantments, and with the multitude of thy sorceries, wherein thou hast labored from thy youth: if so be thou shalt be able to profit, if so be thou mayest prevail. Thou art wearied in the multitude of thy counsels. Let now the astrologers, the star-gazers, the monthly prognosticators, stand up and save thee from those things that shall come upon thee." And Ezekiel, describing the march of the king of Babylon against Jerusalem, says, (chapter 21): "the king of Babylon stood at the parting of the way, at the head of the two ways, to use divination: he made his arrows bright, he consulted with images, he looked in the livers."

The Persians, also, were addicted to the same practices; and it is said that among that people even at the present day, no one commences a journey, or almost any work the most trifling, without consulting an almanac, or an astrologer, for a fortunate moment. It would seem, indeed, as if there were a natural tendency in the human mind to read futurity by certain devices of its own. We hear sometimes of individuals even in our own day, and in our own country, who are so weak as to suffer themselves to become the dupes of designing knaves, who for money pretend by certain signs and omens to foretell what will be the result of matters in which they are interested. One could afford to smile at the absurd credulity which thus allows itself to be imposed upon, if it were not that the cherishing of the desire to know the future, and having recourse to any such means to have it gratified, is denounced in the Scripture as impiety. The Jewish people were solemnly warned against such procedure, that they might not by means of it degrade and pollute themselves as the heathen did. "There shall not be found among you," said Moses, "anyone that useth divination, or an observer of times, or a charmer, or a consulter with familiar spirits, or a wizard, or a necromancer, for all that do these things are an abomination unto the Lord." And to the same effect Isaiah says: "When they shall say unto you, Seek unto them that have familiar spirits, and unto wizards that peep and that mutter: should not a people seek unto their God? To the law and to the testimony; if they speak not according to this word, it is because there is no light in them."

No rational man will suppose, that by casting lots, or by observing the flight of birds, or by inspecting the entrails of an animal slain for sacrifice, or by astrology, or by any of the other methods which were employed to discover what day or hour would be suitable for an undertaking, or what would be the issue of it, a true result could be obtained. Yet, as all these things formed part of the instrumentality by which Satan kept up his dominion over the minds of men, we can conceive that sometimes in the divine providence they might be permitted to take effect, to punish those who were given over to a blind and reprobate mind, and that, as in the case of Haman's lots, there might be an overruling of human sin and folly to work out the purposes of the divine government.

But without enlarging upon this, let us take home and improve for a moment the lesson so plainly contained in the passage above quoted from Isaiah: "To the law and to the testimony; if we speak not according to this word, it is because there is no light in us." The future, in so far as particular events affecting ourselves and others are concerned, is mercifully and wisely hidden from our view. As has been already said, it is natural to us to desire to lift up the veil; and sometimes, in pressing emergencies, we would give much to be enabled to do this. But since the word of God tells us that all events are under His control, and that His eye is ever on His people, and all that concerns them, for their good, we may well wait patiently for the evolution of His purposes.

Let it be here remarked, however, that the Scripture does not leave us utterly in the dark with respect to futurity; on the contrary, it sheds a strong and satisfactory light upon it with regard to our secular as well as our eternal interests. Here, for example, is a passage— and it is but one of a few that might be quoted to the same effect—a passage which we say makes the future absolutely certain, even as to things temporal: "Godliness is profitable unto all things; having the promise of the life that now is, and of that which is to come."

Let any man entering upon life take the truth contained in this passage for his guidance, and it will certainly conduct him to respectability and comfort. If he frame his actions according to the principles of godliness which the Lord has prescribed in His word—if his life is what may be properly called a godly life—then he will find that all things are made to work for his good. He may have to encounter trials and troubles of an external kind, like those which overtake the ungodly, but he will find outlets from them all; and he will have the continual luxury of a conscience void of offense toward his fellowmen, and void of offense toward God, through the peace speaking blood of Christ. It needs no divination to predict—for the unerring Word of God has predicted it— that "wisdom's ways are pleasantness, and her paths peace."

Lecture 6: Esther 3:6-11

And more especially upon matters of eternal moment, the Scripture has invested the dark future with absolute certainty to us. We know the result of the last judgment, and the unchangeable destiny of men thereafter, as clearly as if the whole were already past. To them who believe in Christ, and who, by patient continuance in well-doing, seek for glory, honor, and immortality, there is reserved eternal life; but to them who reject Christ, and obey not His gospel, there remaineth nothing but a fearful looking for of judgment and fiery indignation, which shall devour the adversaries. Seeing, then, my friends, that in everything which it really concerns us to know for our good, we may be lifted above all doubt and uncertainty, if we only submit to the teaching of God's word, and embrace and follow the Savior whom He hath sent, let us take His word to be a lamp to our feet and a light to our path, and pursue our way, looking unto Jesus, the author and finisher of our faith. Thus assuredly we shall obtain the end of our faith—the salvation of our souls.

But we must now proceed to consider verses 8-11: "And Haman said unto king Ahasuerus, There is a certain people scattered abroad and dispersed among the people in all the provinces of thy kingdom; and their laws are diverse from all people; neither keep they the king's laws: therefore it is not for the king's profit to suffer them. If it please the king, let it be written that they may be destroyed: and I will pay ten thousand talents of silver to the hands of those that have the charge of the business, to bring it unto the king's treasuries. And the king took his ring from his hand and gave it unto Haman the son of Hammedatha the Agagite, the Jews' enemy. And the king said unto Haman, the silver is given to thee, and the people also, to do with them as it seemeth good to thee."

It might have been supposed that Haman, before he proceeded to cast the lot to ascertain what would be the favorable time for wreaking his vengeance upon the Jews, would have been at pains to ascertain whether or not he would be empowered to carry his design into effect. But it seems he had felt satisfied that he would obtain whatever request he asked from the king, and he was not disappointed. Wherever there is favoritism, the master really becomes the slave; and it might be truly said, that it was on Haman, while his season of power lasted, and not upon Artaxerxes, that the destinies of the whole empire depended.

It is not expressly mentioned in the text that Haman specified the Jews by name as the people whom he sought to have exterminated; yet it can scarcely be thought that this was not done. It would not, indeed, be in the least degree inconsistent with the ordinary habits of such a prince as Artaxerxes, to suppose that he should never have taken the trouble to inquire who those were who were represented as enemies to the peace and good government of his kingdom.

In an affair of this kind, his indolent temper might have led him at once to give Haman the liberty which he craved to destroy them; yet we can hardly imagine that he should not have asked some information regarding a race that he was requested thus summarily to cut off. And if he did know that it was the Jews, then the difficulty occurs—how, when he had but very few—perhaps about five—years before shewn such favor to the Jewish nation through Ezra (as we learn from his book) he should all at once have been influenced by Haman to consign them to be massacred without pity. But even this circumstance need not astonish us. The Jews and their concerns would occupy but for a short time the thoughts of a luxurious prince, who lived in intemperance and sensuality; and the same caprice that elevated a man to the highest dignity one day, and sentenced him to be strangled the next, would lead to similar dealing in the case of the people of a whole province. This is one of the miseries of despotic government, that no man can feel himself secure under it. The slightest breath of suspicion, the most unfounded calumny, puts his life in peril, while he has not opportunity to speak a word in self-defense.

In order to draw the king over to his purpose the more readily, Haman offers to pay ten thousand talents of silver into the king's treasury. This was a vast sum—above two million dollars of our money. But I do not think it is necessary for us to suppose that Haman offered to pay it from his own resources, although this is the view taken of the subject by

Lecture 6: Esther 3:6-11

many. There would be nothing, indeed, beyond the bounds of probability in the supposition that this is what was meant, as the favorites of those great Eastern princes had it in their power to accumulate immense treasure, which was wrung under various pretenses from people of every rank; and we read of a case in the reign of the father of this Artaxerxes, where the offer of a sum much larger than that mentioned in the text was made to that king by a nobleman of Lydia for a certain purpose. But with all this, we conceive the meaning of the offer of Haman to be, that he would guarantee the payment of ten thousand talents of silver to the king from the spoils of the Jews who were to be slain.

But whether this be the meaning of his proposal or not, it is very evident that it was not so much the desire of gain as the thirst for blood that influenced this wicked man. It is seldom that such naked cruelty is exhibited; but the evil spirit had full possession of him, and he was thus converted into a savage beast of prey. The king, without any expression of reluctance, granted the request of his favorite, gave him his signet-ring, with which public documents were sealed, that the necessary edicts might be issued with due authority; and when he thus made himself an accomplice in this horrible transaction, he gave at the same time a display of munificence, saying, "The silver is given to thee, the people also, to do with them as it seemeth good to thee."

And thus was the fate of the great body of the Jewish nation apparently left in the hands of two individuals, of whom it is not easy to say which was the more culpable—Haman, who projected the bloody design; or the king, who, apparently without scruple, assented to it and sanctioned it.

But now, while we wonder that there should have been men found so destitute of every feeling of humanity, as in cold blood to consign to destruction so many thousands of their fellow-creatures who had been guilty of no crime, we have not the consolation at the same time to think that their conduct is without parallel. In one sense, indeed, the many examples which history records of ambition pursuing its way from conquest to conquest, through blood and devastation and ruin, may be regarded as much the same in point of atrocity with that which we have in the text. And yet, there is a difference in the feelings with which we contemplate the one series of acts and the other. There is a false halo of grandeur shed around the path of the conqueror, and there is not so palpable a connection between his exploits and absolute revolting ferocity, as there is between the decree of Artaxerxes and Haman, and the execution of it. But looking away from the cruelty which is glossed over by the name of military glory, we even find cool unmitigated atrocities in the records of civilized nations, which are as disgraceful to humanity as Haman's—yea, which surpass them.

Haman was a heathen—a stranger, therefore, to the softening power of religion, and we see in him only an illustration of what human nature is, when left to itself, without the control of any pure and heavenly influence. But what shall we say of the indiscriminate massacre of the Protestants (1572) in Paris, and other parts of France, wherein at least 70,000 persons in a brief space fell victims to the bigotry and cruelty of the king and his advisers? That was a tragedy contrived in cold blood, and advised by favorites, to glut the revenge of Papal Rome. Day and hour were fixed here, as they were by Haman. But in this case, unhappily, day and hour were kept, and the true worshippers of God, the lovers of His truth, the best friends of religion and morality, the excellent of the earth, were massacred, because they would pay homage to Christ himself, and not to the Roman Antichrist.

And what shall we say of the cruelties, *that* is too tame a word, what shall we say of the horrible barbarities which, by the command of the Romish tyrant, whose hands are red with the blood of the saints, were perpetrated in the valleys of the Waldenses, when not only men, but feeble women and helpless children, were savagely tortured and slain by a brutal soldier, for no other reason than that they would worship God, as His word commands? And are there not scenes of equal atrocity set before us in the history of our own country, when wholesale murder was

Lecture 6: Esther 3:6-11

authorized by royal edict, because our forefathers would not take their religion and forms of worship from the enactments of the civil power, but would serve God, as they believed the Bible required, and as their consciences approved? Haman's character is one of the blackest in history. But, on a calm review, and with full allowance for the time and circumstances in which he lived, he is pure as compared with the infamous king of France, who looked from his palace window and enjoyed the scene of slaughter in his capital; with the savages who shed the blood of the noble martyrs in the valleys of the Alps, and with the last monarchs of the Stuart line and their wretched accomplices, who persecuted to the death the resolute defenders of civil and religious freedom. But will not God visit for these things? Nay, should we not rather say, hath He not visited already? The visitation of Haman we shall soon have before us.

Deeply has France already paid for the innocent blood which her rulers shed long ago, and her soil, it is to be feared, is not yet cleansed from the pollution. Other persecutors have had their award also. And the great central persecuting power—Rome herself, will in due time have her foretold destiny fully accomplished. As she hath done, it will be done to her. Even if the word of God were silent on the subject, we could not but anticipate that that anti-Christian power, to whose direct influence may be traced persecution and bloodshed, such as heathenism never was stained with, will have the measure meted to her, which she has meted out to others. But we need not speak doubtfully here. The divine word has fixed the doom of Papal Rome. And if she seems to be raising herself in our day, it is assuredly only to give the greater impulse to her final ruin, that she may fall from the greater height, when, like the great millstone cast by the angel into the sea, she shall be engulfed in the abyss of the wrath of God.

But I would now go back, to call your attention to one point in the verses before us, which has not been referred to, and which deserves to be noticed, e.g.—the description which Haman gives of the Jews in verse

8: "There is a certain people," he said to the king, "scattered abroad, and dispersed among the people in all the provinces of thy kingdom; and their laws are diverse from all people; neither keep they the king's laws; therefore, it is not for the king's profit to suffer them." In this account of the Jews, given by their most determined enemy, it is natural to suppose that there would be exaggeration, but at the same time, it must be acknowledged to be highly honorable to them.

It had been their characteristic, and the great cause of their dispersion among the heathen, that, previously to the destruction of Jerusalem by Nebuchadnezzar, they had adopted the usages and the worship of the heathen nations around them, and had ceased to be what Jehovah designed them to be, separate from every other people, and His special witnesses in the world. But now, according to Haman's testimony, which there is no reason to call in question, they had become sensible of their former trespasses, when in the state of captivity, and had refused to take part in the prevailing idolatry. It might have been supposed that, scattered as they were throughout an immense range of country, and deprived of the opportunity of worshipping God according to the requirements of His law, they would have fallen away either into utter infidelity, or into the false forms of worship which they saw practiced by their conquerors. But instead of this, they clung to the maxims and usages of the Mosaic law, as far as they could. They kept themselves separate from the pollutions of the heathen among whom they lived, and were, what their descendants are at the present day, a people distinct from every other people on earth.

Haman brings against them the charge, that "they kept not the king's laws;" *i.e.,* that they were of a rebellious spirit; but this was no doubt a misrepresentation. If the king's laws had been like the commandment of Nebuchadnezzar, that all should worship his gods, then there might have been some of the Jews of the same heroic spirit with the three youths who would endure any torment rather than obey such a commandment. But it does not appear that the kings of Persia were so intolerant, or that

Lecture 6: Esther 3:6-11

they enacted any religious service from the Jews which was inconsistent with their creed. And in all probability, Haman's charge against them was founded merely upon their strict adherence to such distinctions as the law pointed out between things clean and unclean; and perhaps, upon their endeavor to keep holy the Sabbath day. These things would give color to an accusation against them, that they refused to be subject to the laws of the empire, and when this accusation was laid before a monarch too devoted to self-indulgence to inquire whether or not it was well-founded, it would be strong enough to incline him to leave the Jews in the hand of his favorite, to deal with them according to his pleasure. Thus far, however, the narrative is satisfactory, that nothing could be said against God's ancient people, at this time, by their mortal enemy, really tending to their discredit. And when they could only be charged with observing their own laws, which made them diverse from all other people, and with not keeping the king's laws, we must acknowledge that they only occupied the position which the word of God commanded them to occupy. But you will observe how singularly striking the analogy is between the reasons which Haman gave for destroying them, and the reasons which popery and arbitrary power assigned in the instances we have already alluded to, for cutting off the friends of true religion and liberty.

Adherence to the principles of Scripture has always been the great offense of God's people, and the cause of the world's enmity against them, and of its desire to crush them, In this respect, however, they have only experienced the treatment which Christ warned His disciples to expect, when He said: "If the world hate you, ye know that it hateth me before it hated you. If ye were of the world, the world would love his own; but because ye are not of the world, but I have chosen you out of the world, therefore the world hateth you."

Now, in concluding the present lecture, I would take, as the ground of the practical lesson which you are specially to carry away, the description which the wicked Haman gives of the Jews. They are to be regarded as representing the church of God. At many periods of their history, they were as a body unfaithful to the great trust committed to them; but there never was a time when there were not found among them some devoted witnesses for the truth. On the occasion referred to in the text, while they were externally in a depressed condition, captives in a foreign land, they were almost all true to their religion, and zealous for the law of God. They were known to be Jehovah's people, not merely by their language and dress and manners, but particularly by their adherence to His law.

They were scattered through all the provinces of the empire, but they were diverse from all the people among whom they lived. Even so it should be with the followers of Christ in the world. They must be known as His, because while they are in the world, they are not of it. They must give evidence of their heavenly birth, by keeping themselves free from the world's pollutions. In striving to exhibit the same mind which was in Christ, in cultivating the graces which form their proper ornament, in habitually aiming at conformity to His will, they must be known as His. The reality of their faith must be evidenced by their love and their purity. And then they most effectually honor Him when, like Daniel, and like the people referred to in the text, they are only subject to this accusation on the part of the world, that they refuse to be guided by any other principles than those prescribed by the law of their heavenly Lord. Yet, my friends, let us carry along with us the whole truth which requires to be stated here. The Jews were a distinct race—the seed of Abraham. Their separation from the heathen was to be traced up to their birth, and to their determination to be known as Abraham's children—the worshippers of Jehovah. Let not this consideration be overlooked.

We can conceive many reasons operating to lead men to shun what may be called worldly society, and worldly amusements and follies, while at the same time they are strangers to the power of true religion in the heart. Observe, then, that we must be of the separate race—*born of God;* we must be new creatures in Christ Jesus, ere we can give proper evidence of separation from the world. But if we are partakers of the quickening Spirit, certainly this will form a proof of it, that we strive to keep ourselves unspotted from the world.

Amen.

Lecture 7: Esther 3:12-15 and 4:1-9

IN the last lecture we saw Haman's plot laid for the destruction of the Jews. Incensed against Mordecai, because he would not pay homage to him like the rest of the king's servants, he determined to wreak his vengeance, not merely upon the offender himself, but upon the whole race to which he belonged. Having ascertained, as he thought perfectly, by some superstitious practice then usually employed, what would be the most fitting time for carrying his design into execution, he easily obtained from the king the requisite authority. And not only so, but he also received in gift the spoil which would be gathered from the slaughtered Jews. It was a high-handed scheme of iniquity which this wicked man had contrived—a gigantic atrocity, as we may well call it. But the Lord watches over His own and defeats the purposes of their enemies.

Let us proceed to consider verse 12-15: "Then were the king's scribes called on the thirteenth day of the first month, and there was written according to all that Haman had commanded unto the king's lieutenants, and to the governors that were over every province, and to the rulers of every people of every province according to the writing thereof, and to every people after their language; in the name of king Ahasuerus was it written, and sealed with the king's ring. And the letters were sent by posts into all the king's provinces, to destroy, to kill, and to cause to perish, all Jews, both young and old, little children and women, in one day, even upon the thirteenth day of the twelfth month, which is the month Adar, and to take the spoil of them for a prey. The copy of the writing for a commandment to be given in every province was published unto all people, that they should be ready against that day. The posts went out, being hastened by the king's commandment, and the decree was given in Shushan the palace. And the king and Haman sat down to drink; but the city Shushan was perplexed."

Lecture 7: Esther 3:12-15 and 4:1-9

Now the principal thing that requires comment here, as involving a difficulty, is the time that intervened from the issuing of the edict for the extirpation of the Jews—which took place, as we see, on the thirteenth day of the first month—till the day when the crime was to be perpetrated, which was to be the thirteenth of the twelfth month; that is to say, a period of eleven months was to elapse between the notification of the cruelty and the execution of it. And this circumstance has been alleged as an objection to the truthfulness of the whole narrative—it being altogether improbable, it is said, that Haman, if he really wished to do what he is represented as bent upon doing, would have given notice so long beforehand of his design. Now, in answer to this objection, it must be at once admitted that the arrangement of the whole affair illustrates rather the fiendish spirit than the sagacity of Haman; but at the same time, there are some considerations which deserve notice in connection with the plain statement which is here presented to us.

First, I would observe, that the very circumstance which is urged as an objection to the truth of the narrative is rather to be regarded as an evidence of its trustworthiness. The Book of Esther does not contain any record of miraculous events. There are no wonders and prodigies in it, at which infidelity might carp, and with reference to which it might say that the writer must have drawn so largely upon his fancy in some places, as to render suspicious what appears to be the record of simple matters of fact. The whole tenor and style of the book indicate that the writer of it acted the part of a historian who was concerned only to relate what actually took place; and if he had been a deceiver, he certainly would not have laid himself open to an objection so very palpable as that under review, when it was in his power, by the mere alteration of dates, to make the whole narrative so plausible that not a flaw could be found in it. In a word, I consider the difficulty before us as an argument for the truth of the history. But farther, in the second place, it must be kept in mind, that though the king's scribes were called on the thirteenth day of the first month to write the decree, it does not follow that the work was finished in a day. King Artaxerxes reigned over one hundred and twenty-seven provinces, as we read in the first chapter. Diverse languages and dialects were spoken in many of these provinces. The edict was given forth, we are told, "to the rulers of every people of every province, according to the writing thereof, and to every people after their language." The document had to be translated, then, into different languages, and a translation sent with the Persian original; and besides, there would, no doubt, be private communications, dictated by Haman to the governors of the different provinces, containing directions as to the manner in which the bloody work was to be executed, and the spoils of the Jews disposed of; so that some considerable time would elapse before the royal decree could be sent out to the provinces. We learn, indeed, from the eighth chapter, that it was the twentieth day of the third month before Mordecai obtained permission to counteract the design of Haman; and making allowance for distance and modes of travelling, we may suppose that the sentence against the Jews had not even reached the more remote parts of the empire, when the remission of it was resolved upon. But again, in the third place, and more particularly, it is very obvious that we have to regard the whole transaction here as overruled in the providence of God for the good of His people and the confusion of their enemies. It is easy to say that there is an air of improbability in the whole story, because, even with a few months' warning, the Jews would have had time to remove from the places where they were doomed to perish. But whither could they have gone? is one question. The Persian empire was so extensive, that it would have been difficult for them to escape beyond its bounds and find a refuge elsewhere. Besides, how could they have fled, when no doubt there were orders issued to prevent their flight? We know that in persecuting times in France, and in our own country also, while the victims of persecution were warned that within a certain period no mercy would be shown to them, there were steps taken to prevent their escape; and even the attempt to escape was denounced as criminal.

Lecture 7: Esther 3:12-15 and 4:1-9

In the case which we have before us in the text, the whole matter turns upon this point—that Haman got what he considered the favorable day for his enterprise fixed by a superstitious practice, which he revered, and believed to be infallible. Then, after this, he felt as if all were secure; and with a recklessness—or, as we might call it, an infatuation—such as there are many examples of in the perpetrators of heinous crimes, he proceeded to accomplish his purpose in a way which one would say was calculated to render it abortive, and to ruin himself.

Perhaps I have spent too much time upon this topic; but this is the reason, that it is one of the points which have been specially dwelt upon as subverting the divine authority of the Book of Esther; and on this ground, therefore, it would have been inexcusable to pass it over without particular comment. The only other subject that requires to be noticed in the verses before us, is the concluding sentence: "The king and Haman sat down to drink; but the city Shushan was perplexed." These words of course refer to the time when the king's proclamation was published in Shushan. In this place, where the court was kept, the notice would be first given of what was purposed against the Jews; and very probably it would be when preparation had been fully made to send the edict into all the provinces, that it was publicly made known in the royal city. This could not be done, however, without exciting a strong sensation. The subjects of Eastern despotism are not easily moved by the procedure of their masters. The will of the one man is so absolute and irresistible, that there is nothing left for them but submission. There is no such thing known among them as that which we call public opinion, which is one of the strongest bulwarks between the governing power and the governed- preventing arbitrary and hurtful measures on the part of rulers, and sudden ebullitions of impatient discontent on the part of the populace. Yet the severest despotism cannot repress all feeling; and when the decree was published that the Jews were to be destroyed throughout the empire on a certain fixed day, men's minds were agitated. There was a great number of Jews located in Susa. They were exiles from their homes, but they were an inoffensive race. They had gradually come to take part in such trade and commerce as was carried on in Susa. They had not become amalgamated with the native population. They stood aloof from them in religion, and in the common habits of life, but they mixed with them for the transaction of ordinary business. They formed a part of the community; and this edict, dooming them to destruction, could not but make all men wonder, while to the Jews themselves it must have been like the shock of an earthquake.

There is certainly no apparent exaggeration in the language of the text, when it is said that "the city of Shushan was perplexed." But the king and his favorite were beyond the reach of popular feeling. No breath of it, no symptom of excitement out of doors could penetrate the royal palace. They sat where the groans and secret murmurings of the oppressed people could not be heard, and where no one could have ventured to echo them. Sensual indulgence was their pursuit; all serious thought, all concern for the good of the empire, was drowned in the wine-cup: "the king and Haman sat down to drink, but the city Shushan was perplexed." It is a humiliating view of human nature, that is presented to us in these words. But the picture, although dark and revolting, is not a solitary one. If history speaks truth, some of the proclamations issued for the destruction of our covenanting forefathers were issued when the persecutors were so much under the influence of wine that they scarcely knew what they did; and many a sufferer died, when the judges who passed sentence were incapable through intoxication of affixing a legible signature to the death-warrant. We cannot be thankful enough that we live in an age when such indecent atrocities would not be tolerated.

But I would now proceed to make some practical application of the verses which have been reviewed.

Lecture 7: Esther 3:12-15 and 4:1-9

First

In the first place, then, we see how enmity to God's truth and His people displays itself with restless activity for the accomplishment of its ends. It is very likely that applications made to Artaxerxes through his chief favorite, or as we would say in modern speech, through his vizier, Haman, for the due administration of justice, for protection against oppression, and for restitution where wrong had been done, would be slowly enough listened to and followed out. In all such cases, a bribe was necessary to quicken the procedure of the minister. But when the Jews are doomed to perish, and revenge is to be glutted by their destruction, then there is no listlessness or sloth in the court; edicts are written out, and couriers dispatched with a promptitude that would have been most exemplary in a good cause. And so always, as is plain from what the Scripture tells us, there is incessant stir and action in the kingdom of darkness, for the purpose of opposing the cause of truth and godliness. And what should this teach us, but that there must be corresponding activity put forth to counteract the deep designs of Satan's agents, and to promote the interests of the kingdom of righteousness? If the desire to spread mischief and misery among men be so intensely cherished, and eagerly followed out, by those who are enlisted in the service of the great adversary, when they have nothing to expect at the utmost in the form of reward beyond the present life; how intense and concentrated should be the desires and endeavors of those who love Christ to glorify Him upon earth, when they have set before them the reward of living and reigning with Him forever! Surely, my friends, if we really believed the Bible, and felt the influence of its truths upon our heart, we would not be so indifferent to the spread of Bible principles, while the enemies of Christ are so busy in spreading their soul-destroying errors. Let us remember that the love of Christ constrains those who feel the power of it to live not unto themselves but unto Him, and that the people made willing in the day of God's power, are *willing* to spend and to be spent for Christ.

Second

In the second place, you will notice how self-indulgence renders men callous to the distresses and sufferings of their fellowmen. "The king and Haman sat down to drink, but the city of Shushan was perplexed." Give the votary of sensuality or intemperance the opportunity of gratifying his craving, and he cares not what misery he may occasion to those whose well-being he is bound to take the deepest interest. Let the sensualist have his will, and it costs him not a thought that he may be destroying the happiness of families and ruining for time and eternity the victims of his ungodly lust. Strong carnal appetite, when it is excited, sets at defiance the law of nature as well as the law of God.

One can scarcely think without shuddering of the conduct of the two men referred to in the text. They had resolved to shed innocent blood without measure; but they could sit down as boon companions to enjoy themselves over their wine and could contrive to drown any remonstrances of conscience with the flowing goblet. Could there be a more thorough personification of evil in one of its most revolting forms than we have here? And yet, my friends, it finds its counterpart, although on a smaller scale, in the procedure of multitudes who live under the light of the gospel! Is that individual one whit better than the infamous pair referred to in the text, who, forgetting the claims of home, and his responsibilities as a father and a husband, spends his earnings in debauchery, and thus reduces what might be a happy family to wretchedness and poverty? While he is enjoying himself with his companions, all reckless of his obligation to protect and provide for his wife and children, they are sitting in absolute want, with no prospect for the morrow but what is still more gloomy than the experience of today. Then, if there are any here to whom these remarks are in any respect applicable, let them bethink themselves of their sin and folly; let them judge themselves by the same rule whereby they would judge the king and Haman. Then they will acknowledge that they have been unfaithful

Lecture 7: Esther 3:12-15 and 4:1-9

to a sacred trust committed to them, and they will endeavor, by the help of the grace of God, to be no longer the destroyers, but the protectors of those whom they have solemnly vowed to protect. And let me conclude my remarks upon this part of the subject, by again saying, that the excessive indulgence of any forbidden appetite makes men selfish, and regardless of the rights of others. So that, as the followers of Christ, we must all strive to keep the desires of our animal natures in subjection, else we forfeit all claim to belong to Him with whom the will of His heavenly Father was paramount in everything. But we now go on to chapter iv.; and we shall consider first verses 1-3: "When Mordecai perceived all that was done, Mordecai rent his clothes, and put on sackcloth with ashes, and went out into the midst of the city, and cried with a loud and a bitter cry; and came even before the king's gate: for none might enter into the king's gate clothed with sackcloth. And in every province, whithersoever the king's commandment and his decree came, there was great mourning among the Jews, and fasting, and weeping, and wailing; and many lay in sackcloth and ashes."

It is not unlikely, that while the proclamation for the destruction of the Jews was published in Susa, and in this way made generally known there, some of those who had reasoned with Mordecai in vain as to the disrespect which he showed toward Haman, had furnished him with a special copy of the edict, in order that they might make him bitterly regret his obstinacy in not having listened to their remonstrances. At all events, it is evident from verse 8 that he had a copy of it; and it is not to be wondered at that the effect which it produced upon him, when he read it, was at first so overwhelming as to render him almost unconscious of what he did. Grief vents itself differently in different individuals, according to their natural temperament. In eastern nations generally it is accompanied with passionate outcries and violent gestures, which would be regarded as altogether extravagant among the nations of the west. "Mordecai," it is said, "rent his clothes, and put on sackcloth with ashes, and went out into the midst of the city, and cried with a loud and a bitter cry;" and among the Jews in other parts where the edict was published, "there was great mourning, and fasting, and weeping, and wailing, and many lay in sackcloth and ashes." We have not the means of knowing with certainty whether or not Mordecai was aware, that it was his own refusal to pay homage to Haman that had directly given occasion to this enactment for the destruction of all his countrymen. If he was aware of it, then his sorrow must have been so much the more intense, when he had to look upon himself as the cause of his brethren's ruin. And surely his conviction must have been very deep that he was right in acting toward Haman as he had done, when we find him in the next chapter persisting in his determination to show no respect to the Amalekite. But whatever was his knowledge or suspicion of the connection that subsisted between the cruel edict and his own conduct toward the king's favorite, he was not ashamed to appear publicly as one of the doomed race. A timid man would have shut himself up in his own house, and would not have ventured abroad except from necessity, when the king's proclamation, denouncing the Jews as it did, might have given encouragement to the populace to insult and injure them, even before the appointed time. But Mordecai, in the garb of a mourner, and with bitter wailing, rushed into the street, thus making himself a marked man, and showing utter disregard of his personal safety. Very probably he designed to betake himself to his usual place in the king's gate, with a vague notion that there he might find some means of obtaining deliverance. But here his progress was arrested, "for none might enter into the king's gate clothed with sackcloth."

There is a reference made to this point in the book of Nehemiah, which may be here noticed. There, that remarkable man, who, some years after the incident referred to in the text, was cup-bearer to the same Artaxerxes who is spoken of in this book, informs us, that on hearing of the desolations of Jerusalem, he was so grieved that he could not even conceal his grief in the king's presence, at the same time saying, "I had not been beforetime sad in his presence." It was contrary to every

Lecture 7: Esther 3:12-15 and 4:1-9

established rule, and an offense highly punishable, for anyone to appear within the precincts of the palace of the Persian kings, in the dress, or with the look of a mourner. There must be nothing seen there to remind the sovereign that trouble and suffering are experienced by mortals. With every luxury to gratify his pampered appetite, with external splendor to please his eye, and sweet music to soothe his ear, and the flattery of courtiers to make him regard himself as something more than mortal, he passed his life in seclusion from all sights and sounds of distress and woe. Mordecai's sackcloth must not appear within the king's gate.

It is well remarked by Henry, in his commentary upon this passage, that, "although nothing but what was gay and pleasant must appear at court, and everything that was melancholy must be banished thence; yet it was vain thus to keep out the badges of sorrow, unless they could withal have kept out the causes of sorrow, and to forbid sackcloth to enter, unless they could have forbidden sickness, and trouble, and death, to enter." "We are reminded by these words of the well-known saying of John Knox to the ladies of Queen Mary's court, when he had been dismissed from her presence with marks of high displeasure, and was waiting to hear the result of his interview with her: "Oh! fair ladies, how pleasing were this life of yours if it should ever abide, and then, in the end, that we may pass to heaven with all this gay gear. But if upon that knave—death, that will come whether we will or not." But it is not to those only who dwell in palaces that our application of the text may be made. People in exalted stations among ourselves—people who might be expected to act more rationally than heathen potentates and nobles were accustomed to do, often exhibit the same desire to have removed out of their sight everything that would remind them of their frailty and mortality; as if in this way they could put trouble and mortality away from them. But it is unavailing. The unwelcome heralds of death, in the varied forms of disease, will find their way into the mansions of the great as well as into the humble dwellings of the poor; and at length the enemy himself will appear, all unceremoniously to drag away from their luxuries and their selfish enjoyments, those who have no portion but in the present life. What I would say here then is, would it not be the best course for all to have their minds directed toward the reality, which must overtake them whether they will or not; and to avail themselves of the means which God has provided in the gospel, to strip death of its terrors? One of the chief reasons which render the death-bed attentions of the physician valuable is, that he can by his medicines allay pain, and smooth somewhat the passage to the grave. But surely the best appliance for this end, is that which comes through faith in Jesus Christ, whereby the soul, in the midst of its pain and tossings, can find abundant comfort, and good hope in the prospect of enjoying the Savior forever. And is it not the most effectual way to disarm us of the fear of death, and to enable us to look forward to it, even when we are in health, without any overwhelming misgivings, to have a real and assured interest in Him who hath destroyed death, and him that had the power of it, that is the devil; and who can deliver those who, through fear of death, would otherwise be subject to bondage?

Before proceeding to consider the verses which follow, there is one remark that I would offer, suggested by the passage which has just been reviewed. It has reference to the indications of sorrow which were exhibited by Mordecai. These, according to our notions, were extravagant, but in that age and country, they would not have been judged to be so much beyond bounds, as we would regard them. There are certain recognized measures of propriety and becomingness in outward conduct, where no moral principle of right and wrong is involved, which must be acknowledged and submitted to. The general customs of a nation—education and position in society, put restraints upon the outward exhibition of feeling; so that allowance must be made for the different degrees of excitement which people of different classes manifest, when their sensibilities are very deeply stirred. I advert to this subject, because sometimes there is too little sympathy shown by some people with the sufferings and sorrows of others, and their mode of

Lecture 7: Esther 3:12-15 and 4:1-9

giving vent to them. There are some who seem to imagine that the gospel of Christ is designed to deaden all human feeling, and that it is a proof of high Christian attainment when great domestic calamities and bereavements can be borne without a tear, or a single indication of mental anguish. Now, with this notion I cannot sympathize. Such coldness and apathy are not a proof of submission to the will of God, but rather of heartless indifference to it.

The conduct of David, when his infant died, is referred to as an example to be followed by those who suffer under bereavement, as to the moderation of their feelings. But this case, when it is fully examined, does not bear out the inference drawn from it, that all signs of sorrow must be suppressed. And certainly, that father's agony and tears, when he heard of the death of Absalom, teach a different lesson. But to take a higher example: did not Christ himself sympathize and weep with the mourning sisters of Lazarus? And does not His apostle exhibit the same spirit, when he says to the Philippians, "Epaphroditus was sick, nigh unto death, but God had mercy on him; and not on him only, but on me also, lest I should have sorrow upon sorrow." Let us then respect the indications of grief which God's visitations cause His people to manifest; and while we speak words of comfort to mourners, let us not coldly and unfeelingly rebuke their sorrow, as if sorrow in itself were sinful. One maxim of Scripture bearing upon the subject, is beautifully expressed in these words: "Remember them that are in bonds, as bound with them; and them which suffer adversity, as being yourselves also in the body."

But we now go on to consider verses 4-8: "So Esther's maids and her chamberlains came and told it her. Then was the queen exceedingly grieved; and she sent raiment to clothe Mordecai, and to take away his sackcloth from him: but he received it not. Then called Esther for Hatach, one of the king's chamberlains, whom he had appointed to attend upon her, and gave him a commandment to Mordecai, to know what it was, and why it was. So Hatach went forth to Mordecai unto the street of the city, which was before the king's gate. And Mordecai told him of all that had happened unto him, and of the sum of the money that Haman had promised to pay to the king's treasuries for the Jews, to destroy them. Also he gave him the copy of the writing of the decree that was given at Shushan to destroy them, to shew it unto Esther, and to declare it unto her, and to charge her that she should go in unto the king, to make supplication unto him, and to make request before him for her people."

Perhaps there was an unwonted stir outside the palace, occasioned by the dress and deportment of Mordecai, so that some of those who were passing out and in, and among others, some of Esther's more immediate attendants, noticed it, and brought her the tidings. It is very likely, that although as yet they did not know the relationship that subsisted between her and Mordecai, they knew that she felt an interest in him, as he had done in her when she was first taken into the palace. And, therefore, they told her how he stood without clothed in sackcloth, and heavily distressed. Ignorant as yet of the evil that was purposed against her nation, and supposing that it was some private sorrow that pressed upon the spirit pf her friend, Esther sent a change of raiment to him, thus expressing her desire, that whatever the cause of his trouble was, she was anxious that he should be comforted. This was one of the ways in which, in those times and countries, sympathy and affection were manifested. And so we learn that when the prodigal returned, the father said to his servants: "Bring forth the best robe and put it on him, and put a ring on his hand, and shoes on his feet." And it is in allusion to the same custom that the Savior says: "The Lord hath sent me to appoint unto them that mourn in Zion; to give unto them beauty for ashes, the oil of joy for mourning, and the *garment of praise* for the spirit of heaviness." It is a very pleasing trait in the character of Esther, that her advancement, and the grandeur and luxury of the palace, had not made her forget the friend of her childhood. His grief touched her heart, and she would have him know this. But his sorrow was too deeply seated to be assuaged even by her kindness. Mordecai refused the raiment which she sent and persisted in wearing his sackcloth. The rejection of such a present would have

Lecture 7: Esther 3:12-15 and 4:1-9

been accounted highly offensive in ordinary circumstances, but it only made Esther apprehend that Mordecai's trouble must be of no usual kind. Accordingly, she sent the chief officer of her household, to inquire why he so mourned, and refused to be comforted. This was probably the very opportunity which Mordecai waited for, as affording some hope that the threatened calamity might be averted. Accordingly, he informed the eunuch of the plot of Haman, gave him a copy of the decree to show to Esther, and sent his own urgent request to her, that she should immediately use her influence with the king, to obtain a revocation of the sentence. He did not know, or he had overlooked the difficulty she might have to bring the subject under the notice of the king. That difficulty was very great, and as we shall see afterwards, could not be surmounted without extreme danger to Esther herself. But Mordecai was so intent upon the accomplishment of his object, and the matter was so pressing, that he could not pause to look at difficulties. It seemed to him that Esther had the power to work out at once the deliverance of her countrymen. At all events, there was no other channel open even for the hope of deliverance; and therefore he intimates what must be done, rather in the way of command than of request. "He charged her to go in unto the king, to make supplication unto him, and to make request before him for her people." As we shall see, it was not without pressing his point hard that Mordecai gained it. But ultimately, he did gain it, although we must defer the further consideration of the subject to the next lecture. In the meantime, this lesson may be drawn from his conduct, that a resolute will, when it is exerted for the accomplishment of any purpose, is usually successful in the end. In the pursuit even of worldly good, when a man keeps his eye steadily fixed upon some one object, and makes that the point toward which his efforts directly and indirectly tend, he commonly succeeds. There are, indeed, providential interpositions which overthrow the most promising and best laid schemes and show the insufficiency of human wisdom and power to effect their ends, apart from the blessing of God. But generally, when there is no impious disregard of the order of

Providence—a resolute will, combined with activity, sweeps all difficulties out of its path, and succeeds in accomplishing its aims. Some of the greatest movements in worldly affairs are, humanly speaking, to be traced up to this. The triumphs of the Reformation for example, in our own country and in other lands, where it did triumph, while they are really to be ascribed to the overruling providence of God, are instrumentally to be attributed to this, that God raised up and qualified for the work certain men of determined will and unflagging energy, who kept before them the great purpose which they sought to effect, and would be turned aside by no danger or difficulty from working it out. And I would remark, that in things spiritual—in things affecting the eternal salvation of man—resoluteness of will and indomitable energy, are as indispensable as in the pursuit of temporal good. Nothing must be allowed to obscure the great cardinal truth, that salvation is of grace, and that "it is not of him that willeth, nor of him that runneth, but of God who showeth mercy." But still, it is only when men, by the grace of God, set themselves resolutely to contend with their spiritual enemies—when, looking to God for help, they will not be driven from the path of well-doing by obstacles which they meet with in pursuing it; it is only then that they are treading the course which will terminate in the rewards of a glorious victory.

Now, in conclusion, the parting lesson which I would leave with you, is founded on Mordecai's grief and Esther's sympathy. Gladly would she have removed the sorrow of her friend, and willingly would she have mingled her tears with his, had it been permitted. Her sympathy he could not doubt. But there are griefs deeper than human sympathy can reach; and Mordecai's were beyond Esther's power to assuage them. She could only be helpful by speaking to the king. It was the king alone that could change the sorrow into joy.

You see the application, my friends. The mourners in Zion have the sympathy of their brethren, and that sympathy is sweet. But still it cannot heal the wounds of a spirit that is troubled by the sense of sin, nor of a

Lecture 7: Esther 3:12-15 and 4:1-9

heart that is sore pierced by God's afflictive dispensation. But the King of Zion can heal these wounds. And He is touched with the feeling of His people's infirmities—He breaketh not the bruised reed: He will heal them. Cast yourselves upon Jesus, ye mourners, with simple-hearted faith, and ask of Him the comfort which ye need, and you will receive the oil of joy for mourning, and the garment of praise for the spirit of heaviness. Amen.

Lecture 8: Esther 4:10-17

In the last discourse, after some remarks in answer to the objection which has been raised against the truthfulness of this book, from the circumstance that so long a period was suffered to elapse between the publication of the decree for destroying the Jews, and the day on which it was to be executed, I adverted to the conduct of the king and Haman, who, reckless of the horror and distress which their cruel design could not fail to produce throughout the empire, sat down to drink. And while they were drowning reflection in debauchery, there was weeping and wailing, sackcloth and ashes, in all the families of the Jews.

The history, however, while it indicates the feeling which was awakened and prevailed generally, concentrates our interest upon the conduct of Mordecai. While others were prostrated by the decree which had been issued and shut themselves up in their own houses as utterly bereft of hope, he rushed forth into the street in his sackcloth, giving vent to his feelings "in loud and bitter cries. Hardly knowing whither he went, and yet, as if guided by some unseen hand, he ran to the palace! He was not permitted to enter the gate to occupy his usual place, because he wore the dress of a mourner. But he remained near enough to arrest the attention of some of the eunuchs who were passing, and, among these, of some whose service was appropriated to Queen Esther.

From them she learnt what was passing without; and not knowing the cause of Mordecai's mourning, she took the method of expressing her sympathy which the custom of the country sanctioned. She sent him an ornamental dress, thereby signifying that she would have him put away his sackcloth and be glad. But even the interest which she took in his trouble could not assuage his sorrow. As Jacob, when he heard of the supposed death of Joseph, put sackcloth upon his loins and mourned for his son, and when all his sons and daughters rose up to comfort him, refused to be comforted, so Mordecai, even at Esther's bidding, would

Lecture 8: Esther 4:10-17

not put away his sackcloth. This led to farther inquiry, indeed to the very inquiry which Mordecai desired to be made. When a second message came to him from the queen, requesting him to tell the special cause of his mourning, he informed her of what she did not then know, of the plot for the destruction of the Jews, which was certified by the publication of the royal edict; and at the same time he sent her a copy of the edict, and laid upon her his command that she should use her influence with the king to avert the threatened catastrophe.

It did not occur to him that any difficulty lay in the way of her doing so. He supposed that she possessed the power of swaying the king's mind, if she would but use it; and hence his urgency in pressing her to lose no time in doing what he thought she could so easily accomplish. It is one of the penalties which those who occupy stations of influence have to pay for their elevation, that there are demands made upon them which are sometimes wholly beyond their reach, and very often far more difficult to answer than those imagine who look on from a distance. In this latter situation Esther felt herself to be placed; and however anxious she was to comply with the wish of her best and earliest friend, she was obliged to let him know that he calculated too largely upon the extent of her influence. This brings us to consider the verses which form the subject of the present discourse. Verse 10-12: "Again Esther spake unto Hatach, and gave him commandment unto Mordecai; all the king's servants, and the people of the king's provinces, do know, that whosoever, whether man or woman, shall come unto the king into the inner court, who is not called, there is one law of his to put him to death, except such to whom the king shall hold out the golden scepter, that he may live: but I have not been called to come in unto the king these thirty days. And they told to Mordecai Esther's words."

That part of the message which Esther sends to Mordecai, contained in verse 11, is so inconsistent with all our ideas and customs, that we wonder at first if there could have been a law so absurd as the one which is here referred to. But ordinary history completely verifies the words of the text. In all the despotic governments of the East, for many ages, and much farther back than the period to which this book refers, it seems to have been the practice to regard the monarch as altogether a being of a superior order. Access to his presence was attained only by a few favored ones.

Certain domestics, whose services were indispensable to his personal comfort, of necessity had liberty to come near him, but all besides were excluded, except when it was his express pleasure that they should be admitted. And even the members of his own family could not present themselves before him unless they were sent for, or when leave was specially asked and granted. Such was the law and usage, particularly, in the Persian court. And one of the Greek historians relates the case of a Persian nobleman, who, because he would force his way into the royal presence, when he was informed by the doorkeepers that he could not enter, was put to death, and most of his family with him. The law may not be so severe, under similar forms of government at the present day, but it is well known that personal interviews with the sovereign in Persia, in China, and in smaller principalities, can only be obtained with extreme difficulty, as if a sight of these potentates were too high a privilege for ordinary mortals. But besides the standing order by which such matters were regulated in the Persian court, Esther mentioned that she had not been called to come in unto the king for thirty days.

With the fickleness which characterizes such princes, and under a system which destroyed all real family ties and endearments, Artaxerxes had for some time neglected his queen, whom at first he seemed to love so tenderly. In all probability he was engaged from day to day in those intemperate excesses which Haman encouraged and shared. Esther had no more power therefore, for the time, than any menial in the palace; and thus she felt the more that if she were to present herself before the king, uncalled for, she might, according to the established law, be condemned to die, were he in one of his angry moods. It is evident, then, and it is not

Lecture 8: Esther 4:10-17

surprising, that in this pressing difficulty she craved delay. For this seems to be the purport of her answer to Mordecai by Hatach.

If she had been freely admitted to the king's presence as in former times, she could have found an opportunity to intercede for her people; and should she be again fully restored to the royal favor and confidence, she would then be able to seize an auspicious moment to follow out the request of her friend. Meanwhile, however, she could do nothing. All this, we think, is manifestly implied in the message which she sent to him. Now there are two remarks which may be offered in the way of practical application of these verses:

1. In the first place they furnish us with an illustration of what is not unfrequently observable in the arrangements of the divine providence, that the affairs of God's people assume a darker and darker aspect, just before a favorable interposition comes—in order, no doubt, to make the truth more palpable, that it is by His hand that their deliverance is wrought out, and that therefore they should never distrust Him, nor think that He has forgotten to be gracious. In the instance before us, when the prospects of the Jews appeared to be so gloomy, or we might rather say desperate, the only gleam of hope that Mordecai had arose from Esther's advancement to her high dignity. But now, when he sought to avail himself of the aid which he might reasonably expect from that quarter, his hope seemed to be extinguished. He found that an unforeseen obstacle had occurred to make his fond expectations fruitless. If the cruel decree had been published two months earlier than it was, Esther, then in the full sunshine of royal favor, could have easily interposed to arrest the execution of it; but now she was herself neglected, and the king was wholly guided by the wicked Haman, whose object evidently was to engage him so deeply in sensual indulgences, that he should have no time for calm reflection. Everything, then, connected with the circumstances of the Jews, was portentous of evil, and seemed to

render their deliverance utterly hopeless. Yet, as we shall soon find, this dark and stormy night of trouble was to be chased away by the dawning of a bright and prosperous day. There was to outward appearance a similar concatenation of adverse incidents in Jacob's history, when Simeon was detained in Egypt as a pledge for Benjamin's being brought down, and when the patriarch thought that all these things were against him, and that his sons were to be forever torn away from him. But his mourning was soon turned into gladness, and the issue of these trials was the restoration to him, not only of Simeon and Benjamin, but of the long-lost Joseph also. Now I doubt not that there are some here, in whose experience there have been providential dealings somewhat of the same kind. One difficulty or trial has been succeeded by another, as if some fatality had been in your lot, and as if you had been marked out for disappointment and trouble. Incidents which, in certain circumstances, would hardly have been felt as evils, have occurred at the very time when you were least prepared for them, and then your minds have been depressed, as if it were vain and useless for you to continue the struggle against adverse fortune. And yet in brief space you have been extricated from your difficulties by some turn of providence, as unexpected as that which occasioned them. And what does this teach you, whether your trials have been worldly or spiritual, but to take encouragement from past deliverances if your path shall again become clouded? "The Lord hath been mindful of us, and He will still bless us:" "hitherto hath the Lord helped us," are precious maxims for faith to rest upon; and if you would remember the outlets from trouble which were opened up to you formerly, when you were ready to suppose that all things were against you, you would commit your way to the Lord for the future, without those distracting cares and anxieties which so often disturb the quiet even of God's children.

2. In the second place, there is a very obvious lesson suggested to us, in the way of contrast, by the message which Esther sent to Mordecai.

Lecture 8: Esther 4:10-17

She could not venture into the king's presence in the inner court of the palace, but at the hazard of her life. She must die, except the king should hold out the golden scepter to her. How blessed, then, is our condition, in that we have at all times freedom of access to our heavenly King, with the assurance that our requests, if made in faith, will obtain a gracious hearing. It is true, indeed, that we must not presume upon the divine forbearance, and thrust ourselves rashly and unpreparedly into the presence of the Holy One. The awful punishment inflicted on the two sons of Aaron, for offering strange fire before the Lord, with the accompanying sentence for the warning of others: "I will be sanctified in them that come nigh me, and before all the people I will be glorified," may well impress the lesson upon us, that there must be preparation of heart and solemnity of mind conjoined with our approaches even to the mercy seat. Let us guard against presumptuous sin; for if, under the dispensation of Christ, there have not been such outward exhibitions of the divine displeasure on account of such sins, as were given under the law, when the worship was made up so much more of externals, yet it must not be forgotten, that there may be spiritual judgments inflicted, really more terrible than any bodily punishment, whereby the sanctity of prayer and other divine ordinances is maintained.

But, with all this in our view, we can still say to everyone who desires to go to the footstool of God, in sincerity and with humble heart, to make his requests known there, that there is no obstacle in his way.

It is indeed with the Great King you have to deal, and life and death are at His disposal; but you may go to Him without fear, if you go with a true heart. The path for a long period seemed to be barred up, at least the path which led into the holiest of all; but when Christ died, the veil of the temple was rent from top to bottom, for the purpose of teaching us, that through the rent veil of Christ's flesh sinful men everywhere might draw near to God.

There was all the formality of priestly services under the law, between the worshippers and Jehovah, to make them feel that they could not come nigh personally; just as there were functionaries to prevent Esther from coming into the presence of the king, when she merely felt the wish to do so. Now, however, God invites us to come to Him at all times, and what prevents us from having full communion with Him is not our personal unworthiness, but our unbelief. His word tells us that every blessing we need, from our daily wants up to life eternal, is to be had, if we only seek it in faith. And what other language, therefore, can I address to all than this which the word furnishes, when it says: "Let us come boldly to the throne of grace, that we may find mercy to pardon, and grace to help us in time of need."

But now we must prosecute our examination of the narrative. Verses 13-14: "Then Mordecai commanded to answer Esther, Think not with thyself that thou shalt escape in the king's house, more than all the Jews. For if thou altogether holdest thy peace at this time, then shall there enlargement and deliverance arise to the Jews from another place; but thou and thy father's house shall be destroyed: and who knoweth whether thou art come to the kingdom for such a time as this?"

We see illustrated in these verses, what was adverted to in the last lecture—the resolute and determined will of Mordecai, who would not be turned aside from his purpose by formidable difficulties. The answer which was returned to his urgent request might at once have silenced him, when he perceived that Esther might only endanger her own life, without obtaining the deliverance of her countrymen. Natural affection, if he had listened to its voice, would have made him at least irresolute, prompting the reflection: "Why should I be the instrument of destroying the beloved of my heart before the time?" But the interests at stake were so vast, that he felt as if everything must be hazarded. The course which he had pointed out was the only one that promised the possibility of success, and perilous although it was, it must be taken. Private affection must be sacrificed to the high claim of public duty. We may, however, be

Lecture 8: Esther 4:10-17

assured also that Mordecai knew thoroughly the temper and character of Esther, and that he was fully satisfied that she would not be afraid to do what she was convinced was right, be the issue what it might.

It was but natural that in the first instance she should shrink from the task which he would have her undertake, of going in to the king to make intercession for her people, because it might cost her her life. It did not imply either selfishness, or a lack of true courage, that she should hesitate to take this step. On the contrary, we think that the whole transaction, as here recorded, brings beautifully into the light her generous and truly heroic spirit.

There are two kinds of courage—the mere *animal* courage, which results from well-strung nerves, and is exerted by impulse rather than by reflection; and the *moral* courage, which, on a calm calculation of difficulties, and of the path of duty, will face the difficulties and prosecute the path of duty at any hazard, even at the risk of life itself. It will often be found that men are deficient in the latter of these qualities, while they are remarkable for the former. It will be found, for example, that soldiers who will rush fearlessly upon an enemy, braving death without one symptom of alarm, are incapable of submitting to the calm endurance of trouble, and are like others alarmed when they have to meet death quietly after lingering illness.

It is courage of the highest and noblest order, then, we say, which braves danger and death upon cool reflection. Such was the courage of the martyrs, and such was the courage of Esther. As a timid female, she drew back at first from the hazardous enterprise to which Mordecai called her; but when she had fully weighed the matter, and perceived the real path of duty, although the danger was not in the least degree diminished, she resolved, in the strength of God, to encounter it.

These remarks, however, anticipate the course of the narrative; but they have been suggested by the circumstance that it was by the use of plain argument that Esther was moved, and not by sudden impulse. Had she consented at the moment to do what she was urged to do, we must have said, "Here is an example of unselfish devotedness to a perilous undertaking." But the courage manifested may have been, after all, rather the result of a momentary excitement, than the fruit of firm and steady resolution. But when reasoning was used and listened to, and acted on, and when the mind was thus nerved for the enterprise, it was moral courage in all its dignity, and not a mere specimen of boldness, that the subsequent conduct of Esther exhibited. But, passing from this, we come to look at the arguments which Mordecai employed to engage the active co-operation of Esther. His arguments, it must be confessed, are unceremoniously stated; but they are quite in keeping with the relationship he bore to the queen, the claim he had upon her services, and his own unselfish and noble character.

First, he says (verse 13): "Think not with thyself that thou shalt escape in the king's house, more than all the Jews." It does not appear that Esther had as yet made known her kindred or her people to the king; but Mordecai intimates that this could not fail to be discovered; and indeed, this present correspondence now revealed it to those who before were ignorant of it. So that when the time for destroying the Jews came, the queen herself would be at the mercy of any of her attendants who might choose to reveal the secret. Then she, like others, would fall a victim to the royal edict, according to the principle that the law of the Medes and Persians was unalterable.

There would be additional force imparted to this argument by the circumstance to which Esther herself had alluded—e.g. that she seemed to have lost for a season the affection of the king. She might, therefore, become the victim of his cruelty, through the same fickleness and caprice which had raised her formerly to be the object of his tenderest affection.

Then Mordecai's second argument is founded upon a conviction or presentiment of his own, that in some way or other God would interpose for the deliverance of His people, and that if Esther did not perform the part which her high position seemed to call for, retribution would overtake her. Verse 14: "If thou altogether holdest thy peace at this time,

Lecture 8: Esther 4:10-17

then shall there enlargement and deliverance arise to the Jews from another place; but thou and thy father's house shall be destroyed." This statement, as I have said, was based merely upon Mordecai's own conviction or presentiment; and when he made it, we may suppose that he would have been altogether unable to advance any solid reason in defense of it. Yet the whole past history of the Jewish nation might well suggest it to him, and give it a coloring of strong probability.

On many occasions, when all human hope seemed vain, the Lord had raised up deliverers to free His people from the hand of their enemies; and His word contained bitter imprecations against those who, like the inhabitants of Meroz, would not come to the help of the Lord against the mighty.

In former ages, women, such as Deborah and Jael, had been made the instruments of saving Israel. Esther might have a place among those whose memories, after so many generations, were still fragrant among their countrymen. But if she suffered herself to be deterred from making the attempt to save her people, then some other individual would be raised up for the purpose, and she would be punished for her selfish timidity.

There was much in this mode of putting the case to make an impression upon a generous mind like Esther's, and the concluding argument was more powerful still. "Who knoweth," said Mordecai, "whether thou art come to the kingdom for such a time as this?"

This was the right way to estimate the design of her advancement to her high dignity, and to enforce the responsibility which was thus laid upon her. So extraordinary a movement of providence as that which had raised a poor unknown exile to share the throne of the most powerful monarch in the world, must surely be intended to serve some higher end than merely to promote the temporal interests and gratify the pride and vanity of that one individual; and she herself must feel that it could not have been for her own sake alone, but to afford her the opportunity of doing good upon the widest scale, that she had been so singularly favored. In fact, it was only now that light was beginning to be cast upon the whole of her previous history; and Mordecai would have her think of this. A special providence had watched over her cradle, when she was left in the world a helpless orphan. More remarkable still had been all the steps by which she had reached her present elevation. It was evident that God had marked her out for some great enterprise; and now the time seemed plainly to be come when she must with all earnestness and self-devotion respond to the call of providence.

These considerations, then, Mordecai pressed upon the attention of Esther, to engage her in the work which lay nearest to his heart, and the effect of them we shall soon see. Meanwhile, let us make a practical improvement of the topics which have been referred to.

The great lesson which they unitedly teach, is that of the obligation which rests upon each of us to employ the talents and influence, and other means which God in His providence has bestowed upon us for the good of His church and people, and generally for the advancement of the cause of truth and righteousness in the world.

I think it may be safely affirmed, that while the grand design of the gospel of Christ is to restore sinners to the enjoyment of God's favor and to the divine likeness, the two chief obstacles which it has to encounter in the human heart, are unbelief and selfishness. Under the power of these evil principles, men reject God's testimony in His word, respecting their guilt and sinfulness, and the means of salvation, and live on in self-indulgence and self-will, regardless of the calls addressed to them to turn to God, and to live for the advancement of His glory. And not only do those who despise the gospel exhibit the spirit of unbelief and selfishness, but even Christ's own people, of whom better things might be expected, afford many melancholy proofs that they are not wholly emancipated from the influence of the same spirit. "Oh ye of little faith," is language which requires often to be addressed now, as it was by the Lord Himself, to His followers. And the great maxim enforced by the apostle needs to be equally enforced in our own time: "Christ died for all,

Lecture 8: Esther 4:10-17

that they who live should not henceforth live unto themselves, but unto Him that died for them, and that rose again."

It was practically to prevent Esther from sinking under the influence of unbelief and selfishness, that Mordecai urged upon her attention the two truths, that deliverance would be wrought out for the Jews as God's covenant people, and that the very reason of her being advanced to the kingdom was, not that she might live in luxurious ease, but that she might exert her power for God's glory, and the benefit of her countrymen. And it is for a similar end that we inculcate upon you the lesson which this part of the history suggests. You may be disposed to imagine, that when, in the providence of God, you are put in possession of wealth and other advantages, which at one period you could have scarcely looked for, you are at liberty to employ them as you think fit yourselves, for your own gratification, and without any reference to the interests of Christ's kingdom. And you may be ready to plead, when you are reminded of the need there is, amid prevailing indifference, that energetic and active effort be put forth for the advancement of its interests, you may be ready to plead that you are not qualified for such work, and that it involves difficulties and sacrifices greater than you can submit to. We set the words of Mordecai then before you, and ask you seriously to ponder them. Assuredly the kingdom of Christ will prosper, whether you put your hand to the work or not. Its progress and triumph are secured by the word of truth. And if in a spirit of unbelief, deterred by apparent difficulties, you will not help it onward, then from some other quarter help will come. But then, as you cannot be numbered among those who are on the side of Christ, you must be numbered among those that are against Him, and their lot must be yours in the end.

But farther, and more particularly, do you think that the bounties of providence have been conferred upon you for the mere purpose of enabling you to pass your days in the enjoyment of comforts and luxuries which are denied to many others, while so much remains to be done for the spread of the gospel in the world, and for promoting the best interests of mankind? If you do, you form a conclusion altogether at variance with the teaching of the word of God. "No man is at liberty to live unto himself," and God will call us all to a reckoning for the use we have made of the good gifts of His providence, as well as of the means of grace. The advantages which He has bestowed upon you, are given for a special end, e.g.—that He who gives them may be glorified.

A worldly-minded and selfish man may reason in this way, when his schemes have prospered, and all his affairs are flourishing: "I may now accomplish objects which I have long sought in vain to accomplish, I may now say to my soul, soul, take thine ease, eat, drink, and be merry." But a Christian cannot reason thus. He feels that he has got his blessings, that he may make them available for some good purpose. He will find some praise-worthy Christian object languishing for lack of aid, when he is able to impart aid, and will act upon the principle, that this is one of the very designs for which Providence has so blessed him. And this is the right mode of reasoning. For then a man is twice blessed; blessed in having the means of doing good, and blessed in having the generous heart rightly to employ them.

But we must now proceed to consider the remaining verses of the chapter. Verse 15-17: "Then Esther bade them return Mordecai this answer, Go, gather together all the Jews that are present in Shushan, and fast ye for me, and neither eat nor drink three days, night or day: I also and my maidens will fast likewise; and so will I go in unto the king, which is not according to the law: and if I perish, I perish. So Mordecai went his way, and did according to all that Esther had commanded him."

Here we have a most interesting light shed upon the character of Esther. She felt the force of Mordecai's arguments, and although they did not make her danger the less, they satisfied her as to the path of duty, and determined her to follow it at all hazards. Her conduct displays a mixture of that moral courage of which we have already spoken, and of genuine piety. She was now resolved to brave all the consequences of an act which, by the Persian law, was most perilous, even to hazard her life in

Lecture 8: Esther 4:10-17

the attempt to save her countrymen. But still she felt that she was but a weak woman, and that she needed divine strength to uphold her. She felt also, that without the blessing of God, her endeavor to deliver her people could not be successful, whatever might be the issue to herself. And, therefore, she commanded Mordecai to engage all the people of God in acts of solemn worship in her behalf, that the divine blessing might rest upon her enterprise. Prayer, indeed, is not expressly mentioned in the text; but the reason is, that it was so uniformly an accompaniment of fasting, that it was not judged necessary to specify it by itself.

It is very probable that, as the Jews had hitherto been tolerated in the Persian empire, they would have their synagogues for prayer. The secret fasting, then, and the public assembling for prayer for three successive days, formed the exercises on the part of the people which Esther looked to as the means of drawing down from heaven the help she needed: and she herself was not to be wanting in the same exercises. "I also, and my maidens, will fast likewise," she said. It forms a proof of the ascendancy she had gained over the minds of her attendants, by her gentleness and kindness towards them, that she could so readily promise that they would submit to this self-denial, because she imposed it upon herself. There is no reason for supposing that they were Jewish maidens who waited on her, because her own religion was not yet known. But she concluded, from their proved attachment to her, that when they saw her in distress, and abstaining from her ordinary food, they would sympathize with her, and follow her example. And thus, while in one part of the palace, the king and his favorite were engaged in their revels, the latter rejoicing in the prospect of having his vengeance glutted with the blood of the Jewish race; in another part there was humiliation and sorrow, with earnest cries to the God of Abraham, that He would interpose as of old, for the protection of His own. All the power seemed to be lodged where the revelers were, but it was not so in reality. The supplications of Esther, and of her apparently helpless countrymen, ascended as a memorial to the throne of God, and omnipotence was thus engaged on the side of the distressed.

There is something well worthy of remark in the concluding words of Esther: "So will I go in unto the king, which is not according to law; and if I perish, I perish." This is not the resolution of a fatalist, who acts upon the principle, that what is destined to be must be, and that therefore it is useless either to attempt to ward off evils, or to complain when they have been inflicted. Neither is it the resolution of a person wrought up to a state of absolute desperation and acting under the impulse of the feeling—"matters cannot be worse, and to have done the utmost may bring relief, while it cannot possibly aggravate the evil." Neither is it the resolution of a person prostrated under difficulties, and yet, with a vague hope of deliverance, saying: "I will make one effort more, and if that fail, and all is lost, I can but die." Esther's purpose was framed in a spirit altogether different from that of any of those persons, although her language appears to be almost the same as they would have used. And there is an actual case recorded in the Scriptures which illustrates the difference.

When Samaria was besieged by the Syrians, and the people were dying of famine within the walls, four leprous men, that had their dwelling without the wall, said to one another: "If we enter into the city, famine is in the city, and we shall die there; and if we sit still here, we die also. Now, therefore, come and let us fall unto the host of the Syrians; if they save us alive, we shall live: and if they kill us, we shall but die." Here we have men reduced to a state of utter recklessness by suffering, from which, if they did not obtain immediate relief, they must inevitably perish in one way or other, and so they adopted the only course which presented the possibility of relief. But in the case of Esther, we have neither fatalism, nor desperation, nor the listlessness of waning hope, which says: "It matters not what I do."

Hers is the heroism of true piety, which, in Providence, shut up to one course, and that full of danger, counts the cost, seeks help of God, and calmly braves the danger, saying: "He will deliver me if He hath pleasure in me," if not, I perish in the path of duty. Her noble resolution entitles her to a place among the most eminent of those who wrought out deliverances for Israel.

And now, in conclusion, have not her words peculiar significance when applied to the case of those who, under the burden of their sin, are afraid to come to Christ lest He reject them? Some such we have known. There may be some of them here. Do you feel that you are lost? Do you acknowledge that Christ might justly throw you off, even were you to cast yourselves upon His mercy? And are you now almost without hope? Still we say, His invitations are addressed to sinners, and none need them more than you. You are lost without Him: then make the great effort to lay hold of Him. Job said: "Though He slay me I will trust in Him." You may say: "If I perish, I perish, but it shall be at the foot of the cross, looking to Jesus." And I can tell you, my friends, that none ever perished there, putting all their trust in the Lamb of God.

Amen.

Lecture 9: Esther 5:1-8

In the last lecture, we saw Mordecai urgent in requesting Esther to go to the king and plead for her countrymen. His arguments were very weighty, and to this effect, that if the royal edict were put in execution, she herself would not be exempted from the general massacre; that even if deliverance came from some unexpected quarter, she would certainly suffer for her timidity and selfishness: and that she should regard her advancement to the throne as brought about just to render her useful in the present emergency.

These arguments produced the desired effect upon her mind; but she knew, at the same time, that in a case where matters so momentous were at stake, and where the success of her undertaking depended upon the temper and feeling of the king when she presented herself before him, something more was needed than a brave heart. The blessing of Jehovah—who, in the language of His own word, "has the hearts of kings in His hand as the rivers of water, and turneth them whithersoever He will"—she felt to be indispensable toward the prosperous issue of her enterprise; and therefore she would have Mordecai engage all the Jews in Susa in the exercises of prayer and fasting, while she herself was to be occupied in the same way for three successive days, so that unitedly they might implore the blessing which alone could work out for them deliverance and enlargement. Then she would face the danger, and perish in the attempt to save her people, if such should be the will of the Lord.

This brings us now to the subject of the present discourse. Verse 1-2: "Now it came to pass on the third day, that Esther put on her royal apparel, and stood in the inner court of the king's house, over against the king's house: and the king sat upon his royal throne in the royal house, over against the gate of the house. And it was so, when the king saw Esther the queen standing in the court, that she obtained favor in his

Lecture 9: Esther 5:1-8

sight: and the king held out to Esther the golden scepter that was in his hand. So Esther drew near, and touched the top of the scepter."

It is impossible for us to understand precisely the arrangements of these royal palaces, which were the abodes of licentiousness and luxury, and which were so studiously shut up from the view of the multitude without. Thus much is known, however, from the examination of ancient ruins, and from the construction of similar buildings in the East at the present day, that there was such separation between the apartments which the king employed for the transaction of public affairs and those which were occupied by his wives and concubines, that there could be no free communication between the two places except by express royal permission. And what Esther had to do implied the departure from all established usage.

She had to come out of her own special residence, and to tread upon ground which no one might presume to occupy, but with leave granted by the king. This seems very strange to us, but such was the law in Persia; and we must therefore connect with Esther's conduct the idea that it was bold and hazardous beyond what any in her place had done before. When Vashti was degraded, it was because she would not submit to an order of the king which involved the humiliation of her sex. She had, or at least might justly suppose she had, the judgment of all the right-thinking in the kingdom upon her side; and but for the king's intemperate excitement, and the too great facility of his counselors, her case would have borne the fullest examination. But it was against all known law, and in a way hitherto unheard of, that Esther had to act, when she came forth from her own proper apartments, and presented herself before the king, as he sat in the place where none could be received except on leave formally asked and obtained.

But now let us look particularly to the account which is given of this remarkable interview. "It came to pass," it is said, "that on the third day, Esther put on her royal apparel, and stood in the inner court of the king's house." I had occasion to mention, that when the beautiful Jewess was first brought into the king's presence, she made little account of such ornaments as those with which the other competitors for the royal favor decorated themselves. Having a better taste and a more modest bearing than they, she sought no extraneous adorning to enhance her charms; and though perhaps she herself was of all the least sensible of this, she needed none. But now, on the occasion referred to in the text, she pursues a different course. She arrays herself in her queenly attire, and is decked in all the splendor which the most giddy-minded votary of fashion could have selected to set off to advantage the graces of her person.

And why this change? Had Esther become corrupted by the prevailing manners of the court, and learned, like those among whom she lived, to put an undue value upon things which were dazzling to the eye, and which she had formerly regarded as among the vanities of life? No! There were other and more satisfying reasons for her acting as she did on this occasion. Two of these are very obvious. In the first place, it would have been altogether unlawful for her to appear in a mourning garb, and unbecoming in her to have dressed herself in mean apparel, when she was to go into the king's presence in public. There is something due to rank and station, which is felt among ourselves, that would prevent anyone from waiting upon a superior without some attention to dress and outward equipment generally. It would indicate, not superiority to vulgar prejudice, but absolute coarseness of mind and feeling, to overlook such arrangements, trifling though they may appear intrinsically to be. And at the court of Persia there was still more attention paid to such matters: so much so, as we have seen, that Mordecai could not even sit in the king's gate clothed in sackcloth. For Esther, then, to have gone in humble attire into the presence of the king, would have been to put an affront upon the sovereign, and at once to defeat the very object which she had at heart.

Then, in the second place, the royal apparel which she put on was all the gift of the king to her. Her ornaments were his love-tokens, bestowed when she was the chief object of his confidence and affection, and, as

Lecture 9: Esther 5:1-8

such, fitted to call up in his mind the remembrance of the days when he had delighted in her presence, and when no designing favorite shut out from her the rays of his royal favor.

We all expect to see any gift we have bestowed upon another applied to its destined use, and the neglect of the gift is regarded by us as equivalent to a contempt of the donor. Now it was in presents of dress, and ornaments connected with it, that the Easterns displayed and still display their munificence; so that Esther, arrayed in her royal robes, going to cast herself upon the king's favor, just went to him in the way that would most vividly remind him that she was the creature of his bounty, as she had been the object of his love.

We may take an illustration here from our Lord's parable of the Wedding Garment. There is something in that parable which at first appears inexplicable. The persons who were brought into the marriage-supper were those whom the king's servants had gathered together from the highways; and how, it may be asked, could the man be found fault with who had not on a wedding garment? Here, then, lies the solution of the difficulty. Dresses befitting the occasion were furnished to the guests, according to the custom of the time; and he who had not on the proper dress must have supposed that his own clothing was good enough, and must have rejected the offer of a garment suitable, which was made to him by the keeper of the king's wardrobe. For this contempt, then, he was righteously charged and condemned. And so in the case before us, Esther would have been subject to displeasure, and righteously punishable according to the established law, if, when the king had furnished her with the apparel and decorations suited to her exalted station, she had appeared before him, as he sat upon his throne, in attire more homely. But she had too much wisdom, and too strong a sense of what was becoming and proper, to expose herself to challenge on such a ground; and hence her carefulness to come forth in all the splendor of her queenly dress and ornaments.

Festive clothing often covers an aching heart. And if we could read the feelings of the children of vanity when they are fluttering in all the pride of their rich attire, the lesson might be, that there is more real happiness to be found where there is less vain show. On the present occasion, at all events, we may be sure of this, that there was not a heart worse at ease in the kingdom of Persia than was hid under those gorgeous robes which Esther wore as she passed through the court from her own apartments into the presence of the king—the wonder and the envy of the attendants that followed her.

But now, with life or death depending on every step, and with a timidity that must have made her look more beautiful than ever, she comes within reach of the king's glance. He had not seen her for more than thirty days. The sight of her at that moment, and in that place, was altogether unexpected. Without having time for reflection, or for speaking to Haman, who no doubt was beside him, of this strange disregard of the courtly etiquette, his former love was rekindled in his heart by the sight of the beautiful vision. He smiled and held out to Esther the golden scepter that was in his hand. She felt that she was safe, and so drew near and touched the top of the scepter.

Thus far the simple words of the history conduct us; and those who were spectators of this strange scene, would see nothing more in it than a most daring adventure on the part of the queen, with a singular exhibition of good will on the king's part. But with the help of what is stated in the preceding chapter, we get a clearer light upon the whole scene, and can understand the real meaning of the words: "Esther obtained favor in the king's sight." The prayer and fasting of the three previous days had not been without fruit. A divine influence had been put forth to touch the heart of the king; and, without knowing it himself, by that influence he was led—not only to forgive the queen's unwarrantable intrusion into his presence, but also, as we shall see, to grant her any request which she might make. Here, then, there is the dawning of the day of deliverance for the Jews.

Lecture 9: Esther 5:1-8

Now, let us, before going farther, make some practical application of this part of our subject.

1. In the first place, this lesson is obviously to be taken from it, that when we are to engage in any special work or enterprise involving difficulty or danger, the most effectual way to gain the object we have in view, is to seek help and direction from on high. No man, indeed, whose heart is really imbued with the fear of God, will fail every day to ask direction and a blessing in the conducting of his ordinary affairs. And this is one circumstance which makes a difference between the pursuits of the mere worldling and those of the Christian, although externally they may seem to be engaged in the very same kind of business. But when there are momentous interests at stake, when things have to be done out of the ordinary course, then, we say, there ought to be a special application made for divine assistance and guidance. This is not to supersede the use of such means as prudence and experience may dictate for the accomplishment of the end in view. On the contrary, one of the subjects of prayer in such cases is, that the mind may be enlightened and strengthened so as to lead to the selection of the best means. But then, with all this, the committing of the issue to the appointment of God is the right procedure on the part of all who believe in a divine providence and look up to the God of providence as their Father in heaven. Esther, although she fasted and prayed, did not neglect the duty of arraying herself suitably to her station, and as the honor of the king required her to do. But we doubt not, that as she put on her ornaments, and as she went with throbbing heart across the court which separated her apartments from those in which the throne stood, her thoughts were more in heaven than on earth. And from her example we learn, that the spirit in which we should conduct our most important affairs is, that of committing our way to God, while we endeavor not to be awanting in personal

activity, and in the employment of such lawful means as seem most likely to promote our purpose.

2. In the second place, we learn from this part of the narrative, that there may be divine influence at work upon the heart and will even of those who have no personal regard for religion, by which they are unconsciously rendered instrumental in advancing the interests of God's people and of His cause. As has been already said, we cannot avoid connecting the sacred exercises in which Esther and her friends were engaged, with the turning of the king's heart toward her. And many other examples of the same kind might be selected from the sacred record. There is the memorable one in the case of Cyrus, when he was moved by the Lord to take compassion on the captive Jews, and to permit all of them who chose, to return to their own land and rebuild the city of Jerusalem. There is another in the case of the same Artaxerxes who showed favor to Esther, to which reference is made in the book of Nehemiah. When this patriotic and pious man was troubled on account of the desolations of Jerusalem, he prayed fervently that the heart of the king might be affected so as to lead him to grant assistance for remedying the evils which were felt by the Jews who had gone to repair the waste places of the holy city. And the king was moved accordingly. It does not follow from those cases, that the putting forth of divine influence to incline these heathen monarchs to do what was for the good of God's people, implied any gracious operation upon their hearts in the way of delivering them from their deadly errors. All that can be inferred is, that God's creatures, high and low, are as the clay in the hand of the potter. But this conclusion is very manifest, that as the settlement of numberless affairs, in which the interests of God's people are concerned, rests upon the will of individuals who may not be naturally well disposed toward their cause; this is one direction which their prayers may well take, that God would overrule the heart and will of those enemies, so that the truth may prosper. In this way, in answer to believing and

Lecture 9: Esther 5:1-8

persevering prayer, the words of the Lord may still be, as they often have been, verified, that mountains of difficulty are removed: "The crooked things are made straight, and the rough places plain."

3. In the third place, from the verses under review, compared with the previous history, we may draw an illustration of some important principles in the economy of grace. I must, however, remind you here of a distinction which requires to be kept in view in all comments upon the Old Testament history, and in the illustration of Scripture generally—a distinction between truths evidently deducible from the historical narrative, and directly bearing upon subjects of belief and practice, which are applicable to all times and circumstances; and reflections suggested by certain portions of the history, but suggested by them, rather than manifestly designed to be taught by them. There has often been a tendency exhibited by interpreters of Scripture, to spiritualize all the events recorded in it. And in many cases, it must be acknowledged, this has been so happily done, as to make us feel as if we were refreshed by water from the flinty rock. Yet we must never overlook the difference between truth directly revealed, and truth suggested merely in the way of illustration. Now, with these remarks, the point which I would have you for a moment look at here, as bearing upon the doctrines of grace, is suggested by the contrast between Esther's first appearance before the king, and her appearance now in the manner above described. In the first instance, she sought not the aid of ornament, but appeared in simple attire. And just as she was, she gained the king's heart. But now, when she is about to present an important request to him, a request involving life or death to herself and multitudes besides, she goes arrayed in the dress, and ornaments, and jewels, which were the king's gifts to her, that he might recognize his own love tokens, and be moved to show favor again by the remembrance that he had shown favor before. You will easily perceive the application we make of all this. The sinner at first casts himself upon the mercy of God in Christ, in all his natural

worthlessness, feeling that he has nothing to rely upon for acceptance and favor, but sovereign grace. And God, in accepting him, is moved solely by His own mercy; for many others, who are more highly gifted, and who have many qualities that might seem to give them a preference according to human judgment are passed by. Our heavenly King has no respect of persons, so far as birth and the external circumstances and condition of men are concerned; but, at the same time, His love is bestowed sovereignly. "He has mercy upon whom He will have mercy." But when His believing people go to Him in their difficulties and troubles to implore His aid, then He recognizes in them, amid all their deficiencies, something of His own comeliness which has been put upon them. They may be laboring under fears and doubts almost as depressing as those by which they were weighed down when they first threw themselves at His feet imploring mercy to pardon. But they stand now in a different relation to Him. He has been gracious toward them, and in their distress, although it may be the distress which is the result of conscious backsliding, He perceives His own marks, or, as the Scripture expresses it, "The spots of His own children," upon them, and as His own, He welcomes them, and graciously answers their requests.

The stretching out of the golden scepter referred to in the text, expresses the sense which He imparts to them of His willingness to help their infirmities. And their touching it is the renewal of that acting of faith upon Him on their part, which takes Him at His word, as having promised, and being ready to supply all their wants out of His glorious riches. And they need not fear that He will frown upon them, when they go to intercede with Him either for themselves or others. If faith and love are in their hearts, and they are clothed with humility, they have the passport which will always get admission for them into the presence of the King, and which will always gain for them from His beneficence what is most needful, although it may not always be what they most desire.

Lecture 9: Esther 5:1-8

Much might be said upon this interesting subject; but I must pass on to consider what follows in the narrative. Verses 3-5: "Then said the king unto her, What wilt thou, queen Esther? and what is thy request? it shall be even given thee to the half of the kingdom. And Esther answered, If it seem good unto the king, let the king and Haman come this day unto the banquet that I have prepared for him. Then the king said, Cause Haman to make haste, that he may do as Esther hath said. So the king and Haman came to the banquet that Esther had prepared."

Esther had come into the royal presence, not knowing but that her life might be forfeited by what she did; but all is overruled, so that she has only to express her desire, and it will be gratified. Of course, the words: "it shall be even given thee to the half of the kingdom," are to be understood not literally, but as the exaggerated Eastern form of intimating willingness to confer any reasonable benefit that might be asked. Herod used the same words in promising to the daughter of Herodias a reward when she danced before him so as to please him. Solomon's form of speech, however, was far more appropriate, when, his mother Bathsheba having come to him with a request as he sat upon his throne, he said to her: "Ask on, my mother, for I will not say thee nay." Yet Solomon refused to grant the very request which was made to him at that time; and Esther, notwithstanding the encouragement she received, did not venture to ask the very thing which lay nearest to her heart.

"If it seem good unto the king," she said, "let the king and Haman come unto the banquet that I have prepared for him." This appeared a small matter to have put her life in peril for; and yet it was a proof of her wisdom and sagacity that she thus spoke. Some may think that there was something of artfulness in her procedure; but she had good reason to proceed with caution. If she had at once and broadly stated what she really wished to be done, when the king was engaged in the transaction of public affairs, and when he was surrounded by his officers of state, her request would have struck them all with astonishment. The edict had gone forth for the destruction of the Jews, and could not be *formally* recalled, because the recognized principle was that the laws of the Medes and Persians were unalterable. We see, for example, how, when the enemies of Daniel had craftily led King Darius to pass a decree by which, as they anticipated, the prophet would certainly be placed within their power, and when their scheme succeeded, the king, although he was most anxious to save him, was prevented from altering the decree. So we may suppose, that if Esther had pled for a reversal of the sentence which had been passed against the Jews, the king, however willing he might have been to gratify her, would have found himself hemmed in by the established law of the empire—and that the more especially when he was employed in formally administering the affairs of the kingdom.

The request of the queen, however, as she put it, created no difficulty, and was at the same time flattering to the king himself. He had for a season withdrawn himself from her society, and what she asked was, that he would condescend again to honor her with some share of his regard; and that he might not suppose that she wished to separate him from the society of his chosen favorite, she included Haman in the invitation to partake of the banquet which she had prepared. A petition so reasonable, and at the same time so gratifying, was at once acceded to, and Haman was forthwith ordered to prepare for waiting on the queen.

The question may be considered here, whether there was not artifice, amounting to duplicity, in the conduct of Esther on this occasion? Certainly her expressed desire was not that which she most ardently wished to obtain. And the fact of her requesting Haman to come to the banquet, while at heart she hated him as the cruel enemy of her people, does look like the laying of a snare for him to accomplish his ruin. She was to smile upon the man whom the king honored, at the very time that she was scheming his destruction. Is not this like some of the dark passages of history, in which we read of friendships feigned to throw men off their guard, that they might be slain without resistance, as when "Joab took Abner aside to speak with him quietly, and smote him under the fifth rib, that he died?"

Lecture 9: Esther 5:1-8

In answer to this question, then, we would say, that the conduct of Esther here will bear to be most closely examined. There is nothing in it that bears resemblance to a pious fraud, neither did she do evil that good might come. Enough has been said already, to show that she could not with any prospect of success make known publicly what she was most anxious to obtain. Her whole hope, humanly-speaking, rested upon the influence which she might bring to bear upon the king. Should she succeed in awakening in him the affection which he had formerly shown toward her, and at some happy moment, when he was in most favorable mood, lay her request before him, then her object might be gained, but in no other circumstances. And so her requesting him to come to her banquet, was just the best and the most likely method of accomplishing her purpose. Again, with regard to Haman, the reason why he was outwardly so favored, while in reality evil was designed against him is very manifest. The king was likely to be pleased by this arrangement. And it was of importance that Haman should be present when the full disclosure of the affair was made, in order that he might not have opportunity covertly to defeat the purpose of the queen, by practicing upon the too facile mind of Artaxerxes. Altogether, there was a wise and skillful management of the whole business, which could not have been expected from one so young and inexperienced as Esther was, and which we may safely say, she could not have exhibited had she been left entirely to her own resources.

But let us now make a brief improvement of the verses which have been considered. And here the train of thought suggested to us will have already occurred to the minds of some. It embraces two particulars: the largeness of the king's offer, and Esther's hesitancy at once to avail herself of it.

1. With respect to the largeness of the offer. "Even to the half of my kingdom," the king said, "will thy request be granted." This, we have remarked, was the language of exaggeration. But we have it declared,

in the words of truth addressed by our heavenly Lord to His people: "Verily, verily I say unto you, whatsoever ye shall ask the Father in my name, He will give it you. Hitherto have ye asked nothing in my name: ask, and ye shall receive, that your joy may be full." Here there is no limitation, but whatever is needed to the completion of our true spiritual joy, we are invited to ask, in the name of Christ; and if we ask in faith, as we are elsewhere told, it will be given, "that the Father may be glorified in the Son." "All things are yours," it is said to believers; and it may well be said, since Jehovah gives Himself to them as their God, and Christ is theirs, and the Spirit dwells in them.

2. But then, secondly, as Esther was afraid all at once to ask what she most desired, so God's people are often slow or afraid to avail themselves to the full of their privilege of asking. Many are contented to live from year to year, with little more to uphold them than an indistinct hope that they shall reach heaven at last, when, if they would but take home God's promises in all their freeness and richness, they might be able to rejoice in Him as their portion. Many even seem to think that it would be presumptuous in them to expect such comfort and enlargement of heart as they read that others have enjoyed; whereas the Scripture tells them that the Spirit of the Lord is not straitened, and that they are only straitened in themselves.

But perhaps it may be, that as Esther did not feel herself in a condition all at once to close with the king's most liberal offer, so some among us, for other reasons than the feeling that it would be presumptuous, may be exercised in the same way with respect to spiritual privileges. This point deserves a moment's notice. There are some professed followers of Christ, who are not altogether prepared either to ask or to receive the full measure of privilege which He offers to His people. They have still some lingering desires after the world and its pleasures, which they are unwilling all at once to renounce; and though they seem to have cast in their lot with the redeemed, they would rather have the process of self-renunciation and of sanctification to be gradual

Lecture 9: Esther 5:1-8

than summary. In a word, with their present feelings, they would be, I must say unwilling, or at least afraid, to receive the large communications of grace which Christ has promised to bestow. Now this is a most dangerous state of mind, and cannot be otherwise designated than as a grieving of the Spirit of God. And if there be any here to whom the above remarks are applicable, I would beseech them no longer to sport with offered blessings—no longer to imagine that they can serve Christ and the world together. Esther only deferred craving all she wished, because that was the best way to obtain it in the end. But if you are unwilling to take all that you might have, because in that case you must bid adieu to certain pleasures which you desire to retain, then you provoke the Lord to withdraw from you altogether the sense of His favor, and to leave you in utter darkness.

But we must now glance for a moment at verses 6-8: "And the king said unto Esther at the banquet of wine, What is thy petition? and it shall be granted thee: and what is thy request? even to the half of the kingdom it shall be performed. Then answered Esther, and said, My petition and my request is; if I have found favor in the sight of the king, and if it please the king to grant my petition, and to perform my request, let the king and Haman come to the banquet that I shall prepare for them, and I will do tomorrow as the king hath said."

It would appear from this passage, that the king understood that Esther's inviting him to her banquet was only preliminary to her making some request which she could not with propriety present in public. Hence, he again declares his willingness to grant her whatever she should desire. Whether her heart failed her at the moment, or whether she saw that matters were not yet fully ripe for the disclosure of her troubles, we cannot determine; but from what follows in the narrative, we can see that her reluctance was overruled to answer two purposes—to allow the farther development of Haman's wickedness, and to place the cause of the Jews, in the person of Mordecai, in so favorable a light to the king, that Esther might plead it with less fear than she felt on the occasion referred to in the verses before us. Thus far she had attained the object she aimed at, that she was restored to the king's confidence, and that Haman, the great enemy of her people, was put off his guard, so that he could have no suspicion of her ultimate design. He was left standing upon the brink of destruction, when he never appeared to be more secure. And thus it often is that the wicked are nearest ruin when they are least prepared for it.

But I must now conclude; and I would do so with one remark, drawn from the general bearing of the passage which has been reviewed—e.g., that in all our troubles, the true path of safety is to be found in our having immediate recourse to Christ our King. Esther would have gladly excused herself from making personal application to Artaxerxes; but Mordecai would receive no excuse. She went, therefore, and with God's blessing was successful. Act ye in the same spirit, believers. Listen not to fears and doubts suggested by the feeling of personal unworthiness. Christ will not say nay to any that come to Him in faith, and with sincere heart. He is described as waiting to be gracious; and the only things that will shut out your prayer from Him, are unbelief and the love of sin. From these seek to be delivered. With honest and earnest desire, come to the mercy seat. You will find the way to it open. Your reception is secured there, because Christ is there, and out of His fullness you will receive grace for grace.

Amen.

Lecture 10: Esther 5:9-14

In the last lecture we saw Esther, inspired with a courage which was the fruit of prayer, offered up by herself and by others in her behalf, venturing to transgress the established law of the kingdom of Persia, and braving death that she might save her people, by going into the king's presence in public when she was not sent for. The same prayer, however, which strengthened her for this bold undertaking, was effectual in crowning it with success. A divine influence rendered her superior to those fears which made her shrink at first from the undertaking which was urged upon her; and a divine influence was at the same time put forth to soften the heart of the king toward her. She was saved from the penalty which by the law she had incurred. When she appeared in the royal presence, the scepter was stretched out toward her—a token that she had obtained favor in the sight of the king; and as she came in the character of a suppliant, the large promise was given her that her request would be granted so far as the kingly munificence could satisfy it.

For reasons which are not specified, but which it is not difficult to conjecture, Esther did not presume at that moment to present the request which lay nearest to her heart. She felt that she must be first fully established again in the confidence and affection of the king; and that, in a matter which involved the annulling of a decree which had been formally issued, she would more likely gain her end when she had possession of his private ear, than when he was surrounded by his counselors, and when, for the sake of his own dignity, and of preserving his consistency, he might feel it necessary to say nay to her. She therefore only entreated him to come, along with Haman, to a banquet which she had prepared. This petition was readily complied with, although the king evidently knew that she had something farther to ask, which she could only ask in private. And accordingly, at the banquet he again expressed his desire to gratify her, whatever she might wish him to bestow. Not yet prepared to lay open her mind, and, as we believe, withheld by a special providence, she put the matter off, with a request that the king and Haman should come again on the morrow to feast with her, when she would fully make known what was her desire.

At this point, then, we are brought to consider the passage which forms the subject of the present lecture. Verse 9: "Then went Haman forth that day joyful and with a glad heart: but when Haman saw Mordecai in the king's gate, that he stood not up, nor moved for him, he was full of indignation against Mordecai."

Our attention in the present discourse must be directed chiefly to Haman. He is the principal character in the picture which is presented to us in the remaining verses of this chapter; and we shall find that the study of his feelings and conduct, although it is not pleasing, may nevertheless be turned to some advantage. But Mordecai is also introduced in an interesting light, and we shall first of all make some reference to him. It is very obvious, from what is here said, that after he found he had made that impression upon the mind of Esther which he desired—and no doubt, also, after he had, with the rest of the Jews in Susa, engaged in earnest supplication for her, according to her request—he had laid aside his sackcloth, and resumed his usual place in the king's gate. As has been already said, he could not have appeared there in his mourning dress; and the circumstance of his being there, would thus seem to indicate not only his anxiety to obtain the earliest possible tidings of Esther's procedure, but also his confidence that the Lord would listen to the prayers of His people in their time of trouble.

One thing, however, is peculiarly to be noticed, that with all his consciousness of Haman's power and influence, he still refuses to pay him homage. A man of low and groveling spirit would have crouched at the feet of the favorite, and endeavored to gratify him by any act of submission, so as to mollify his wrath, and to draw him to listen with a favorable ear to any intercession that might be made for the poor Jews

Lecture 10: Esther 5:9-14

who were doomed to destruction. But Mordecai was no fawning flatterer. His opinion of Haman, as one of a race on which the malediction of the divine law lay, and as personally the declared enemy of the Jews, remained unchanged, and therefore his conduct toward him was unchanged also. And thus, when the Amalekite came forth from the queen's banquet, more inflated than ever with a feeling of self-importance, Mordecai looked at him, perhaps with a glance of disdain, as he passed, and sat still as a statue, without doing him reverence.

This fact of itself adds weight to the remarks which were made formerly, when the subject of Mordecai's deportment toward Haman had first to be noticed—e.g., that it was from a conscientious conviction that he, as one of the seed of Abraham, from the first refused to pay respect to one of the seed of Amalek. The conviction was founded upon the statement in the law of Moses, that between the two races there should be war for ever—the Amalekites being the representatives of the enemies of the church of God, and the Jews of its members.

We therefore venerate the memory of Mordecai the Jew, who, when the affairs of his countrymen were in the most desperate condition, would not be moved to perform an act which he felt to be unbecoming, although by doing it he might have hoped to gain some advantage for himself and for his people. He would not have refused to give due honor to any of the nobles of Persia, however much he might have pitied them in his heart for their ignorance of the true God; but that haughty and wicked Amalekite he disdained to pay court to, even when he was reduced to the necessity of feeling that his own life, and that of many thousands besides, lay at his disposal.

We say again, that his memory deserves to be venerated on account of his steadfast adherence to principle. If it had been a question of mere personal liking and disliking, we would have been disposed to say that Mordecai acted irrationally in suffering his dislike to Haman to carry him so far as to confirm that favorite of the king in his hatred of the Jews. If it had been a matter of indifference whether he made obeisance to the royal favorite or not, we would have been disposed to say that he would have been inexcusable to let slip any possible opportunity of advancing the interests of his countrymen; but it was a matter of high principle, and therefore, whatever might be the consequence, Mordecai would not swerve a hair's-breadth from the course which he had formerly pursued.

It would be a blessed thing if, in matters which affect the interests of religion and practical godliness, the followers of Christ would exhibit the same kind of firm determination as we read of in the case of Mordecai. There would then be a more decided separation between the church and the world, and less of that tendency to combine the two services of Christ and the world which prevails among us so extensively. If men were estimated according to their real character, and treated rather as their moral worth merits, than with deference to their wealth—if the true elements of greatness, such as the fear of God, the love of truth, and unbending adherence to Christian principle, were honored by those who profess to follow Christ, and the opposite qualities were visited with the disapprobation they deserve, then the church would occupy her proper ground, and her members, although hated by the world, would be the object of its secret respect. But on this point we cannot enlarge at present.

We turn now from Mordecai to Haman. "When the all-influential man of power saw the Jew in the king's gate, that he stood not up nor moved for him, he was full of indignation against Mordecai." He had come out from the banquet, we are told, joyful and with a glad heart. And no wonder; for the honor which had been conferred upon him, of being invited to such an entertainment, was higher than usually fell to the lot of the most exalted subject. He seemed now to be secure in the possession of his dignities and influence, when he stood so high in the favor both of the king and of the queen. Visions of still greater grandeur and wealth than he had yet attained floated before his mind; and as he passed along, receiving the profound homage of the servile crowd of attendants, who knelt as he approached, and shaded their eyes, as if it had been

Lecture 10: Esther 5:9-14

presumptuous to look upon the face of so great a man, he was the more puffed up with a sense of his own preeminence. But all at once he comes to the spot where Mordecai sits, and here his triumph ends. The Jew takes no more notice of him than if he were the humblest officer about the court, excepting that there is in his countenance an expression of contempt, and perhaps of dislike. This scorn is like a dagger in Haman's heart. All the feelings of self-congratulation which he had so pleasingly cherished, and the visions of yet higher honor which he was to attain, are at once dissipated, and he retires to his house, with the mingled passions of anger, and hatred, and revenge burning in his bosom.

It is remarkable, and it is profitable to notice, how completely worldly men lie at the mercy of very trifling incidents for the preservation of their comfort and happiness. A circumstance in itself of no importance, falling out unexpectedly, will have the effect of disturbing and deranging the whole train of their enjoyments. A little matter, which you would think scarcely worth their notice, is poison in the cup of their pleasures, and converts their satisfaction into exquisite misery.

Haman's case finds many parallels. We have referred to the subject before: we may allude to it again. From the banquet and the festive assembly, from which it might have been supposed that all vexation, and care, and trouble would be excluded, the votaries of fashion frequently depart with such bitterness of spirit, as to make them the objects rather of pity than of envy. A supposed slight, a contemptuous glance, a suspicious whisper, a preference shown to some other party over them by those whose favor and patronage are regarded as of consequence, will throw a deep cloud of disquietude and discontent over the minds of those lovers of vanity, which distresses them more than many of the real ills of life would do. In this way it is that the proud, and vain, and frivolous are partly punished, even in this life, for their sin and folly. They carry about in their own breast the materials which, by a just retribution, turn their sweetest enjoyments into gall and wormwood. This point, however, will come to be more fully spoken of afterwards, when we consider the remainder of the chapter.

In the meantime, the chief lesson which is evidently deducible from the verse before us is founded upon the contrast between the two individuals mentioned in it—Mordecai and Haman—between the servant of God and the wicked enemy of God's people. Mordecai occupied the subordinate place; and not only so, but he was, with all his countrymen, doomed to death in consequence of the royal edict. He had done good service to the king, even to the preservation of his life, but for that service he had received no reward.

If he had been of morbid temper, he would have been dissatisfied on this account; and more especially, with the prospect before him of the coming evil, he would have been unfitted for all his ordinary duties. Only three days before he was running about in sackcloth—wailing, and refusing to be comforted. But now he is in his ordinary dress, and in his usual place, as calm and composed as if all his affairs had been most prosperous, and with as independent and manly a spirit, and as unabashed countenance as if he had had nothing to dread. We may truly say of him, then, that in the midst of his trials he was happy.

There, again, is Haman, who is the next man to the king, and who really possesses more power, because he can mold the king to his purposes. Bank, wealth, and honor are his, sufficient, it might be thought, to satisfy the most ambitious mind. Thousands bow before him, his will is law, the lives and destinies of millions are in his hand, he can rule everything but his own spirit. Here, however, he is a slave —a slave to fiendish passions. And in consequence of this, because Mordecai the Jew would not do him reverence, he is frantic with rage. He forgets all the real benefits he enjoys by reason of the slight put upon him by this one man. It needs no argument to prove which of these two persons is truly the greater character, and which of them is most entitled to our respect.

But how, it may be asked, came Mordecai to be able to bear with such equanimity the pressure of real trouble, while his enemy was all

Lecture 10: Esther 5:9-14

discomposed by an imaginary wrong, or by that which, if it was a real injury, he could so well afford to overlook? The answer to this question is easily given. Mordecai's heart and mind were under the influence of the word of God. He had committed to Him the whole issue of that affair in which all the Jews were so deeply interested. He could thus look forward with good hope to a happy deliverance from danger, through the interposition of the God of Abraham, who had told His people that He was the shield and the reward of all who trusted in Him. Mordecai, therefore, possessed his soul in patience, assured that some outlet would be found from the threatened danger.

Haman, on the other hand, was destitute of all fear of God, and unaccustomed to lay any restraint upon his passions, except when self-interest prompted him so to do. His success in life had only stimulated the evil principles of his nature, and rendered him haughty, imperious and revengeful, where he had power to gratify his dispositions. He was therefore capable of any villainy, and incapable of enjoying the blessings of his condition, as all must be who are strangers to self-government. So that upon the whole, when we contrast the two men, we would rather cast in our lot with Mordecai than Haman. To the despised Jew belonged true greatness and true happiness, because he was influenced by the fear of God.

But we must proceed now to consider verses 10-13: "Nevertheless Haman refrained himself: and when he came home, he sent and called for his friends, and Zeresh his wife. And Haman told them of the glory of his riches, and the multitude of his children, and all the things wherein the king had promoted him, and how he had advanced him above the princes and servants of the king. Haman said moreover, Yea, Esther the queen did let no man come in with the king unto the banquet that she had prepared but myself; and tomorrow am I invited unto her also with the king. Yet all this availeth me nothing, so long as I see Mordecai the Jew sitting at the king's gate."

"Haman refrained himself." It is a circumstance not unworthy of notice, that even those persons who are habitually self-willed, and destitute of the power of self-government, can nevertheless, when occasion requires it, exercise a wonderful control over both their speech and their passions. Thus, for example, a man who is addicted to the sin of profane swearing, will be found to put such guard upon his words in the presence of a superior who detests that sin, that not one oath will escape from his lips. A man who has no command of his temper at ordinary times, will appear smooth and unruffled in his intercourse with those on whom he is dependent, or whose good opinion he desires to gain. A man given to excess in the indulgence of his appetites, will be careful not to transgress in company where it would be accounted shameful.

Now there is an important principle involved in all this, deeply affecting the moral responsibility of such men for all their conduct. For if they can lay themselves under such restraint—when it serves their purpose—that long-formed habits can be checked and mastered, then we think that even they themselves must admit that they are deprived of all excuse when they suffer themselves to be usually governed by these habits. And if regard for the opinions and feelings of their fellow men exerts a power over them which the law of God does not possess, then manifestly they are chargeable with the guilt of standing more in awe of men than of God.

These remarks have been suggested by the words of the text, that "Haman refrained himself." Sorely galled as he was by Mordecai's contemptuous look and attitude, he did not openly give vent to his passion. It must have been a hard struggle; but he contrived to conceal his wrath, so as to appear in the sight of all the king's servants calm and dignified, as became his exalted station. And very probably it was this feeling, that he had a character to sustain, and that it would have been beneath his dignity publicly to notice the affront that he had received from a Jewish slave: it was this that prevented him from giving way to the rage that swelled in his breast. And besides, it would contribute to

Lecture 10: Esther 5:9-14

keep him from openly exhibiting his anger, that the day was not far distant when his revenge would be gratified to the full.

"Let the Jew sit," he could say to himself, "and shew his contempt for his superiors; his punishment shall only be the more severe. He may suppose that his place at the palace will save him from the fate which is to overtake his countrymen; but he will soon learn his error. Nothing shall save him from my hand. And of all that doomed race he shall suffer the most fearful punishment." I believe it is no uncommon thing, that when an unprincipled man feels that he has his enemy wholly in his power, he can control his passion, and afford to protract the time of vengeance, deriving gratification from the thought of the vengeance during the interval; just as the epicure gladly prolongs his banquet, instead of devouring it like a famished man. That this should be so, gives us a gloomy picture of human nature; but where unholy passions dwell, Satan has his throne; and what can be expected but the manifestation of Satanic feelings and deeds?

But in whatever way it is to be accounted for, Haman *was* able to refrain himself, so that none could learn from his look or speech the dark thoughts that were working in his mind. When he reached his own house, however, he felt himself at liberty to throw off all disguise; and it is when disburdening his heart to his family that we have him presented to us: "He called for his friends, and Zeresh his wife, and told them of the glory of his riches, and the multitude of his children, and all the things wherein the king had promoted him, and how he had advanced him above the princes and servants of the king." But he wound up the recital by adding, "Yet all this availeth me nothing, so long as I see Mordecai the Jew sitting at the king's gate."

It was noticed by anticipation in a previous lecture, that the only redeeming quality in Haman's character appears to have been his retaining family affection, and his having around him a certain circle composed of persons who are called his friends. He was not a being utterly isolated, and incapable of the interchange of social feeling. He could unbend and throw off reserve in the presence of certain parties; and he had his own home, with such kind of home-enjoyments as the manners and usages of the age afforded and sanctioned.

Now I would observe that this circumstance is not to be undervalued. It is not to be regarded as of little importance in estimating the character of a man that he is not a stranger to the exercise of the domestic affections.

So much of the happiness of human life depends upon their exercise—so much of the light by which we would desire to see every home gladdened must emanate from him who is the head of the family—that when we find a man mindful of his responsibility in this respect, we say he is justly entitled to our approbation. But then, on the other hand, the mere fact that a man is not insensible to the claims of family duty, and that he acts with kindness, and tenderness, and affection toward his wife and children, and other relatives, must not be overestimated. It is a mere instinctive feeling of our nature that prompts to all this, and not any high principle, for the exhibition of which anyone deserves peculiar praise or credit.

Yea, sometimes we can see the domestic affections very pleasingly manifested by those who, in every other respect, are regardless of the great duties they owe toward God and toward their fellowmen. Thus in many cases it happens, that persons who, in the bosom of their own families, and within a certain range of friendship and acquaintanceship, are to be commended for their amiable and kindly dispositions—are noted, beyond that circle, for everything that is repulsive, and mean, and dishonorable. While, therefore, we admit that there is one softening light in the dark portrait of Haman which is set before us in this book, we would not have too much made of it.

Any man who is possessed of wealth and power, and who is fond of display as well as of self-indulgence, will gather some others around him that he may enjoy himself in their society, and have them to witness and admire the splendor with which he is encircled. And to these he may

Lecture 10: Esther 5:9-14

perform some acts of generosity, while yet his intercourse with them may be utterly unworthy of the name either of true affection or of real friendship. This we are inclined to suppose was the case with Haman; and the text seems to justify this supposition. For now, when he is in the midst of his family and friends, and opens up his mind freely to them, what is the burden of his speech? He dilates upon the riches he had acquired, the power and dignity to which he had been raised, and the special marks of royal favor and confidence which had been conferred upon him, together with his domestic comforts, so as to impress all who heard him with a sense of his surpassing importance and grandeur. And then he will have them sympathize with him, because, although he is so great a man, there is yet one thing that embitters his life and makes him wretched, e.g., that a Jew, Mordecai, sits at the king's gate, and will not pay homage to him. It is very evident from all this that he did not desire to have friends and relatives about him that he might make them partakers of the blessings he enjoyed, but rather that they might be dazzled by his greatness, and that they might minister to his caprices and his selfishness.

But now we may advert for a moment more particularly to the qualities and dispositions which are indicated by Haman's address to his friends. These are vanity, pride, and ambition, accompanied with arrogance and violence of temper, cruelty and revenge. The last two, revenge and cruelty, were the natural produce of the others, in a heart wholly destitute of the guidance of right principle. The spirit of Haman was not perhaps so ferocious as that of the Emperor Nero, and some others we read of, who delighted in deeds of savage cruelty, apparently because to inflict pain and to witness human suffering formed really a pastime to them. But then, when anything occurred to wound his pride and vanity, or to disappoint his ambition, he would not scruple to have recourse to any means to gratify his revenge. Witness his scheme to destroy a whole race, without distinction of age or sex, because he felt aggrieved by one man. There are few, if any, more aggravated cases of revenge on record than this; and therefore, we say, there are few worse characters delineated in history than that of Haman.

The divine providence, however, as we have repeatedly said, is in many respects retributive, even in the present life. This wicked man, with all his wealth and greatness—with his flourishing family, and with all his luxuries—was miserable.

His pride, and vanity, and ambition had been so largely gratified, that it might have been supposed he was beyond the reach of all the ordinary troubles of life, unless he had been visited with bodily disease, or stripped of the comforts and privileges which he enjoyed. But strange to say, when there was nothing really to cause him a moment's pain, and when the foundations of his happy fortune seemed more securely laid than ever, he is compelled to cry, "All this availeth me nothing, so long as I see Mordecai the Jew sitting at the king's gate." Yes; it is so ordered that the evil passions of men frame the very scourge with which they are to be punished. It is a proverbial saying, that the man trembleth at his own shadow when his conscience is awakened; and it is equally true, that incidents as trifling as shadows have power to mar all the enjoyments of those whose sources of happiness are sought for in the lust of the flesh, the lust of the eye, and the pride of life. But we must now endeavor to draw from these verses some of the lessons which they suggest.

In the outset, however, I would remark, that it is not to be supposed that these lessons are to be inculcated as if there were any here present who can properly be likened to Haman. The point which I would select as leading to the remarks that follow is this—that you have in the text a man described, who was possessed most amply of all the elements which in this world are usually supposed to constitute happiness, and who yet, by his own evil passions, was prevented from being happy. One thing was awanting to give him full satisfaction, and for the lack of that, all the other great and good things he had within his reach ceased to have any power to please and satisfy. Now, while Haman's *wickedness* is not exemplified among us, we fear that there are to be found examples of his

Lecture 10: Esther 5:9-14

folly, and it is with reference to this view of the subject that I offer a few practical observations.

1. In the first place, in the case of men worldly-minded and destitute of the fear of God, there is generally some dominant principle or passion which destroys their comfort and precludes them from reaping the full benefit of the blessings which God has bestowed upon them. Thus, the man whose heart is full of covetousness can never be happy. "What he has, although it is far more than sufficient to supply his wants, is yet so far beneath what he desires, that he will not take full use of it, just because it is not so much as he would have. What Mordecai was to Haman, some imagined amount of wealth is to him; and thus his present acquisitions avail nothing, so long as he cannot get all he aims at. Again, the envious man cannot be happy. Oh, with what malignant eye he looks upon his neighbor's good, and marks his advancement, and observes the success of his schemes, and his growing prosperity! He may be thriving in the world himself beyond what he could have anticipated, and may have all the substantial comforts of life in abundance; but he cannot find enjoyment in them, because this other man stands so much higher than he. What Mordecai was to Haman, his neighbor's worldly advantages are to the man in whose heart envy dwells; for it eats out all happiness. Again, the victim of pride and vanity cannot be happy. The self-importance to which these passions give birth cannot escape unruffled in the world. Men are not always measured by their own pretensions; and when any respect or honor is withheld from them to which they think themselves entitled, they are far more deeply troubled than they would be by any temporal loss. They deem themselves insulted and degraded; they cannot look with patience upon objects which formerly pleased them; and they long for an opportunity to make retaliation for the wrong or slight they have received. This is a case analogous to that of Haman; and those who are animated by these

feelings must, like him, be necessarily wretched. I might protract these remarks, but enough has been said to illustrate the principle, that whatever amount of worldly good men who fear not God may have, yet, by allowing some evil passion or propensity to obtain the mastery over them, they destroy their own comfort, and pierce themselves through with many sorrows.

2. But now, in the second place, I would advert for a moment to the danger to which such people expose themselves. That which the covetous spirit feels to be lacking to satisfy its desires, it will often strive to attain by most unwarrantable means. Hence the sins of dishonesty, deceit, falsehood, and, when opportunity serves, violence and rapacity, are superadded to the sin of covetousness, and men, ere they are well aware, are drawn into courses from which at one time they would have shrunk back with horror. So also, the cherishing of the spirit of envy leads to the sins of uncharitable judging, malice, detraction, slander, all of which are destructive of a man's personal happiness, as well as of the peace of society. In the same way vanity and pride stand not alone, but bring in their train hatred and revenge, as we see in the text, and as all history testifies. And thus, by the indulgence of forbidden passions and desires, men not only deprive themselves of the comfort which they might derive from the blessings of a kind providence, but, as one sinful propensity leads to another, they lay themselves open on every side to many positive evils, from which, with better regulated hearts, they would have been completely free.

3. But in the third place, there is another and more general application that may be made of the text to matters bearing more directly upon the spiritual interests of men. Haman, describing to his friends his wealth, his grandeur, his various possessions, and his vast influence, had to conclude by saying: "All this availeth me nothing." There was still a something needed to complete his happiness. Now, we say this is a true picture of the feelings of worldly men, who are destitute of

the fear of God, even when it cannot be affirmed of them that they are in any marked manner the slaves of evil passions. There is always some dissatisfaction with their present lot which needs to be removed; there is a want—a something which the soul requires to its full and thorough well-being, which all the world's good cannot supply. That want originated in man's apostasy, when he ceased to have God as his friend and as his chief good. It makes itself felt often in the midst of such profusion of earthly enjoyment as would lead one to think that there could be no want there. It will make itself be felt awfully when the soul hovers on the brink of eternity. Now this want the gospel of Christ supplies. Through the acceptance of Him by faith as the Redeemer of the lost, the light of God's countenance shines upon the soul, and God Himself comes again to be enjoyed as the soul's chief good and portion. Then providential blessings, and chastisements also, are felt to be good; yea, all things work together for good to them that believe in the Son of God, for they are heirs of God and joint heirs with Jesus Christ.

Yet let me here, before concluding the present lecture, remind you that the feeling of dissatisfaction with earthly good does not of itself indicate a spiritual mind, although sometimes it is unhappily mistaken for it. I have referred to the soul's want as felt and expressed not unfrequently when death approaches. And so it is, that under deep suffering, and after long protracted illness, the confession will be made that the world cannot satisfy, and that the strength has been spent for that which is not bread. But, my friends, do not wait till that time 'ere you make the confession and seek the better portion.

Why should you live under the pressure of a felt want which can be at this moment supplied? Why should you, under the dominance of some evil principle, deprive yourselves of the right relish for the good gifts of God, by saying: "All this availeth me nothing, while the very thing I long for is not given me?" Does not the Savior declare, with reference to earthly good: "He that drinketh of this water shall thirst again, but he that drinketh of the water that I shall give him shall never thirst?" Trust His word, then, and take Himself, and your soul will have substantial and imperishable realities to feast upon.

Amen.

Lecture 11: Esther 6:1-14

The last lecture was chiefly occupied with a review of Haman's character and conduct, and with the practical lessons suggested by that subject. We saw in his case, what is so often illustrated in real life among ourselves, how insufficient the highest worldly advantages in themselves are to render men truly happy; and how, when evil and violent passions have the mastery, they make those who are under their influence incapable of enjoying the best gifts of providence. Next to the king himself, no man in Persia was possessed of such power and wealth as had fallen to the lot of Haman, and none had fewer real troubles to vex and annoy him; but his vanity and pride created imaginary miseries sufficient to embitter all his enjoyments. He had just received the highest mark of royal confidence which could be conferred upon a subject, in being invited by the queen to a banquet, at which none but the king and himself were permitted to be present. He estimated the honor duly, and felt as if he had now reached the highest pinnacle of earthly glory; but as he retired, Mordecai the Jew, who sat in the king's gate, refused to rise up to pay homage to him; and that single circumstance drove from his mind all sense of the privilege which he had just enjoyed, and filled him with deadly wrath and fury.

Hastening home, and summoning together his wife and his friends, that he might get their sympathy, he drew to them such a picture of his wealth and honor and greatness, as to satisfy them that no subject in the kingdom was his equal; "but," he added, frantic with rage, "all this availeth me nothing, so long as I see Mordecai the Jew sitting at the king's gate." Now, if he had been surrounded by wise counselors, who felt themselves at liberty to express their real sentiments, he would have been reminded that the slight shown him by one man, and especially by a person of so little consequence as Mordecai, was unworthy of his notice; and that one who had so much to contribute to his happiness as he possessed should not demean himself by permitting a matter so trifling to ruffle his temper and make him miserable. But his friends chose rather to stimulate his resentment than to attempt to allay it. And I would say it is not improbable that they did so in all honesty.

The conduct of Mordecai might appear to them so heinous and so inexpiable an insult to a man of Haman's rank, as to justify the strongest indignation and the severest vengeance. Accordingly, they would not have him wait till the day came that had been fixed for the extermination of the Jews; they would have Mordecai singled out for special punishment by himself. As we read in the last verse of the fifth chapter: "Then said Zeresh his wife and all his friends unto him, let a gallows be made of fifty cubits high, and tomorrow speak thou unto the king that Mordecai may be hanged thereon: then go thou in merrily with the king into the banquet. And the thing pleased Haman; and he caused the gallows to be made." Although there is nothing in this verse that requires special comment, yet the incident is so prominently connected with what follows in the narrative respecting the destiny of Haman himself, that we cannot pass it by altogether without notice.

As Mordecai's offense had been presumptuous above measure in the view of Haman and his friends, so the punishment of it was to be conspicuous. The gallows on which he was to be hanged was to be upwards of forty feet in height, so that the victim might be exposed to the view of the whole city—so that all might learn that it was no slight matter to provoke the vengeance of the favorite of the king. And mark how the thirst for vengeance converts men into fiends. Far more gratifying than any of the luxuries which he could taste at the table of the queen would be the sight to Haman of Mordecai hanging on the gibbet.

"Have everything ready to feed your revenge," his friends said to him, "and then go in merrily with the king unto the banquet." Generally a deed of cruelty and bloodshed for a time destroys, even in wicked men, their relish for their usual pleasures. But there are monsters in human form, as the recent massacres in India shew us, indeed as all history

Lecture 11: Esther 6:1-14

shews us, and as we see here in the case of Haman. There are human fiends who, when their passions are inflamed, riot in cruelty, and feel as if the exercise of it gave a zest to all their other enjoyments. Some philosophers talk of the innate dignity and excellence of human nature, but it may be safely said that there is no enormity which men will not perpetrate when they are left to themselves, and destitute of the softening and elevating influence of true religion.

But passing from this topic, we may suppose now, when Haman was comforted by the suggestion of his friends, that the two things which chiefly occupied his mind and pleased him, were the preparation of the gallows for Mordecai, and the thought of the interview he should have with the king on the morrow, when he felt sure he would obtain the request he was to make. "Behold the wicked," says the Psalmist, "he travaileth with iniquity, and hath conceived mischief: he made a pit and digged it, and is fallen into the ditch which he made: his mischief shall return upon his own head, and his violent dealing shall come down upon himself." That night was spent in Haman's house—by his slaves in making all ready for the murderous deed of the morrow, and by himself, in joyous anticipation of having his victim fully within his power.

But the following chapter introduces us to a different scene, and to a very different class of incidents. We have now to notice how the night was spent in the royal palace, and what unlooked for issues *that* led to on the morrow. Chapter 6:1-3: "On that night could not the king sleep, and he commanded to bring the book of records of the chronicles; and they were read before the king. And it was found written, that Mordecai had told of Bigthan and Teresh, two of the king's chamberlains, the keepers of the door, who sought to lay hand on the King Ahasuerus. And the king said, What honor and dignity hath been done to Mordecai for this? Then said the king's servants that ministered unto him, There is nothing done for him."

Every appliance which luxury could furnish was wont to be employed to lull to sleep such monarchs as the king of Persia. The softest and sweetest music fell upon the ear, soothing the spirit, and driving away by its charm all thought of the busy world and its cares. But on this night these appliances were unavailing. There was an unseen influence put forth upon the king's mind to counteract the effects of the music, and in spite of himself, he was led to think of the past transactions of his reign, and to endeavor to call up some of its most stirring incidents. Like other despotic princes, he had been nominally the arbiter in numberless affairs more or less important, which had not dwelt on his memory a day after they were settled.

And thus he lay tossing upon his couch, attempting in vain to recollect some of these things, as one tries in the morning to recall and arrange the shadowy remembrances of a confused dream. There would be nothing very remarkable in all this, perhaps, either to the king himself, or to those who were nearest to his person. No doubt the same thing had happened before, as there are times, we all know, when, without any assignable reason, sleep will not visit our pillow, and when the earnest wish for it only seems to drive it farther away. But in the present instance, we perceive the operation of a special providence.

In many cases recorded in the sacred history, the purposes of providence were effected by sending sleep, and then working on the mind by dreams and visions. Thus it was with Nebuchadnezzar, and thus with Eliphaz the Temanite, who, in the Book of Job, tells us of instruction he received in "thoughts from the visions of the night, when deep sleep falleth upon men." But it was otherwise ordered in the case of Artaxerxes, as described in the text. Sleep was banished from him, and he was troubled with anxious thoughts, suggested to him he knew not how. When he had thus lain for hours, we may suppose, in vain courting repose, his feverish mind could tolerate such trouble and disquietude no longer. He could not be longer alone with his own thoughts; and before morning light he summoned his attendants and commanded the keeper of the records of the kingdom to be called for, with the chronicles of his reign.

Lecture 11: Esther 6:1-14

When the mind is agitated and restless, as the kings then was, it does get some relief by turning from its distempered fancies to the contemplation of actual facts. The time passes more tolerably in this way than when we have nothing to grasp which is real and palpable.

The Assyrian and Babylonian kings had been accustomed to preserve the memory of the leading events of their history by inscriptions, of a particular form, graven on their palace walls, and on other places. Some of these, as you know, have very recently been disinterred, after having lain buried for ages amid the ruins of ancient greatness, and have already cast much light upon the transactions of those remote times. The Persian monarchs, however, appear to have caused the chief incidents of their reigns to be carefully written out. In this way the review of them was brought more easily within their own reach, although unhappily the materials of transmission to posterity were more destructible. It was the book of the chronicles of his reign, then, that Artaxerxes commanded to be brought and read to him, that he might escape from the sleepless and nervous fit which had come over him and get something for his mind to rest upon. It was so ordered that among other events which were read to him out of the record, that one was brought up respecting the service rendered to him by Mordecai, in discovering a conspiracy against his life. All recollection of this, or at least of the man who had been the instrument of preserving him from destruction, had been effaced from the king's mind by that perpetual round of sensual pleasures in which his time was spent. But now he is touched with better and nobler sentiments; and begins to feel what it was becoming of him as a king to do.

Upon inquiring what honor had been conferred on Mordecai for his faithfulness, the king learned that no recompense at all had been bestowed. And from what is said afterwards in the chapter, it would appear that they had at the same time mentioned that he was a Jew, and that his place was to sit in the king's gate. Upon all this the king meditated deeply, communicating his thoughts to no one. Gratitude toward his preserver was now awakened in his heart, and his purpose was formed in what way his gratitude should be manifested, as soon as the hour for transacting business should arrive. And thus we see how the righteous and humble-minded Mordecai, all unconscious of it himself, was an object of deep interest, and the chief subject of conversation, at the same time, in the palace of the king and in the house of the king's haughty favorite. But this was with very different designs and results. Intense hatred and death were connected with the thought of him in the one place, and gratitude and honor in the other.

Now let us make some practical application of the statements contained in these verses. There are two lessons deducible from them:

1. In the first place, we see from what is here written of the king of Persia, that no external advantages and appliances can secure for a man that refreshing rest which is so indispensable to the health both of mind and body; and the question arises, What will be found most conducive to this end? We may advert to the subject for a moment, although to some it may appear somewhat out of our proper province. Yet we would endeavor to keep within our province. With bodily derangements, which make the hours of night sometimes so painful and oppressive, we have nothing at present to do, farther than to observe, that the sentiment expressed in the Book of Ecclesiastes will be found to hold good in very many instances—that while "the sleep of a laboring man is sweet, whether he eat little or much, the abundance of the rich will not suffer him to sleep." There are other things, however, than those of an external kind, which rob men of their rest, to which we may with propriety here refer. Those who go to court repose having their minds burdened with worldly cares, and their thoughts occupied with the prosecution of their worldly schemes: and yet more especially those who lay themselves down with a heavy weight of guilt upon their conscience, carry with them what will almost certainly drive sleep away from them. Never so vividly as in the night watches, when the sinner feels all the

Lecture 11: Esther 6:1-14

helplessness of being alone, will he realize the misery of his condition as a sinner, and the evil of any peculiarly heinous transgression of which he has been guilty. In these circumstances he will seek rest, and will not find it. It is very easy to understand, then, what will tend most effectually to free the mind from those troubles which give it power to act upon the bodily frame so as to banish sleep. We must wash every evening in the fountain of Christ's blood. Thinking over the incidents of the day and confessing without reserve the sins and shortcomings of which we have been guilty, we must carry the whole burden to Christ, and cast it upon Him, believing in Him as the all-sufficient Savior. It is thus only that the wounds of conscience can be healed, and that we can obtain rest undisturbed by its weighty charges against us. With the feeling that through Christ we are reconciled to God, we can use the Psalmist's words: "I will both lay me down in peace and sleep; for thou Lord only makest me dwell in safety." Or, to use the language employed in another place: "Thus God giveth rest to His beloved." The subject is beautifully put before us in the Book of Proverbs, when the wise man, after inculcating the pursuit of heavenly wisdom, whose ways are pleasantness and her paths peace, goes on to say: "Her counsels shall be life unto thy soul, and grace to thy neck. Then shalt thou walk in thy way safely, and thy foot shall not stumble. When thou liest down thou shalt not be afraid; yea, thou shalt lie down and thy sleep shall be sweet." But if it should be so—and it may be—that Christ's people have their restless nights, and their tossings when in trouble, like other men, still they have a remedy peculiarly their own. They, like Artaxerxes, and to higher purpose, can turn their thoughts to the study of the chronicles of the Kingdom. They can summon memory to bring up before them the leading incidents in the history of redemption, and the wonderful dealings of God toward His people, and thus pass the hours of darkness in the enjoyment of the light of the Lord. In the night watches, then, as well as throughout the day, Christ is a sanctuary and a rest to His believing people.

2. In the second place, from the peculiarity of the part of Mordecai's history which has just been surveyed, e.g., that he should have been an object of such interest for good and evil at the very same time in Haman's house and in the palace—an encouraging and instructive lesson may be drawn for the benefit of all the true followers of Christ. At every moment there are two principles in operation in the heart of every believer—the principle of grace, which saves, and the remnant corruption of the old nature, which would destroy. Corruption is sometimes strong, but, like the house of Saul, it waxes feebler and feebler; while grace advances, and, like the house of David, waxes stronger and stronger—being ultimately destined to gain the victory. But besides this, *externally* there are two powers set in opposition to one another and contending for the mastery over every child of God. Our Lord brings this before us in His address to Peter, when He said to him: "Simon, Simon, Satan hath desired to have you, that he might sift you as wheat; but I have prayed for thee that thy faith fail not." We cannot actually see the procedure of the spiritual world; but these words teach us this, that as Haman was erecting the gallows for Mordecai while the king was devising honor for him, even so Satan is plotting the ruin of believers, while Christ, the King of Israel, who neither slumbereth nor sleepeth, is watching to counteract the designs of the enemy, and to advance the interests of His own people. This, then, being the state of matters, so far as the followers of Christ are concerned, there is evidently a twofold course of duty incumbent on them. They must be ever on their guard against their deceitful enemy; and they must place implicit confidence in their protector and be ever ready to implore His help.

The two opposing powers, indeed, may be engaged, as in the case of Mordecai, while those about whom the conflict is waged may be altogether unconscious of the fact. Even then, as all authority belongs to

Lecture 11: Esther 6:1-14

Christ the King, the enemy must be defeated. But we would say, that generally the believer may perceive the temptation by which he is assailed; and if, seeing and feeling it, he raises his voice for promised aid, his deliverance and triumph are certain; for the promise stands unchangeable, that when His people cry in faith to Him, Christ will hear and save them in time of need.

The same train of remark might be pursued with reference to the opposition which Christians have to encounter from mere worldly sources. But it is unnecessary to dwell on this; for if Christ has pledged Himself to make His people conquerors of Satan, much more will He save them from all that is hurtful in this present evil world. "In the world ye shall have tribulation," He says; "but be of good cheer, I have overcome the world."

But we must now go on to consider what follows in the narrative. Verses 4-11: "And the king said, Who is in the court? Now Haman was come into the outward court of the king's house, to speak unto the king to hang Mordecai on the gallows that he had prepared for him. And the king's servants said unto him, Behold, Haman standeth in the court. And the king said, Let him come in. So Haman came in. And the king said unto him, What shall be done unto the man whom the king delighteth to honor? Now Haman thought in his heart, To whom would the king delight to do honor more than to myself? And Haman answered the king, For the man whom the king delighteth to honor, let the royal apparel be brought which the king useth to wear, and the horse that the king rideth upon, and the crown royal which is set upon his head: and let this apparel and horse be delivered to the hand of one of the king's most noble princes, that they may array the man withal whom the king delighteth to honor, and bring him on horseback through the street of the city, and proclaim before him, Thus shall it be done to the man whom the king delighteth to honor. Then the king said to Haman, Make haste, and take the apparel and the horse, as thou hast said, and do even so to Mordecai the Jew, that sitteth at the king's gate: let nothing fail of all that thou hast spoken. Then took Haman the apparel and the horse, and arrayed Mordecai, and brought him on horseback through the street of the city, and proclaimed before him, Thus shall it be done unto the man whom the king delighteth to honor."

The incidents related here are full of interest, and the whole scene is so picturesque, that even the most sluggish fancy might realize it. It is an eventful morning that is now ushered in. The king, perhaps sooner than usual, is ready for the dispatch of business; for although sloth and negligence are the characteristics of despots, yet, when they are moved to activity, everything must be done according to their will at the instant. From morning to night, and even during the night, there were always some in waiting to receive the commands of the Persian monarch; and therefore, as soon as he was in fitting attire to hold conference with any one, Artaxerxes asked who was in waiting in the court, and he was told that Haman was there.

The hour was not yet come when the king, according to established custom, could be seen by anyone; but Haman had been determined to be early at the palace, that he might attract the notice of some of the attendants, and have his name mentioned to the king, in the hope that he might be called for, and then he would accomplish the ruin of Mordecai without difficulty.

"Woe to them," says the prophet Micah, "that devise iniquity, and work out evil upon their beds! when the morning is light, they practice it, because it is in the power of their hand." Haman is one personification of the prophet's words. All night he had lain brooding over his scheme of vengeance, and in the morning he is ready for the full execution of it, thinking it to be "in the power of his hand." "But the Lord disappointeth the devices of the crafty, so that their hands cannot perform their enterprise. He taketh the wise in their own craftiness; and the counsel of the froward is carried headlong. But he saveth the poor from their sword, from their mouth, and from the hand of the mighty." While the wicked Amalekite is moving to and fro impatiently in the outer court, breathing

Lecture 11: Esther 6:1-14

vengeance against his adversary, a summons is brought to him to come into the royal presence. Never was that summons heard by him with greater delight. This seems to bring him to the very crowning point of his wishes. He could not have desired anything more opportune than the arrangement, brought about without any previous contrivance on his part, that when he was earlier at the palace than usual, he should be thus called to a private conference with the king.

It may be noticed here, that often in the career of those who have given themselves over to work iniquity, there are strange facilities opened up to them for a time to prosecute their schemes of wickedness, as if everything were made ready to their hand, until at some unexpected moment the whole train of their evil devices is overturned, and they themselves receive the visitation due to their iniquity. It is with reference to this that the Scripture says: "Fret not thyself because of evildoers, neither be thou envious against the workers of iniquity; for they shall soon be cut down like the grass, and wither as the green herb."

But now we pass from the court into the palace, where Haman is admitted to hold converse with the king. There, too, all at first seems most favorable to his views. The question is proposed, evidently in such a way as to indicate that some action was to follow it: "What shall be done unto the man whom the king delighteth to honor?" This question is so wide, and holds out such prospects, that for a moment Haman is taken by surprise, and forgets the affair of Mordecai; or, if he remembers it, it is with the feeling that he will obtain some mark of the royal favor so much higher than he has yet received, as that the crushing of the poor Jew will be a very easy matter. He could not imagine that there was any other man more deserving of promotion, or more likely to be promoted than himself; and therefore, he speaks freely, and taxes the royal munificence very largely. "For the man whom the king delighteth to honor, let the royal apparel be brought which the king useth to wear, and the horse that the king rideth upon, and the crown-royal which is set upon his head; and let this apparel and horse be delivered to the hand of one of the king's most noble princes, that they may array the man withal whom the king delighteth to honor, and bring him on horseback through the street of the city, and proclaim before him: Thus shall it be done to the man whom the king delighteth to honor."

Now, it may be noticed here, that there has been some difficulty felt in fixing precisely the meaning of Haman's words. As we read them, they seem to imply that it was literally with the king's robe that he would have this favored individual decorated, and that he should ride upon the king's horse, and wear the crown royal. But this way of understanding the passage seems repugnant to all that history teaches of the customs of the East, and of the jealousy with which eastern monarchs regarded all their prerogatives. The scepter, indeed, was the great emblem of royalty; but the robe, and the diadem, and the horse, were all very closely connected with it. And therefore, it has been supposed by some, that the words of Haman are not to be interpreted literally, which would be extravagant; but that what he meant was, that the man whom the king delighted to honor, should be clad with a robe similar to what the king wore, and should wear a coronet, and ride on one of the king's horses. It is of little consequence, however, whether we understand the words in this way or not. Certainly there is nothing improbable in the supposition, that Haman, who was intoxicated with vanity, and who now thought that he had the opportunity of gratifying his desires to the uttermost, should have asked such marks of distinction as had never been granted before, and as no one had presumed to ask before. But be this as it may, he received the recompense that was due.

Then the king said to Haman: "make haste, and take the apparel and the horse as thou hast said, and do even so to Mordecai the Jew, that sitteth at the king's gate, let nothing fail of all that thou hast spoken." Who can conceive rightly the terrible tumult that was excited in Haman's bosom when he heard these words? If the king had known all his most secret feelings, and had lain on the watch to wound him in the point on which he was most sensitive, and had chosen the most fitting opportunity

Lecture 11: Esther 6:1-14

to make the wound deep beyond endurance, he could not have issued a command so calculated to make Haman writhe under it as this one. And the command at the same time was so peremptory, that he durst not say nay to it. He could not venture to utter a word to the prejudice of Mordecai. He could not say: "I came hither to ask as a boon that the life of that man should be at my disposal." He knew too well the temper of the king to venture upon such ground. It only remained for him to bow to the royal will, and go and do as he had been commanded.

It is said that those who are accustomed to be in kings' courts, acquire a command even over the muscles of their countenance, so that they can conceal what is passing in their minds, and appear calm when their breast is like a volcano. Haman verily needed such self-possession on this occasion, and no doubt exercised it. But who can describe the struggle of passion that was going on in his breast? We could not sympathize with him when he said (describing his possessions and his grandeur): "all this availeth me nothing, so long as I see Mordecai the Jew sitting at the king's gate." But we can see now that he had some reason for calling himself wretched. But there is no escape for him. The king does not know his feeling toward Mordecai, and he ventures not to tell it. So he must go forth with the retinue required to carry the king's gifts, and to join in the procession: he must proceed to the gate and pay homage to Mordecai, and array him in the costume which was fitting.

And while the Jew rode on horseback in the royal attire through all the principal thoroughfares of the city, Haman had to walk on foot at his side with the servants, who proclaimed: "thus shall it be done to the man whom the king delighteth to honor." No doubt they would pass within sight of the gallows which had been erected in Haman's courtyard; and that would cost him a pang like the bitterness of death. Perhaps the thought might then come across his mind: "who can tell, amid these changes of the times, whether I have not reared that gibbet for myself?" But if his anticipations were not so gloomy, the anguish of his spirit must certainly have been intense beyond conception, during the whole time that he led that procession in honor of Mordecai. You can almost fancy that you see the train passing along from street to street, amid the acclamations of the multitude who delight in such spectacles; and the strange thing which most excites their wonder is, that Mordecai the Jew should have the honor paid to him; and that Haman, the great lord, the king's favorite, should be found walking beside him as one of his attendants.

In making a practical improvement of these verses, I would notice:

1. That we see here the working and the punishment of vanity and pride. "Whom can the king think worthy of special honor but myself," thought Haman. The vain man is always occupied about himself. He thinks about himself; he speaks about himself; he is all in all to himself. The idea never crossed Haman's mind, that there could possibly be anyone besides himself whom the king could desire to distinguish by any particular mark of favor. But then how crushing was the order: "go and do as thou hast said to Mordecai the Jew." "Pride goeth before destruction, and an haughty spirit before a fall." This is a general statement. And as we all know, that when there is any part of the body weak and wounded, there will always be something from without to cause uneasiness in that part, even so it is with pride and vanity. The humiliation will fall just where it is most difficult to be borne. And, apart from this, there is scarcely another way in which a man places himself and his happiness so much at the mercy of the minutest trifle, as when he is filled with vain thoughts of his own importance. He is sure to be ruffled and chafed, and that exactly in proportion to the estimate which he forms of himself. And when the humiliation comes, he is loaded with ridicule instead of meeting with sympathy, and the higher his pretensions have been, the more degrading is his fall.

2. But in the second place, and as suggested by the text, rather than directly taught by it, there is encouragement here for the humble-

Lecture 11: Esther 6:1-14

minded. Perhaps there was not an individual in the whole city of Susa, who thought more meanly of himself than Mordecai. Yet there was a book of remembrance kept by the king in which his good deeds were recorded, and although the recompense was not soon made it was made in due time. When he was least expecting it, and when he was thinking whether there could possibly be a way of escape from death opened up to him, he was singled out by the king as worthy of the highest honors. He learnt by experience, that it is better to be of "an humble spirit with the lowly, than to divide the spoil with the proud." And so it holds good in higher matters, my friends, when you form a true estimate of yourselves as utterly unworthy of the divine favor. I do not say when you express this in words, but when you feel it, then the Lord casts a gracious eye upon you. "God resisteth the proud, but giveth grace unto the humble." The self-emptying spirit is just that which Christ the King rejoices in. And those who look up to Him, feeling that they have nothing, are in the direct way to obtain more than they could have ventured to ask, out of His glorious riches. Whether for well-being in time or in eternity, then, humility is our proper ornament. Pride and vanity must be cast away.

But we must now look for a moment at the remaining verses of the chapter. Verses 12-14: "And Mordecai came again to the king's gate. But Haman hasted to his house mourning, and having his head covered. And Haman told Zeresh his wife and all his friends everything that had befallen him. Then said his wise men and Zeresh his wife unto him, If Mordecai be of the seed of the Jews, before whom thou hast begun to fall, thou shalt not prevail against him, but shalt surely fall before him. And when they were yet talking with him, came the king's chamberlains, and hasted to bring Haman unto the banquet that Esther had prepared."

We have here to notice again, what has been referred to before, the humility of Mordecai. After all the honor that had been paid to him, he comes to occupy his old position, as if nothing extraordinary had taken place. We may suppose, indeed, that the strange incidents of the day had inspired him with hope that the Jews would yet escape from the plot which had been laid for their destruction; but there was no haughtiness expressed in his deportment, and if any further advancement was designed for him, he was contented to wait for it in his usual place of service. But it is Haman we have principally to look at. He had retired to his house before, a miserable man for a foolish reason. Now, however, as we have said already, he has some cause to be mortified and dejected, to cover his head and to mourn. Yet who can pity him? It is a just retribution that has overtaken him; it is his own wicked heart that has prepared for him this cup of bitterness. He would have one of the king's most noble princes lead the horse of the man whom the king delighted to honor. He conceived himself to be the very noblest of all, and it was only fitting, therefore, that, as a punishment of his pride, he should have this duty to perform to Mordecai.

In his former trouble, his wife and his friends had been able to administer at least temporary comfort to him, but now they can suggest no remedy. On the contrary, his wise men, e.g., the astrologers whom he kept and consulted, strangely enough, spoke so as to add to his misery. "If Mordecai be of the seed of the Jews, before whom thou hast begun to fall, thou shalt not prevail against him, but shalt surely fall before him." The language is somewhat obscure, but the purport of it evidently is, that the advancement of Mordecai was not only in itself an omen of no good to Haman, but that it was an indication that his scheme to destroy the Jews would fail, and that his own ruin might be the consequence. How they came to speak so, has been the subject of many conjectures. Some have supposed that as Balaam and Caiaphas were enabled to prophesy truly, so these astrologers may have been unconsciously guided at this time by a divine influence. But conjecture is vain. No doubt Haman was alarmed when he heard their words, but he had not time to ask an explanation. The king's chamberlains broke up the conference, by coming to bring him to Esther's banquet.

Lecture 11: Esther 6:1-14

Now, the concluding remark which I would leave with you on a survey of the whole subject we have reviewed, respects the security and advancement of God's people amid all the troubles to which they are exposed. There is nothing miraculous in this part of the narrative. Everything falls out in accordance with the ordinary laws of nature. And yet there is such an arrangement and piecing together of events as is equivalent to a miracle, if I may so speak. Even so still, the Lord can provide for the safety and honor of His own in the common course of His providence. See to it, my friends, that you can claim Christ as your brother, and have your names written among God's children, and then you need be exercised by no anxious and depressing cares, for all things work together for good to them that love God and are members of His family.

Amen.

Lecture 12: Esther 7:1-10

The last discourse brought under our review a wonderful change in the affairs of Haman and Mordecai, in which, though unseen, the hand of a special providence was immediately concerned. The wicked Amalekite had left his house early that morning, and repaired to the palace, that he might obtain from the king a warrant for the death of Mordecai. He was admitted to an audience of the monarch sooner than he could have expected. But ere he had time to make the request which he was so anxious to submit, and which he had hoped would be granted without inquiry or difficulty, the king anticipated him, by asking what should be done to the man who was entitled to receive the highest honors which the sovereign could confer.

Haman, full of vanity and self-importance, could not for a moment doubt that he himself was the person whom the king had in view; and accordingly, under this impression, he proposed such honors for the favored individual as no one else would have ventured to name. His counsel fell in with the present humor of the king, and he was directed forthwith to go and confer this honor upon Mordecai the Jew, and to wait upon him personally as his attendant, until everything had been done which he himself had suggested.

Haman was compelled to comply with the king's commandment, to decorate the man whom he hated with a royal robe, and walking before him, while he rode in something like kingly state through the city, to proclaim that this was the man whom the king delighted to honor. After this duty, humiliating to him beyond description, was gone through; we saw Haman hastily returning to his own house, with his head covered up, as if he had been ashamed to meet any one who knew him, or to be seen by any who had formerly paid him reverence. He had gone out in the morning confident that he would come back to see Mordecai hung on the gibbet which had been ready made for him; but instead of this, it is to tell

Lecture 12: Esther 7:1-10

the strange adventures of the day, Mordecai honored and himself degraded.

At home he got but little comfort. The sudden change which had taken place in the fortunes of Mordecai was startling to all the members of Haman's family. Even his wise men, as they are called, that is, the astrologers whom he kept about him for consultation, were, for the time, driven from their usual resources of flattery and servile accommodation to his wishes, and constrained to acknowledge that the whole aspect of affairs was ominous of evil. It was in these circumstances that Haman was summoned by the chamberlains of the king to Esther's banquet. This brings us to consider verses 1-4: "So the king and Haman came to banquet with Esther the queen. And the king said again unto Esther on the second day at the banquet of wine, What is thy petition, queen Esther? and it shall be granted thee: and what is thy request? and it shall be performed, even to the half of the kingdom Then Esther the queen answered and said, If I have found favor in thy sight, O king, and if it please the king, let my life be given me at my petition, and my people at my request: for we are sold, I and my people, to be destroyed, to be slain, and to perish. But if we had been sold for bondmen and bondwomen, I had held my tongue, although the enemy could not countervail the king's damage."

It was evident now that the king was really desirous to grant the request of Esther, whatever it might be, since for the third time he thus urged her to make it known. And as she now felt herself secure in the enjoyment of his favor and confidence and saw that his curiosity too was so awakened that it might have been dangerous to sport with it, she proceeded to lay her petition before him. We have probably only the substance of what she said recorded here, but brief as the narrative is, it illustrates very fully, both the tenderness of her heart and the clearness and maturity of her judgement. The wisest counselors of Artaxerxes could not have enforced the adoption of a right system of policy by sounder argument, and an accomplished orator could not have pled a cause more touchingly. She had concealed her kindred hitherto, but now, in the pressing hour of danger, she avows it, as prepared to die with her people if she could not save them: "If it please the king, let my life be given me at my petition, and my people at my request. For we are sold, I and my people, to be destroyed, to be slain, and to perish."

She uses the expressions which had been employed in the edict for the destruction of the Jews; and the king and Haman come to know for the first time that she was of the seed of Abraham. "We are sold," she says, "I and my people," referring apparently to the vast sum of money which Haman had offered to pay into the royal treasury, if he was permitted to accomplish his purpose of vengeance: "We are sold," "to be destroyed, to be slain, and to perish;" for the edict issued by Haman's order was in these words: "to destroy, to kill, and to cause to perish all Jews, both young and old, little children and women, on the twelfth day of the month Adar." But it is not this part of her address that is most remarkable. She states here only the cruel purport of the decree, which would have awakened the sympathy of any tender-hearted man or woman, even if personal safety had not been at stake. It is the following part of her statement that is most impressive and touching, while it is at the same time singularly illustrative of her sagacity and fitness for the high place which she occupied. "If we had been sold for bondmen and bondwomen," she said, "I had held my tongue, although the enemy could not countervail the king's damage."

The tone of quiet submission which is breathed in these words is first of all noticeable. If it had not been a question involving life or death, Esther would not have troubled the king with any petition or complaint. Seeing the edict had been published in his name, she would have beheld without murmuring her people, and herself along with the rest, yet farther degraded than they had been, reduced even to the condition of slavery, although that would have been hard to bear. The intimation of the royal will would have sealed her lips, so long as the life of the unhappy people was not aimed at. And this statement must have gone to

Lecture 12: Esther 7:1-10

the king's heart; for even despotism and cruelty are not always steeled against every feeling of generosity. But the concluding words were calculated to draw his attention to the subject as affecting the interests of his kingdom.

The Jews were an industrious race. Dispersed throughout the kingdom of Persia, they had devoted themselves to the pursuits of agriculture and commerce. They were captives, but not properly slaves, having their settlements here and there, for the cultivation of the soil or for merchandise, as their inclination led; and, although foreigners, yet mixed up with the general population of the country, and in the character of quiet, peaceful subjects, contributing toward the general wealth and prosperity. That they were not burdensome for their support, but, as to temporal matters, in a flourishing condition, is very manifest from Haman's offer to pay out of their spoil so large a sum into the royal treasury as we saw in a former lecture. To have swept away, then, by a wholesale slaughter, a race so active and industrious as the Jews were, would have been to inflict a heavy blow upon the prosperity of the kingdom. Their spoils might be a present benefit to the royal exchequer, but the loss entailed upon the national wealth would be permanent and irreparable. And the difference would not be great as to the national loss, if they were not to be destroyed, but merely reduced to the state of slavery. If sold as slaves and carried away into other countries by the slave merchants of Tyre and Sidon, the price paid for them would be a poor return for the fruit of their continued industry as the subjects of the Persian king. And if they were made slaves in his own dominions, there would be the loss to his revenue of so much active enterprise on the part of a people who paid all the public taxes and increased the national resources by the cultivation of the soil and foreign trading. Esther seems to have known better than the king did, and better than some modern politicians have done, or yet do, the secret of the wealth of nations. To annihilate an industrious and peaceful people, she represents as an act equally cruel and impolitic. To substitute slave-labor for the labor, and vigorous and persevering industry of freemen, she speaks of as also most opposed to the real interests of the state. This is the meaning of her words: "If we had been sold for bondmen and bondwomen, I had held my tongue, although the enemy could not countervail the king's damage." The sentiment here expressed is far in advance of the age in which Esther lived, and the truth and significance of it have often been illustrated since her time, although only illustrated so as to indicate that its importance was not yet estimated, nor the wisdom of it practically felt. Thus, for example, when persecution against the friends of Protestantism raged fiercely in France and Belgium, and those who preferred the religion of the Bible to popery, had to choose between remaining at home to be massacred, or seeking a refuge abroad, a vast number of the most intelligent and industrious of the population took refuge in England and Scotland, bringing their skill and industry with them to benefit the land of their adoption.

History settles it as a fact beyond all question, that these refugees for conscience sake contributed more largely to the industrial and commercial advancement of this country than it would be easy to calculate. For in those days we were far behind our continental neighbors in the practice of the mechanical and useful arts; and thus the bigotry and cruelty which drove multitudes to seek an asylum in this island, dried up the sources of the wealth of the countries from which they came, while Britain, on the other hand, was rewarded for opening her arms to shelter the oppressed, by obtaining all the benefit of their intelligence and labor, as not only skillful artisans, but peaceful and religious citizens.

And then again, with respect to the difference between the exertions and enterprise of free men for the real advantage of a country, as contrasted with slaves, Esther's judgment was far more correct, for instance, than that of the Americans, who boast so much of their liberty and their political wisdom; and her judgment is corroborated by the sentiments of all intelligent travelers, who have recorded their experience in passing through those states of America where slavery is legalized.

Lecture 12: Esther 7:1-10

The labor which is exacted by the lash is neither so well performed nor so great in amount as that which is paid for.

There is no inducement to the slave to cultivate his intellect. When he sees that he cannot better his condition, he naturally sinks into a state of apathy, or endeavors by craft and cunning to over-reach his taskmasters. And thus altogether, the just law of providence comes in to punish the avarice and cruelty of those who trample upon the rights of their fellowmen. For while the strength of a country consists, humanly speaking, in the amount of its industrious population, with a full supply of the means of subsistence—every man being free to employ his mind and his labor in the field which he thinks will be most profitable—the increase of a slave population is a source of positive weakness, as well as a growing cause of insecurity. Apart altogether from the evils and sinfulness of the system of slavery, as opposed to the great law of love which Christ came to enforce and establish, and apart from the danger which results from the preponderance of a class between whom and those above them there cannot be any real good-will and sympathy, slavery is a positive loss to a community in all respects, whether moral or social; and Esther spoke the truth when she denounced it as calculated to work damage to the king.

Now let us endeavor to make some practical application of the verses which have been reviewed. They suggest three lessons, which we shall give without reference to the precise order in which they are put before us in the text.

1. In the first place, we are here taught that adherence to the rules of justice and benevolence tends to the advancement of our temporal interests. It is on the wide scale, as bearing upon the well-being and prosperity of kingdoms, that the words of the text are principally applicable. The Persian monarch is taught by his queen that the exercise of severity toward the Jews, either for their destruction or to enslave them, would be hurtful to the true advantage of his empire,

whatever present profit it might appear to promise him. Now we say that the same principle holds good in matters of smaller moment. When in the prosecution of their ordinary business, men forget the sacred claims of justice, integrity, and benevolence, they may appear for a season to prosper, but usually in the end they find, in their sad experience, that what they imagined to be for their profit turns out to their hurt and damage. Exceptional cases there may seem to be; but all experience bears testimony to the truthfulness of the scriptural maxim, that "righteousness exalteth a nation." And equally explicit is the teaching of providence in individual cases, that the path which leads to real comfort and prosperity, even in worldly things—I do not say the path which leads to wealth and grandeur, but to *real* comfort and prosperity—is that which is marked out by justice and benevolence. Many short ways there may seem to be to the gaining of present advantage, but the way to permanent prosperity lies in the direction we have just indicated; and the apostle expresses the same sentiment when he says: "Godliness is profitable unto all things, having promise of the life that now is, and of that which is to come."

2. But secondly, the conduct of Esther deserves notice, in her identifying herself with her people at this crisis of their affairs. Even if she had heard of the marvelous change which had taken place in the condition of Mordecai—which is doubtful—still the cruel decree remained in force which doomed the Jews to destruction, and nothing stood between that decree and the execution of it but the arbitrary will of the monarch. And it was a question, as we shall afterwards have to notice, how far even he could alter it, without violating the standing rule, that the laws of the Medes and Persians could not be changed. There was no imperative necessity requiring Esther to compromise her own safety by declaring herself one of the doomed race. She might have pled for them without committing herself, and, whether with or without good reason, she might have thought that she could escape without being detected as one of them. But such selfish

Lecture 12: Esther 7:1-10

notions never for a moment suggested themselves to her mind. Fearlessly, as regardless of the issue, she made it known that she was a Jewess, prepared to live or die with her people. She had not told her kindred before. She declares it now, when the declaration must either bring enlargement and safety to them or lead to her perishing along with them. Now there is something truly noble and heroic in this, and we have to learn a lesson from it. To an exercise like that of Esther on this occasion we are called by the gospel of Christ. It is easy enough to take our place among God's people, and cast in our lot with them, when the truth is well spoken of, and our profession of it leads rather to comfort and honor than to any sacrifice either of feeling or of interest; but it does require an exertion of high courage to take part with the people of God when there is affliction or obloquy thereby incurred, and to speak of Christ among those who despise His gospel and dishonor His name. To confess Him before men, when there is nothing to be gained by the confession but discredit and worldly loss, is one of the noble achievements of faith; and it is in this respect that Esther stands conspicuous in the text. At the same time, my friends, it must not be overlooked, that there are many encouragements to Christ's followers thus to act. This is one, which should of itself be sufficient to animate even the weakest believer: Christ is not ashamed to call His people brethren. Esther's pleading for her people before the king is but a poor representation of the work of our great High Priest, who wears our nature in heaven, and in the holy place not made with hands interposes in behalf of the sinful children of men, and counts the weakest and meanest of those who have truly committed their interests to His keeping as His friends, His kindred, the very members of His body. If such is His feeling and acting toward them, what should be theirs toward Him? Surely they will not grudge to suffer somewhat for His sake, and to avow in all circumstances their connection with Him, when He is thus engaged in their behalf in the presence of the Father.

3. In the third place, Esther's *earnest* pleading for her people suggests a lesson to us. It is true that her object was to save them from temporal destruction, and she says that if their lives had not been in jeopardy she would have remained silent. Now thus far it may be admitted that the parent will be ready to interpose for his child, or the friend for his friend; and beautiful it is to mark the working and the strength of mere natural affection—to witness the sacrifices which parental love will submit to without a murmur, in the attempt to ward off disease or death from the object which is dear to it. But the religion which we profess demands from us something yet higher. Esther said that she would not have pled for her people, if it had not been that thus only there was the hope of saving them from massacre. Smaller evils she could have borne to witness; but when their life was at stake, she could not be silent. Her argument commends itself to our reason so far as it goes; but let us carry it out fully. What is the temporal well-being, or even the temporal life of those we love, contrasted with their spiritual prosperity and eternal life? Do we feel the preciousness of our own souls, and the preciousness of Christ to our own hearts? Then we cannot but feel an irrepressible desire that the members of our family and our friends be brought to Christ and made partakers of His salvation. The natural instinct which would lead us to shield them from danger, or to save their life, purified and refined by the gospel, will prompt us at the least to fervent and persevering supplication in their behalf, that they may be delivered from the power of Satan, and obtain a place in the family of God. Surely it would be a sad reflection to a parent, when a child is torn away from him by death, and has given no indication of being under the influence of grace, that for that child's soul he never wrestled at God's footstool, and that its spiritual condition seldom if ever cost him any real anxiety. Save yourselves, then, my friends, from all such dismal reflections, and from the terrible self-accusation which the neglect of sacred duty will occasion you, by being truly God's remembrancers now in behalf of

Lecture 12: Esther 7:1-10

those you love; and then, whatever the ultimate issue may be, you will be free from the blood of souls.

But we must now pass to consider verses 5-7: "Then the king Ahasuerus answered and said unto Esther the queen, Who is he, and where is he, that durst presume in his heart to do so? And Esther said, The adversary and enemy is this wicked Haman. Then Haman was afraid before the king and the queen. And the king arising from the banquet of wine in his wrath went into the palace garden: and Haman stood up to make request for his life to Esther the queen; for he saw that there was evil determined against him by the king."

Dignities and luxuries, however eagerly they are sought after, do not necessarily bring heart's ease with them. It was in great heaviness of spirit that Haman came to this banquet, and it must have required all his power of self-possession to wear an unruffled countenance, after the humiliation which he had received in the former part of that day. Yet, when an artful and designing man is driven from one position of advantage, he cherishes the hope that by some dexterous stroke of policy he will retrieve himself and regain the ground he has lost. There was no connection, so far as Haman yet knew, between Mordecai and Esther; neither could he have the slightest conception that she was of the Jewish race—since, with his well-known enmity to that people, he had been so specially honored by her. Yea, we may suppose, that as honor never comes more acceptably than when it overtakes a man who thinks himself disgraced, so the summons to the queen's banquet may have contributed somewhat to soothe the spirit of Haman, and to awaken in him a hope that after all he might get his purpose effected in the destruction of Mordecai.

The king was fickle, the queen seemed evidently willing to render him (Haman) any service of kindness, and perhaps he might yet find opportunity, during the freedom of the entertainment, to make known his wishes, and get Mordecai within his grasp. But if with such thoughts as these he contrived in some measure to dissipate the gloom which the transactions of the morning and the words of his astrologers had spread over his mind, and if the blandness of the queen, and the friendly looks of the king, during the first part of the banquet, helped to reassure him, that whatever dignity Mordecai had gained, his own place and influence were still as secure as ever, his hopes were doomed to be awfully and in a moment shattered. The queen, at the king's command, told her pathetic tale, and Haman's countenance fell as she proceeded.

As we have had occasion before to remark, Artaxerxes had forgot the whole matter concerning the destinies of the Jews. Very probably he had been under the influence of wine when he consented to the request of Haman for their destruction, and all the circumstances had escaped his memory. This is of the very nature of despotic rule. Sometimes it performs acts of justice, and benevolence too, more speedily than they could be performed under a free government. But its guide is mere caprice, and its occasional acts of justice and benevolence give no security to the great multitude of the distressed and suffering. It pities one day and oppresses the next. Thus it was that affairs were carried on under the government of the Persian monarch. He was taken by surprise with Esther's statement. The cruelty of the enactment affected even his mind, and he exclaimed in a voice of thunder, "who is he, and where is be that durst presume in his heart to do so?"

The answer might have been given by his own conscience, "thou art the man;" and Esther might have said truly, "the deed is thine own, and the cruel edict is signed with thine own signet." But she spoke more to the point, when she replied, "the adversary and enemy is this wicked Haman;" for it *was* Haman who took advantage of the king's weakness, and used his name and his signet for the nefarious purpose which the king had never taken time to consider in all its naked cruelty. And now the plot is discovered, and the plotter is unmasked. Now Haman trembles before the king and the queen. Guilt brought out into the light of day overwhelms the guilty with confusion. What then will it be when the secrets of all hearts are disclosed, and the judgment of omniscience and

Lecture 12: Esther 7:1-10

of inflexible justice is pronounced upon the transgressors of God's law, the impenitent and unbelieving? Refuge will then be sought in vain.

But we must follow our narrative. It would appear that Esther's statement, and her charge against Haman, had brought to the king's recollection the edict for the destruction of the Jews. He now saw how he had been drawn in a moment of weakness to sanction a design, which was at once as notable for its cruelty, as it was injurious to the interests of his kingdom. His determination accordingly was taken. "He arose from the banquet of wine in his wrath and went into the palace garden." It is said that this is the way in which the eastern monarchs were accustomed, and are still accustomed, to show their resolution to inflict capital punishment. The act of rising and going out seems designed to indicate that no pleading will be listened to on behalf of the criminal, that his fate is sealed. When the king is in such mood, no one dares follow him to soothe him by plea or argument. What he has purposed must take effect. Haman knew this full well. He had witnessed similar scenes without pity for the victims of royal indignation. But now when it is his own turn to suffer, his anguish is acute enough. He has no hope but in the intercession of the queen, and like the drowning man catching at a twig, he falls down before her, as she reclined upon her couch, takes hold of her robe and begs for mercy. Thus we have the enemy of God's church and people humbled, and the mischief devised by the wicked man returned upon his own head.

Let us now in a few sentences improve this part of the narrative. There are two lessons which it suggests, first, one respecting the instability of earthly greatness: and, secondly, one bearing upon the solemn subject, that there may be no place found by the wicked for repentance.

I. As to the first, the instability of worldly greatness, little needs be said. In Haman's case it was illustrated in a day by the suddenness of his fall and by his being subjected unexpectedly to the wrath of the king.

But these are mere accompaniments of the wicked man's history. They strike us, because we have himself before us subjected to accusation, and placed beyond all hope of mercy. Yet it would have been the same thing virtually, if he had fallen down in the way to the banquet and died under the influence of disappointed pride and ambition. It would have been the same thing if the king had merely banished him from his presence and left him to linger out his life in poverty and wretchedness. The great equalizer is death. It puts kings and subjects on a level. And when we trace the path of the most prosperous to the end, in whatever way the end comes, we may well say, "man walketh in a vain show." A year or two makes little real difference in life, and the suddenness of the removal makes less: the reign of death marks the instability of human things, and the fixed realities of the eternal world laugh to scorn the attempts of men to place themselves in this world beyond the reach of accident.

2. But in the second place, the text shews that there may be no place found by the wicked for repentance. No doubt Haman would have consented to the recalling of the edict for the destruction of the Jews, and would have given all the wealth which he had unrighteously accumulated, to purchase his own life. But the king had turned his face against him, and the queen would not listen to his entreaties. No doubt he would have gladly professed himself an Israelite at that time, if thus he could have saved himself. But his doom was sealed; and let the enemies of the truth take warning from his fate. They may cast themselves beyond the reach of salvation. They may cry and not be answered. It is an awfully rash statement to say that there are any here who are in this condition. But the possibility should make us all think in earnest whether or not we have escaped from the wrath to come.

We come now to verses 8-10, "Then the king returned out of the palace garden into the place of the banquet of wine; and Haman was fallen upon the bed whereon Esther was. Then said the king, Will he force the queen also before me in the house? As the word went out of the

Lecture 12: Esther 7:1-10

king's mouth, they covered Haman's face. And Harbonah, one of the chamberlains, said before the king, Behold also, the gallows fifty cubits high, which Haman had made for Mordecai, who had spoken good for the king, standeth in the house of Haman. Then the king said, Hang him thereon. So they hanged Haman on the gallows that he had prepared for Mordecai. Then was the king's wrath pacified."

The movements of the king were perfectly understood by his attendants. His angry reference to Haman pleading for his life at Esther's knees, as she lay upon her couch according to the eastern fashion, made his determination more clear: and probably by some minute signal with his hand, he motioned to the servants to take away the wretched man to the punishment he deserved. That signal was enough for the eunuchs. They covered Haman's face. This seems to have been a mode of procedure in the case of capital punishments, very generally adopted. The reason of it cannot be given with certainty, although there is always some reason for such universal practice. It may have been to prevent the condemned person from using any farther pleading in his own behalf: or it may have been to prevent him from exciting the sympathy of the bystanders by the woe imprinted on his countenance, or by any words he might utter. But whatever may have led to the practice, Haman like other malefactors was carried away with his face muffled, to bear the penalty which his crimes merited. As he was being removed, one of the chamberlains, one of those probably who had been sent to conduct him to the banquet, and who had seen the gallows erected in the courtyard for Mordecai, mentioned this circumstance, and accordingly the king gave orders that Haman should be hanged upon the gibbet which he himself had set up.

Altogether we have presented to us in the text a strange banquet scene, a curious specimen of an eastern royal palace. Wine and every luxury which heart could desire, society select even to fastidiousness, pleasant intercourse for a time, and then the whole wound up by an accusation and a condemnation to death, without anything like what we call the usual forms of justice. We wonder at all this, but similar transactions have a place in the annals of our own country and may not be altogether without parallel in some of the despotic governments even of Europe at the present day. Let us be thankful that we have escaped from such tyranny, and that nothing affecting either our life or fortune can be decided without open trial.

But this remark is only thrown out in passing. The chief lesson to be taken from the verses before us, is founded upon the suggestion of the eunuch that Haman should be hanged upon the gallows he had raised for Mordecai. That man had no doubt bowed to the favorite when he was in the plentitude of his power: but now he deserts him: yea, he becomes his accuser. And thus it will be with the wicked at last. Ah, how many accusations will conscience bring at the very time when they are least prepared to answer them! See the sinner after his course is run, arraigned, convicted, and condemned by all around him and within him. The things that ministered to his pleasure will condemn him. A rush of terrible convictions from his own conscience will condemn him. The law of God will condemn him. Everything will condemn him. And the retribution with which he is visited will be felt to be just and righteous. Oh, my friends, these are solemn realities. And if they do not meet the wicked and impenitent in this life, certainly they will meet them hereafter; wherefore we say, cast your guilt and the whole burden of your sins upon Christ, and receive Him and follow Him, and then, not with muffled face as criminals, but with open face as God's children you will be able to contemplate the realities of death and judgment.

Amen.

Lecture 13: Esther 8:1-14

The interest excited in our minds by the Book of Esther lies chiefly in the first seven chapters, which we have now commented on, although in the remaining portion there are some points of difficulty, and disclosures of personal feeling, which somewhat perplex the expositor. We have seen how, by the special providence of God, a poor orphan Jewess was exalted to the dignity of being queen of Persia, at a time when her people were exposed to greater danger than had almost ever before impended over them as a nation. We have seen how her relative, to whom she owed so much, when he had been doomed to an ignominious death by the powerful enemy of the Jews, was unexpectedly raised to the highest honors which could be conferred upon a subject. And we have farther seen how the wicked Haman, whose blood-thirsty desire could only be satiated by the annihilation of a whole race, received the doom which he merited by being hanged upon the gallows which he had erected for Mordecai. In all these events, and in the circumstances which led to the evolution of them, we have had opportunity to trace the operation of God's hand as clearly as if He had employed the elements of nature to counteract the designs of the enemy, and to advance the interests of His covenant-people.

Now, in the concluding chapters of the book, we have to mark the consummation of the series of incidents which secured for the Jewish people deliverance and enlargement, when they had nothing to look for but utter destruction.

Look first at verses 1-2: "On that day did the king Ahasuerus give the house of Haman the Jews' enemy unto Esther the queen. And Mordecai came before the king; for Esther had told what he was unto her. And the king took off his ring, which he had taken from Haman, and gave it unto Mordecai. And Esther set Mordecai over the house of Haman."

The sudden changes which are here recorded—the advancement of certain parties at the expense and on the ruins of others who had been immediately before in possession of large influence, and wealth, and dignity—are things of common occurrence in despotic governments. The will of the king being arbitrary, and his rule of action being usually nothing else than his own fancy, or the impulse of the moment, the person whom he most trusts for the time can turn him to his own purposes; while, on the other hand, influences *from without* may in an instant overturn that person's schemes, and subject him to all the consequences of the royal displeasure. Hence the suddenness of Haman's rise and fall, and the as unexpected promotion of Esther and Mordecai.

It was also in accordance with the usual procedure of the age and country, that when the old favorite was degraded and punished, the new should succeed to the enjoyment, not only of his honors, but also of his possessions. It would excite no surprise, therefore, that the king should give the house of Haman unto Esther the queen—that is, that he should endow her with all Haman's wealth, in whatsoever it consisted, whether in houses, or lands, or money, or slaves, or all combined. This vast property, much of which, no doubt, had been acquired by oppression and bribery, she was thenceforth to account her own, and was at liberty to employ it according to her own pleasure. It was the common practice of the kings of Persia to assign to their queens and favorites whole cities, or villages, or tracts of country, the revenues of which they had absolute power to dispose of as they saw fit, for the purchase of jewels and ornaments, or luxuries which might please their fancy, or, in a word, to maintain their state and dignity. And so Esther became Haman's heir, and was able henceforth to perform acts of benevolence toward her countrymen and dependents, as her own inclination might prompt her. "Thus," says Henry, quoting from the book of Proverbs, "'the wealth of the sinner is laid up for the just;' and what Haman would have done mischief with, Esther obtains to do good with."

Lecture 13: Esther 8:1-14

But we have now to notice farther how her gratitude is manifested toward Mordecai, and how, by the expression of it, she still farther provides for the accomplishment of her great object—the deliverance of her people.

Freed from the presence of the wicked Agagite, "the Jews' enemy," she now feels herself at liberty to relate her whole personal history to the king. And never could the time have been more appropriate. The previous restless night which he had passed had led to the remembrance of the important service which Mordecai had rendered to him, and to the singular honor which was paid to him in the morning through the unwilling agency of Haman. The banquet, however, with its exciting accompaniments, had again effaced from the mind of the fickle monarch the recollection of what he owed to his faithful servant. But now he hears with astonishment of the relationship which this excellent man bore to the queen, and of the tenderness with which he had watched over her in her infancy, when she had no other earthly friend to look to. Mordecai is immediately summoned from his place at the gate, which he had modestly resumed after his triumphal procession through the city and is brought into the king's presence. What passed *in words* we are not informed; but it is evident from the whole bearing of the narrative that he was honored to occupy Haman's seat at the banquet, as he was promoted to his place in the administration of the affairs of the kingdom. "The king," it is said, "took off his ring which he had taken from Haman, and gave it to Mordecai." And while he was thus invested with the great powers which had belonged to the former unworthy favorite, the queen now finds herself in a position to make some return to him for all the kindness which he had shewn to her when he could expect no earthly reward. She assigns to him the management of the estate of Haman, thereby providing at once for his worldly interests and her own.

Now, before pausing to draw any special lessons from this part of the narrative, it may be as well that we look at the following verses, as they bear upon the great work which Esther was by providence raised up to perform. Verses 3-8: "And Esther spake yet again before the king, and fell down at his feet, and besought him with tears to put away the mischief of Haman the Agagite, and his device that he had devised against the Jews. Then the king held out the golden scepter toward Esther. So Esther arose, and stood before the king, and said, If it please the king, and if I have found favor in his sight, and the thing seem right before the king, and I be pleasing in his eyes, let it be written to reverse the letters devised by Haman the son of Hammedatha the Agagite, which he wrote to destroy the Jews which are in all the king's provinces: For how can I endure to see the evil that shall come unto my people? or how can I endure to see the destruction of my kindred? Then the king Ahasuerus said unto Esther the queen and to Mordecai the Jew, Behold, I have given Esther the house of Haman, and him they have hanged upon the gallows, because he laid his hand upon the Jews. Write ye also for the Jews, as it liketh you, in the king's name, and seal it with the king's ring: for the writing which is written in the king's name, and sealed with the king's ring, may no man reverse."

The removal of the wicked from this world does not all at once remedy the evils which they have planned and perpetrated. Most significantly may it be said, that "the evil which men do lives after them." One profligate, unprincipled, and designing man often bequeathes to posterity such a legacy of wickedness, that all the efforts of the good for many years cannot repair the miseries which he has wrought. Men's actions are like seeds committed to the soil. They grow in secret, and bear their fruit, for good or evil, long after those who sowed them have been summoned either to their reward or to their punishment.

In the case before us, Haman had suffered the penalty due to his crimes; but still the royal decree for the destruction of the Jews, which he had deceitfully got the king to issue, and had sealed with the royal signet, remained in full force. This Esther knew; and it was to have this evil remedied that she again knelt as a suppliant at the feet of the king. It is one of the most interesting traits in the character of this princess, that in

Lecture 13: Esther 8:1-14

the midst of all the grandeur and dignity by which she saw herself surrounded, and by which her head might have been made giddy, she never allowed herself to be carried away by such feelings of pride and self-importance as would have filled the minds of most others in her place, and at her time of life.

Let us not forget what is past in her history, for it comes in at this point to illustrate her present feeling and conduct, although the reference to it is only a repetition of what has been said. When she was taken from the house of Mordecai into the palace, and had all the luxuries there, and all the honor which she could have desired, she never forgot her benefactor. When the crown royal was put upon her head, she was still as submissive to Mordecai's commands, in whatever way they reached her, as if she had been living under his humble roof. When the crisis came which rendered it necessary for her, in compliance with his admonition to hazard everything, even life itself, for the safety of her people, she made the adventure. All along, the warm affection which she had cherished toward the protector of her infancy, and which he had taught her to extend to the whole nation to which they both belonged, remained in all its strength and freshness when she was raised to her exalted place, and surrounded by the fascinations of royal state and power, and waited on as if she had been a superior being, by the menials to whom her look was law.

Now it is just the illustration of the same strong affection and simplicity of heart which had already triumphed over so many temptations, that we have presented to us in the text. With Mordecai beside her, the first among the king's servants, and with more than she could have looked for of the kingly favor toward herself, she feels that her work is not completed, but that another risk must be encountered to undo the evil that Haman had devised, and to secure the safety of her people. The narrative is beautifully simple: "Esther spake yet again before the king, and fell down at his feet and besought him with tears to put away the mischief of Haman the Agagite." We may wonder that she should have felt it necessary to go through such ceremonial when she had the king in her own banquet hall and had already received such manifest tokens of his favor. But it must be remembered that it was about a great affair of state she had to speak, and that in reality the most important part of her undertaking remained yet to be gone through. The king had shewn his personal goodwill sufficiently by what he had done to the chief enemy of her people: but yet she trembled when she thought of the murderous edict which still stood in force. It was this that led her to throw herself weeping at the feet of the king.

She had gained his love when she was first presented to him without any costly ornaments. She had obtained favor in his sight when she ventured unbidden to approach him arrayed in her queenly attire, and now again when she knelt before him, a suppliant in tears, his heart was moved. Having received the token of acceptance, she at once made known her request: "If it please the king, let it be written to reverse the letters devised by Haman, which he wrote to destroy the Jews which are in all the king's provinces: for how can I endure to see the evil that shall come unto my people, or how can I endure to see the destruction of my kindred?" Noble and affectionate heart, that will thus plead for the unfortunate when it has no need to plead in its own behalf! It were strange if it did not gain its object. Yet here there was a difficulty, and the king at once felt it.

It is not, we conceive, with the view of leading Esther to withdraw her request, or with a design to reproach her for asking more, after she had already received so much, that Artaxerxes speaks in answer to her as is recorded in verses 7-8: "Behold I have given Esther the house of Haman, and him they have hanged upon the gallows, because he laid his hand upon the Jews, write ye also for the Jews as it liketh you, in the king's name, and seal it with the king's ring; for the writing which is written in the king's name, and sealed with the king's ring may no man reverse." The meaning of these words, as confirmed by the way in which Mordecai acted upon them, seems evidently to be this, that the king's

Lecture 13: Esther 8:1-14

willingness to comply with Esther's request could not be doubted from what he had already done in the case of Haman; but that it was impossible for him to grant fully what she now sought, on account of the established principle, that the law of the Medes and Persians could not be changed.

The arbitrary prince could put to death the man who had instigated him to publish the decree for the destruction of the Jews, but he could not recall or reverse the decree itself. Even he was fettered by the acknowledged rule of the realm. This is what is intimated in verse 8, which may be thus paraphrased: "Write as you best may in behalf of the Jews, so as to protect them from the consequences of the edict which has gone forth. In this use all liberty. But what you write must not be in such form as to set aside the previous edict. This cannot be; for it has been issued with due authority, and 'the writing which is written in the king's name, and sealed with the king's ring may no man reverse.'"

Here, a second time in the history of Artaxerxes, we have a proof of the felt inconvenience of that law, which despotism itself could not set aside. Gladly would the king be a party to the practical defeating of the object of it; but in its literal acceptation it must stand.

It is said that something like 'the principle of the unchangeableness of the purposes of the kings of Persia' has been preserved in that country even until recent times. And a circumstance may be here alluded to in illustration of this, which although somewhat strange and almost ludicrous, does bear some resemblance to the difficulty in which Artaxerxes felt himself placed between the unalterable law, and the willingness which he displayed at the same time to get quit of the obligation to observe it literally. A Persian king, who reigned not very many years ago, (Aga Mahmed Khan,) having set out upon a military expedition, and encamped in a place convenient for his purpose, gave forth his edict that the encampment should not be removed until the snow had disappeared from the neighboring mountains. The season was severe. The snow clung to the mountains longer than usual, and in the meantime the army became straitened for supplies. Here was an unexpected difficulty. The king's appointment must stand, but the result was likely to be ruinous. To avert the difficulty, then, a vast multitude of laborers were dispatched to clear away as far as they could the snow that was visible from the camp; and with their aid, and the help of a few days of sunshine, the snow disappeared, and then immediately the army was put in motion. Just so in the case before us in the text, Artaxerxes could not revoke his edict for the destruction of the Jews, but he gave power to Esther and Mordecai to make what provision they could for rendering it ineffective and harmless.

Now let us stop at this point to make some practical improvement of the verses we have considered. Many lessons might be drawn from them.

1. In the first place, we see how in the providence of God, the wealth which worldly men would use in opposition to the interests of God's cause and people may be wrested from them and made available for the advancement of these interests. It was painful enough to the proud spirit of Haman to be compelled to conduct Mordecai, whom he hated, through the city in triumph, but it would have been anguish, utterly intolerable to him, if he had been told that this man was forthwith to be his heir, and to have all his wealth placed at his disposal. So not infrequently it happens, that the riches which have been accumulated by those who would grudge the expenditure even of a small part for any purpose purely religious, pass into the hands of those who feel their responsibility as stewards of God's bounties, and who gladly employ His gifts for the promotion of objects by which their fellow-men are really benefited. The conclusion which we draw from all this, and which, without further remark, we leave with you is, that the best and happiest arrangement which a man can make with respect to the good things which have been bestowed upon him is that in his lifetime he seek to be personally the dispenser of good to

others. If he lives and acts in this spirit, then he will have the less anxiety as to the disposal of what he may be able to leave behind him.

2. In the second place, the peculiar providence which we see exercised in the case of Mordecai, teaches us that men may be well content to wait, while they are in the way of well-doing, until they receive their recompense. It was with no view to temporal reward, we most fully believe, that Mordecai assumed the guardianship of his orphan cousin, and brought her up tenderly in the knowledge of the God of her fathers. But if he had any expectation of reward, when he discovered and made known the plot against the life of the king, and such expectation he might have reasonably enough cherished, he had long to wait for the realizing of it. But he waited patiently, and at length his reward came, in greater fullness than his most sanguine hope could have anticipated. Now even in worldly things, although not on the same large scale, we often can mark similar movements of providence. Worth and faithfulness and humility, after they have been long neglected, are brought into the light, and are honored in proportion to the neglect which they formerly experienced.

But it is not with exclusive, or indeed with special reference to the administration of providence in this world, that we speak at present. History sets before us the examples of many, who were the excellent of the earth, persons of whom the world was not worthy, whose deeds of benevolence, and whose faithful services to the Lord and the men of their generation, were never openly acknowledged during their lifetime. Against reproach and obloquy and opposition the most crushing, many have had to pursue their way, compelled to hear even their good evil spoken of. But this does not alter the fact that the reward of all Christ's faithful servants is certain. It is not for reward that they labor in His service. It is from love to Him, and for the glory of God.

Yet as Christ Himself "looked forward to the joy that was set before Him," so His people are taught by His word and His example to have respect to the recompense of reward. Now, as Mordecai had to wait for a season before he obtained what he was well entitled to receive, would it have been a matter of great consequence although he had to wait for a few years longer? If he had received at length, after a very protracted season of delay, what he waited for, while he had still full power left him to enjoy it, would it not have been well? Then may we not say, that although believers in Christ have to wait for their reward until death come to carry them away, or as we may say, until this their last enemy come to lead them in triumph into the presence of the King, clad in the glorious robe of His righteousness, will it not be well seeing that then they shall be in condition to enjoy fully and forever the blessedness of being with Him and rejoicing in His smile?

3. In the third place, from Esther's love for her people we take a lesson. All was now well with her personally, and with her friend Mordecai. Much that her heart craved the king had granted her. As we have already said, he had shown her favor when she appeared before him without ornaments, he had shown her favor when she appeared with the ornaments which were his own gift to her. And now, when as a weeping suppliant, not for herself but for her people she appears before him, he shows her favor still. "How can I endure to see the evil that shall come unto my people?" she said, "or how can I endure to see the destruction of my kindred?'

Love and selfishness are antagonistic. Selfishness grasps, love gives. Selfishness gathers for itself and keeps for itself, love gathers to diffuse the blessings it enjoys. Esther was sorrowful because her people were still under the sentence of death which had been passed on them: and the consciousness of her own privilege, in the enjoyment of the light of the king's favor, could not overcome her feelings of distress, when she looked upon the dark cloud which hung over her brethren. She could not refrain from pleading for them, and she pled successfully.

Then should not this be an example to those among us, who themselves have had their souls gladdened by the grace of God, to be mindful of others who have not been visited so graciously? He who has before stretched out the scepter to you when you went to Him, to make intercession on your own behalf, will not let pass unnoticed the supplication which you present to Him in faith for friends in trouble, or for the church at large. If we have love in our hearts we shall plead for the perishing, and if we plead in faith, Christ will hear us. Never, my friends, rest satisfied with what you get for yourselves. Never let your own comfortable experience of God's love in Christ render you regardless of those who are still strangers to His love.

At no time was Esther more beautiful than when, with tearful eye, at the king's feet, she besought him to pity her brethren. And no prayer of yours will be wafted more acceptably to the heavenly throne than that which, with thankfulness for good you have yourselves received, and pressing, tender desire for the good of others, you present for the salvation of those who will not and cannot pray for themselves.

4. In the fourth place, I cannot pass without noticing specially the lesson which is to be drawn from the conduct of the king as it is here exhibited. It might be viewed under many aspects, but I shall be contented with one remark regarding it.

He saw that he had done wrong in listening to the suggestions of Haman for the destruction of the Jews; he would have most willingly recalled the cruel edict; but there stood between him and the authority which he would have exercised, that irrational enactment, that the laws of the Medes and Persians were unalterable. Now there is nothing analogous to this, we may say with all thankfulness, in the legislation of free countries like our own. There is even less among us now, it may be safely said, than there was half a century ago, to put a barrier to the progress of rational liberty and good government. Laws formerly passed for the benefit of one class at the expense of another class of society, are not now regarded as unchangeable, merely because they are of long standing.

But it is not concerning such matters of mere political and social interest that I now speak. I would call your attention to a subject more important. There is in the heart of almost every man the same principle which influenced the conduct of the king of Persia in the case before us. When once we have taken a side, or given forth an opinion upon any question, we feel ourselves bound to adhere to it, even at the risk of great inconvenience; yes, although we should have good reason to feel that we are in the wrong. There is the *pride of consistency,* if it may be so called, which is strong enough with many to bear down all considerations of reason, and justice, and prudence, and which sometimes influences them knowingly to do what they feel it would be far better to leave undone; and sometimes to persist in courses which they are sensible it would have been wiser for them never to have entered on.

But let not these remarks be misapprehended. It is not meant by them that a man is at liberty to give up an opinion which he has expressed, or to quit the path he is pursuing, merely because his steadfastness will subject him to inconvenience or suffering. By no means. If he is conscious to himself that he is right, he must keep his ground at all hazards. But if he perceives that he is wrong, and only remains steadfast because he is afraid or ashamed to *confess* that he is wrong, then certainly he is both weak and blameworthy.

If one man, for example, has injured another and knows it, but is too proud to acknowledge it, then he is destitute of the true spirit of Christianity. If a man is engaged in a wrong course of action, and is sensible of it, but will put his soul in peril rather than yield to the remonstrance of his friends, then his pride will certainly prove the ruin of his soul. There is, perhaps, more real heroism in confessing and correcting errors and weaknesses, than there is in boldly contending for

Lecture 13: Esther 8:1-14

truth, when we are conscious that we have it on our side. Many voices will cheer us onward in the defense of principles which we defend at some risk. The courage that suffers in a good cause will always get applause. But when I have done wrong, and make confession of the wrong, the men of the world do not sympathize. The humility of spirit, however, which nerves me to acknowledge and correct my wrongdoing has the seal of heaven so much the more obviously graven upon it, for the very reason that it meets not with the world's sympathy.

But we now proceed to consider verse 9-14: "Then were the king's scribes called at that time in the third month, that is, the month Sivan, on the three and twentieth day thereof; and it was written according to all that Mordecai commanded unto the Jews, and to the lieutenants, and the deputies and rulers of the provinces which are from India unto Ethiopia, an hundred twenty and seven provinces, unto every province according to the writing thereof, and unto every people after their language, and to the Jews according to their writing, and according to their language. And he wrote in the king Ahasuerus' name, and sealed it with the king's ring, and sent letters by posts on horseback, and riders on mules, camels, and young dromedaries; wherein the king granted the Jews which were in every city to gather themselves together, and to stand for their life, to destroy, to slay, and to cause to perish, all the power of the people and province that would assault them, both little ones and women, and to take the spoil of them for a prey, upon one day in all the provinces of king Ahasuerus, namely, upon the thirteenth day of the twelfth month, which is the month Adar. The copy of the writing for a commandment to be given in every province was published unto all people, and that the Jews should be ready against that day to avenge themselves on their enemies. So the posts that rode upon mules and camels went out, being hastened and pressed on by the king's commandment. And the decree was given at Shushan the palace."

We may believe, that whether the king was or was not fully aware of the power which he had granted to Haman, when he authorized him to send forth the decree which consigned the Jews to destruction, he would at least take part in the framing of the edict by which, as far as possible, the consequences of that decree were to be averted. But after all, his good intentions and his despotic power could effect nothing more than this, that one class of his subjects who had been doomed to death should be at liberty to stand for their lives, and in self-defense to destroy those who might assail them. It was a strange license which was thus published by royal authority, that the subjects of the same prince should have leave granted them to massacre each other without any interference on the part of the constituted authorities to put an end to the conflict.

Yet, as we have had occasion to remark already in these lectures, as cruel, and if possible, more unreasonable measures have been pursued in kingdoms called Christian. "When the king of Persia, sensible of the error he had committed, but unable to remedy it, permitted the Jews to stand upon their own defense, he at least gave them power to fight for their lives, and withdrew the sanction of his authority from any assault that might be made upon them by their enemies. But some kings professing to be Christians have let loose their murderous bands against their most inoffensive and peaceful subjects, without any warning of the evil that had been devised. These kindled the flame of civil war to exterminate a party. Artaxerxes only permitted a brief conflict, leaving the issue to the combatants themselves. We do not speak thus in excuse of his conduct. But to meet the objection of those who say, as some have said, that it is beyond probability that any prince should have acted as he did, we point to history, comparatively modern, and reply, that there are things recorded there as improbable, and still more revolting.

The only other topic suggested for remark by these verses, has reference to the free and speedy communication which seems to have existed between the several parts of the vast Persian empire at this early period. It is usually ascribed to the policy and sagacity of the great Cyrus, the friend of the Jews, that there were means provided for carrying intelligence with great rapidity throughout his dominions.

Lecture 13: Esther 8:1-14

Public roads were made, and at certain distances there were stages, as we would call them, where the couriers of the king could obtain fresh horses for their journeys, so that in a space remarkably brief, what was done in the capital could be published in the most distant provinces.

When the messages had to be carried through the desert, the animals appropriate for such service were ready, and hence we read, in verse 10: "The letters were sent by posts on horseback, and riders on mules, camels, and young dromedaries;" and in verse 14: "So the posts that rode upon mules and camels went out, being hastened and pressed on by the king's commandment."

The path of war and conquest, in the first instance, invariably leaves behind it traces of misery on every side. Yet it is not without counterbalancing, although certainly un-designed advantages. The immense empire of Cyrus, which could not be ruled without ready communication between its several provinces, made the forming of highways necessary, that means might be used for the preservation of peace and order. And long afterwards the same sagacious procedure was followed by the Romans. The rough paths which at first were trodden by their ambitious and sanguinary legions, became, in due time, the pathways of commerce, and more than this, the openings through which the heralds of the gospel might penetrate with their message of peace to the nations, the inlets for conveying to savage tribes the truth which brings civilization and all other blessings in its train. And if we at the present day, marking the marvelous facilities of rapid intercourse which are now enjoyed from land to land, can smile at what was called rapidity in former days, let us remember that it is for high purposes that we enjoy our privilege, even for the bringing about of the consummation referred to by the prophet Daniel, when he says, "many shall run to and fro, and knowledge shall be increased."

Now in conclusion, the lesson which I would leave with you is suggested by Esther's supplications for her people. In the midst of her own elevation, she thought of the daughters of Judah and their children doomed to die, and she wept and entreated for them. This reminds us of Christ's sympathy with His people. He who in the days of His flesh made supplication to the Father with strong crying and tears, supplicates still. In His exalted state He is still touched with the feeling of His people's infirmities. And the weakest and poorest who believe in Him have His sympathy. Wherefore be not discouraged, believers, but in the midst of all your trouble look up to Him who looks down upon you in love, and who is able to save unto the uttermost all that come unto God by Him. Amen.

Lecture 14: Esther 8:16-17 and 9:1-19

The subject of our last lecture was Esther's intercession for her people, and the favorable result of it. The king could not, indeed, formally revoke the edict which had gone forth for the extermination of the Jews. To have attempted to do this, would have been so contrary to established usage, that it could not even be thought of. "The writing which was written in the king's name, and sealed with the king's ring, no man might reverse." But then, although the edict must remain, something might be done virtually to break the force of it. And accordingly, as we saw, leave was given to the Jews, by a second edict, issued by Mordecai, to stand up in self-defense, and make what provision they best could to resist the attempts of those who might assail them. This, in the circumstances, was a vast boon. It implied that the Jews might regard themselves safe from any violence on the part of the officers of the king; and not only so, but that they might even get assistance from them. At the same time, however, we perceive that by these two enactments the king of Persia authorized, to a certain extent at least, the out-breaking of a civil war in his dominions, which, in whatever way it terminated, could only be productive of much bloodshed and misery, and which must diminish the strength and resources of his kingdom.

No war, indeed, whether civil or foreign, even when it is undertaken on just and necessary grounds, can be prosecuted without immediate consequences so disastrous that the heart of the Christian shrinks from the contemplation of them. The excitement of victory, and the false halo of glory which encircles the conquerors, may for a season dazzle their eyes, and make them insensible of the fearful price which has been paid for their triumph. But when the field of battle is surveyed, and all the other accompaniments of the conflict are noted, which are sometimes as revolting as the carnage of the battlefield itself; then the victors as well as the vanquished have reason to acknowledge that war cannot be waged without tremendous penalties. In no circumstances, indeed, can it be justified, except when it is undertaken in defense of liberty, or for the protection of rights and possessions which lawless ambition would otherwise make a spoil of.

Yet, when we glance at the blood-stained pages of history, we perceive that of all the great wars which are there chronicled, very few can be referred to the class which may be vindicated, most of them having originated in guilty ambition, or in the caprice of despotic rulers, who, like Artaxerxes in the instance before us, sported with men's lives and fortunes, as if they themselves had been free from every kind of responsibility. But we must not enlarge upon this point, important although it be; we must proceed to consider the verses which form the subject of the present lecture. Verse 15-17: "And Mordecai went out from the presence of the king in royal apparel of blue and white, and with a great crown of gold, and with a garment of fine linen and purple: and the city of Shushan rejoiced and was glad. The Jews had light, and gladness, and joy, and honor. And in every province, and in every city, whithersoever the king's commandment and his decree came, the Jews had joy and gladness, a feast, and a good day. And many of the people of the land became Jews; for the fear of the Jews fell upon them."

White and blue were the peculiar colors of the royal apparel in Persia; so that it would appear that when Haman said: "Let the man whom the king delighteth to honor be clothed in royal apparel;" he did not mean merely that he should be arrayed in such costly robes as the king himself might not have been ashamed to wear, but in robes precisely of the same kind as he was accustomed to wear. The coronet of gold, and the garment of fine linen and purple, were not so exclusively the ensigns of royalty, as of high nobility. But the ambition of Haman had soared beyond that of any former favorite. Thinking that the honor was to be conferred upon himself, nothing less would satisfy him than the very dress of the king: and thus it came to pass, that while he received his well-merited reward,

Lecture 14: Esther 8:16-17 and 9:1-19

the unpretending and humble Mordecai came out from the king's presence in such attire as no subject before him perhaps had ever worn.

When it is said that "the city Shushan rejoiced and was glad," this expression, if it is to be understood literally must mean either that there were public rejoicings by the king's appointment, which is by no means unlikely; or that Haman, by his haughtiness and his oppressive conduct, had made himself so many enemies in all classes of the community, that his downfall caused joy and satisfaction so wide-spread, that the whole city might be said to share in it. To one class, at all events, the advancement of Mordecai afforded unmingled delight to the Jews. Only the day before they had had to regard themselves as a proscribed race, who must wait submissively until the fatal day came that had been fixed for their destruction; and from whom all opportunity of flight and means of resistance were alike withdrawn. But now their captivity is turned back in a few short hours, and they are like men that dream. It is not wonderful that they should have had "light and gladness, and joy, and honor." And then, as the king's messengers travelled into the provinces with the decree which brought the tidings of deliverance to the afflicted people, the publication of the good news was hailed with rapture in every place where a colony of them was settled; so that it was as if the old days of the jubilee had returned, as if the outcast and persecuted had felt that a refuge was once more opened up to them from all their troubles.

"In every province, and in every city, whithersoever the king's commandment and his decree came, the Jews had joy and gladness, a feast, and a good day." Then it is added in the concluding sentence that "many people of the land became Jews, for the fear of the Jews fell upon them." It is very probable that during the whole period which had elapsed from the time that Cyrus showed favor to the Jews, and permitted all of them who chose to return to their own land, there had been occasionally proselytes gained to the law of Moses from among the heathen in the Persian empire. And if it was so, those who were not of the seed of Abraham would feel as if they had made an unprofitable change, when

Haman's cruel edict was promulgated. Now, however, when a Jew was advanced to be the chief minister of state, and when the favor of the king toward the whole race was so manifest, many, who had perhaps been even disposed to take part in the contemplated massacre, that they might share the spoil, were moved by the sudden change of the royal will, and were glad to shelter themselves under the protection of the Jewish name.

Now, let us pause for a little, and take from this passage one or two of the important lessons which it suggests.

1. In the first place, the conduct of Mordecai under the strange revolution which had been wrought in his condition and prospects, is full of practical instruction to us. The lesson is this, that advancement in worldly honor and prosperity should be turned to account, by being made conducive to the promotion of the interests of the church of Christ, and to the good of His people. It reflects high honor upon Mordecai, that the first act of authority which he performed in the exalted position to which he had been raised, was one which secured the enlargement of the church, and the safety of his brethren. In other hands the king's signet had been more frequently employed to give effect to decrees of violence and cruelty; but no sooner does it pass into his hands, than it is used in behalf of the oppressed. When he went forth wearing the tokens of the king's peculiar favor, and receiving the homage which had been paid to his haughty predecessor, he carried with him the pleasing consciousness that by the power conferred upon him, he had been enabled to send gladness into many a miserable dwelling, and to revive the spirit of a weak and helpless people.

Worldly honor and dignity in his case were invested with a value which does not intrinsically belong to them, and which never can belong to them, except when they are made subservient to such ends as he sought to promote by means of them. Just think for a moment of the feelings with which he would retire to his house that evening, as contrasted with those which the wicked Haman had cherished. The state of the two men was externally the same. Both had been raised from obscurity by the mere favor of the king, and both had for a time almost unbounded influence. But Haman went to his house miserable, saying: "All this wealth and grandeur availeth me nothing, so long as Mordecai the Jew sitteth at the king's gate." The other went to his house, we are fully confident, with a thankful heart, which is itself a feast, and carried his household with him to the footstool of Jehovah, to bless Him for His goodness, and to adore the Sovereign power which turneth the hearts of kings like the streams of water, whithersoever it pleaseth. Yea, and had Mordecai died that very night, he would have left behind him, among his countrymen, an imperishable name, and the fruit of his labor for their well-being which would have survived him, would have given him a title to be ranked forever among their noblest benefactors.

Now we say that all who have been blessed with wealth and influence may well look to this example and learn from it. The natural selfishness of the human heart prompts men to overlook the miseries of others, when they have gathered about them all that is needful for their own comfort. If they can but obtain the luxuries which gratify the senses, they care not what amount of woe and wretchedness may be experienced by those who live almost at their door. They waste not a thought upon the sad condition of the victims of spiritual darkness. We would remind them, therefore, that there is a luxury, the sweetest and best which wealth can purchase, and which lies fully within their reach, the luxury of doing good. No species of self-indulgence will leave behind it a relish so pleasant as will the endeavor to make the wretched happy; no exertion of power or influence will impart such true dignity to their possessor, as that which aims at the rescuing of Satan's captives from his grasp, and bringing honor to Christ, by extending the boundaries of His kingdom It is in this way that the gifts of providence are used in completest harmony with the will of the sovereign Giver, as well as to the highest advantage of those on whom they are bestowed. We repudiate the notion that men can purchase the divine favor by any act of their own. The folly of such a notion is sufficiently demonstrated by the consideration that when we endeavor to serve God with what we have, we only serve Him with His own. But His word says: "To do good, and to communicate to others, forget not; for with such sacrifices God is well pleased." Then His people have their will in unison with His, when they render these sacrifices of benevolence to which the Scripture summons them; and then they have the comfort of knowing, that all-imperfect as their best services are, they are pleasing, as the fruits of faith and love, to their Father who is in heaven.

2. In the second place, the account given in the text of the feelings of the Jews when the edict was issued for their deliverance, suggests some profitable reflections to us. It caused them light, and gladness, and joy; and the day of its publication was a day of feasting to them, and a good day. All this is natural, and it requires no strong effort of fancy to picture the delight with which the promulgation of the decree would be hailed in every place by the people whom it concerned. But our thoughts are directed by the description to a still higher theme. "How beautiful upon the mountains are the feet of him that bringeth good tidings, that publisheth peace; that bringeth good tidings of good; that publisheth salvation; that saith unto Zion, Thy God reigneth." All mere temporal deliverances sink into insignificance when contrasted with this, which the prophet celebrates. Now the good tidings have been brought to us and proclaimed in our hearing times innumerable. The sentence of doom under which we all naturally lie, as transgressors of God's covenant, has been followed by a message of pardon and life through Jesus Christ to all who will accept God's gracious offer. Surely, then, we are warranted to ask, what has been the effect of this message upon you who have so often heard it? If you have received the divine testimony and welcomed the

Lecture 14: Esther 8:16-17 and 9:1-19

deliverance which Christ has wrought out for sinners, then you cannot but enjoy some measure of gladness and enlargement of heart. If you have realized the awfulness of being alienated from God, and exposed to His displeasure, and have taken home to you the offer of mercy which He makes in the gospel, relying upon it as a faithful saying, and worthy of all acceptation, that Jesus Christ came into the world to save sinners, it is impossible that you should not have felt some relief in your conscience—some joy and comfort, from the reception of this blessed announcement.

What, then, is your experience? Some, if they were to answer the question honestly, would have to confess that they know not what is meant by spiritual joy, and *that* just because they have never been sensible of the misery of their lost estate, and therefore have never seriously sought the salvation which Christ holds out to the guilty. But it is not so much to their case that we allude, as to the case of those who might well be expected to exhibit joy and peace in believing; and with reference to these, we ask again, have they this experience? It must be answered, then, that all have it not.

Now, according to the views of some, where spiritual joy and gladness are wanting, spiritual life must be wanting also. But to this opinion we cannot give our assent. Various causes there may be for the obscuration of the light of divine joy in the soul, while there is no good reason for supposing that the soul is still dead in sin. No one who has had experience of the conflicts of the life of faith, and of the power of temptation, will require any formal reasoning in proof of the fact, that there may be spiritual life without joy, or at least with not a little darkness and disquietude. Yet, my friends, it is unquestionably the duty of all Christ's followers to rejoice in His salvation; and perhaps it would help them to do this more fully than they have yet done, if they would keep the eye of faith fastened more steadily upon the Savior Himself, and habitually bring all their convictions of personal guilt, and unworthiness, and backsliding, and transfer them at once and without reserve to Him who hath said: "Come unto Me, all ye that labor and are heavy laden, and I will give you rest."

3. In the third place, we may take a lesson from what is said in the text respecting the readiness which was shown by multitudes to join themselves to the Jews, when the king's edict in their favor was published. The description which is here given of the effect of the royal patronage extended toward that people, in drawing many to cast in their lot with them, while it exhibits a truthful representation of the whole affair, corresponds completely with the incidents of more recent history.

It may be believed, that in some instances those of the people of the land who professed the Jewish religion were influenced by right motives, and forsook their heathenism because they felt that Jehovah, the God of the Jews, was the true God. Zechariah had foretold such event, when he said (viii. 23): "Thus saith the Lord of hosts; In those days it shall come to pass, that ten men shall take hold out of all languages of the nations, even shall take hold of the skirt of him that is a Jew, saying, "We will go with you: for we have heard that God is with you." A better reason could not be assigned for a change of religion than this—that a man should give up that which he had formerly professed, and embrace a new and altogether different creed and form of worship, on the ground that thus he was brought into communion with the true God. But while, as we have said, there were no doubt some who were animated by this feeling when they became proselytes to Judaism, yet it is very manifest, from the language used in the text, that such was not the generally prevalent feeling.

"Many became Jews, for the fear of the Jews fell upon them." The sunshine of the royal favor was now resting upon the seed of Abraham. They were a numerous body of themselves; and now, when they had liberty of action, by their wealth they could bring over to their side those who would protect them. It was good policy, therefore, to profess to be friendly toward them. And so *not the fear of God,* but the *fear of the*

Lecture 14: Esther 8:16-17 and 9:1-19

Jews, moved many to renounce heathenism, and acknowledge submission to the law of Moses. The church was in one of her prosperous periods, and hence there were strong inducements to the worldly-minded to enroll themselves among her members. Now this, as we have said, is no isolated case. Such things have often occurred, although by no means tending to the advancement of vital religion. For example, it must have often struck the reflective readers of history, as a subject rather of painful than of pleasant contemplation, that the progress of the Reformation in many countries should have been so intimately connected with and dependent upon the belief and practice of the ruling powers. The flowing and ebbing of the tide of religious profession might be calculated too surely from the prevailing sentiments of the court. Thus, for instance, how sudden were the changes which the aspect of the church in England presented during the reigns of three successive sovereigns. In the brief time of the Sixth Edward, when his counselors were Protestant, and Popery was disallowed, how fast did the principles of Protestantism spread through the kingdom? It seemed as if the genial beams of truth had melted at once the old hoary superstition, and as if the land had passed almost in an instant from the dreariness of winter into the freshness and beauty of spring and summer—yea, and into full autumnal fruitfulness. But as sudden was the reverse when Mary came to the throne. Then Popery became rampant again, and the majority were glad to seem to be upon its side. And no less remarkable was the revival of Protestantism during the reign of her successor Elizabeth. The nation appeared to be born in a day; and again, multitudes who had joined in the celebration of the mass cried, "away with it!" and became the friends and promoters of the purer faith. The case of England is not singular. Through changes of the same kind did people pass in other countries, affording melancholy proof of the truth, that a profession of religion may only be a mask to conceal worldliness and selfishness, and even more heinous enormities.

And can we say that these principles have ceased to operate in our own day, and that the laws of toleration now generally understood and observed in our own land have tended to free the church of Christ from the contamination of those who only profess membership in it to promote some secular or unworthy purpose? Alas! We cannot. Although the weight of temporal authority is not exerted to put a strain on men's consciences, and to make them submissive to forms and creeds from which they dissent in their heart, yet there are circumstances of another kind, which influence multitudes to range themselves among the friends of religion, while they are strangers to the power of it. Respectability of character, general trustworthiness, and outward decency are so intimately associated in our minds with a respect for the ordinances of the gospel, that where we do not find the latter, we are not easily persuaded that the former things are to be found. And thus, from regard to character, and with a view to maintain respectability and to forward worldly interests, very many join themselves to the church of Christ without being influenced at all by the love of Christ.

Now, if we examine all the circumstances carefully, we shall perceive that we have as little reason to take comfort to ourselves from the external state of religion among us, as the Jews had from the apparent respect which was shown for their religion in the days of Mordecai, or as the conflicting parties had which alternately sunk or prevailed in many countries at the period of the Reformation. The worldly and selfish element—the fear of man, and not the fear of God—has ever been too prevalent in molding religious profession; the fires of persecution being sometimes employed to compel, and the attractions of self-interest at other times to draw men to confess with the mouth what they did not believe in their heart. And thus it is that the numerical force of Christianity, if I may so speak, is so different a thing from the vital power of it.

If the question were to be formally proposed to us: "Why are you Christians, and why do you prefer the particular denomination with which you are connected to all others?" it is to be feared that many of us would not be able to meet that question with a satisfactory answer. The answer should be: "I am a Christian because I believe in the doctrine of Christ, and in Himself as the Son of God, the Savior of sinners, and because I have obtained from Christ that which I could nowhere else obtain—peace and rest unto my soul. And I am a member of the religious denomination to which I belong, because I believe that its doctrine and discipline are framed in accordance with the word of God." But could all of us give such reason for our Christianity, and for our particular mode of professing it? We fear we could not. Many have no other foundation for their faith than that their fathers so believed before them; and many also pay respect to divine ordinances, merely because they would be regarded with suspicion if they did not. Let me, then, my friends, urge upon you the necessity of being able to give an answer to everyone that asketh you a reason of the hope that is in you.

A profession of Christianity, with some show of reverence for its ordinances, will not carry you to heaven. It will not even abide the trouble of a sifting time on earth, if such time should overtake you. It will not give you solid comfort when you come, as soon you must come, to pass through the dark valley of the shadow of death. Nothing will avail but the faith which rests on Christ, and which, being the substance of things hoped for, and the evidence of things not seen, makes the possession of heaven sure, by the present foretaste of it with which it feasts the soul.

But we must now proceed to review the verses which have been read from chapter 9 verse 1-19: "Now in the twelfth month, that is, the month Adar, on the thirteenth day of the same, when the king's commandment and his decree drew near to be put in execution, in the day that the enemies of the Jews hoped to have power over them, (though it was turned to the contrary, that the Jews had rule over them that hated them) the Jews gathered themselves together in their cities throughout all the provinces of the king Ahasuerus, to lay hand on such as sought their hurt:

and no man could withstand them; for the fear of them fell upon all people. And all the rulers of the provinces, and the lieutenants, and the deputies, and officers of the king, helped the Jews; because the fear of Mordecai fell upon them. For Mordecai was great in the king's house, and his fame went out throughout all the provinces: for this man Mordecai waxed greater and greater. Thus the Jews smote all their enemies with the stroke of the sword, and slaughter, and destruction, and did what they would unto those that hated them. And in Shushan the palace the Jews slew and destroyed five hundred men. And Parshandatha, and Dalphon, and Aspatha, and Poratha, and Adalia, and Aridatha, and Parmashta, and Arisai, and Aridai, and Vajezatha, the ten sons of Haman the son of Hammedatha, the enemy of the Jews, slew they; but on the spoil laid they not their hand. On that day the number of those that were slain in Shushan the palace was brought before the king. And the king said unto Esther the queen, "The Jews have slain and destroyed five hundred men in Shushan the palace, and the ten sons of Haman; what have they done in the rest of the king's provinces? Now what is thy petition? And it shall be granted thee: or what is thy request further? And it shall be done." Then said Esther, "If it please the king, let it be granted to the Jews which are in Shushan to do to-morrow also according unto this day's decree, and let Haman's ten sons be hanged upon the gallows." And the king commanded it so to be done: and the decree was given at Shushan; and they hanged Haman's ten sons. For the Jews that were in Shushan gathered themselves together on the fourteenth day also of the month Adar, and slew three hundred men at Shushan; but on the prey they laid not their hand. But the other Jews that were in the king's provinces gathered themselves together, and stood for their lives, and had rest from their enemies, and slew of their foes seventy and five thousand, but they laid not their hands on the prey, on the thirteenth day of the month Adar; and on the fourteenth day of the same rested they, and made it a day of feasting and gladness. But the Jews that were at Shushan assembled together on the thirteenth day

Lecture 14: Esther 8:16-17 and 9:1-19

thereof, and on the fourteenth thereof; and on the fifteenth day of the same they rested, and made it a day of feasting and gladness. Therefore the Jews of the villages, that dwelt in the unwalled towns, made the fourteenth day of the month Adar a day of gladness and feasting, and a good day, and of sending portions one to another."

These verses contain the portion of the book of Esther which it is most difficult satisfactorily to interpret. We could have wished that some points in this narrative had been different from what they are; but it is one characteristic of the word of God, that it describes with all plainness the procedure of His people as well as of His enemies.

The decisive day at length arrived, when it was to be seen what would be the effect of the two royal decrees respecting the Jewish people. Very particular details are not given, so that we must be guided somewhat by conjecture. Thus, for example, it is not stated that the enemies of the Jews actually commenced the assault, and it is possible that they did not. It may have been that they did not venture to draw together to attack the Jews, but that the Jews, knowing the parties who had been loudest in their threatening against them, when Haman's decree was published, fell upon them and inflicted the punishment which Mordecai's decree gave them liberty to inflict. Or it may have been, on the contrary, that the most daring of their enemies, imagining that the Jews would not have courage to defend themselves, although they were permitted to do so, did assemble together and proceeded to execute their purpose. If it were so, then they were met and destroyed as we read in the text. The procedure, indeed, may have been different in different parts of the empire; but the general result is stated, that in Shushan, the royal city, five hundred men, and throughout the provinces seventy-five thousand were slain on that day. The Jews did not take the spoil of their enemies, and probably neither women nor children were put to death, yet it was a fearful massacre.

At the same time, we can read all this part of the narrative with the feeling that those who fell were visited with a just retribution, and that if it had not been so ordered, the whole Jewish community—men, women, and children, would have been cut off by their relentless adversaries. The difficulty lies chiefly in that which follows. When the account of the number that had been slain in Shushan was brought to the king, he stated it to Esther, adding, "What have they done in the rest of the king's provinces? Now what is thy petition? And it shall be granted. Or what is thy request further? And it shall be done." Esther's reply we read with sorrow. She will have the dead bodies of Haman's ten sons exposed upon the gallows on which their father had suffered, and liberty given to the Jews in Shushan to have another day's vengeance upon their enemies. To the king, this request, savoring so truly of eastern vindictiveness, did not appear strange. He commanded that it should so be done. But we have been accustomed now to associate with the character of Esther so much of what is soft, and gentle, and lovely, that we almost feel as if the charm were dissipated, and as if her memory were less entitled to affectionate regard than we had formerly supposed. It may have been that she had the means of knowing, through Mordecai, that some of the most determined enemies of the Jews, those who best merited death, had escaped. They may have fled from the city in the morning, to return at night, when they supposed the slaughter would be ended. And not anticipating a renewal of it on the day following, they may have only after all received the punishment they deserved. But still, when the thirteenth day of the month Adar was past, the deliverance of the Jews was complete; and it displayed too much of the spirit of dire vengeance, and too little of the softness of the heart that should have animated so fair a form, when Esther sought a repetition of the bloody work during another day. The only apology that can be offered for her is her intense love of her own people, and her unmitigated dislike of all who sought to injure them.

The provocation which she had received was unquestionably great: and the law of loving enemies, and doing good to them that use us despitefully and persecute us, was not so fully known to her as it is to us. Yet we could have even wished that the revengeful request, if it was to

Lecture 14: Esther 8:16-17 and 9:1-19

be made at all, had been made rather by Mordecai than by Esther. It is mentioned as a natural consequence of the triumph which the Jews thus obtained over their enemies, that they celebrated the event with feasting and gladness. To both these points, however, Esther's conduct and the rejoicing of the Jews, we shall take occasion to refer more particularly in the next lecture.

In the meantime, let us make some improvement of the narrative we have just considered.

1. In the first place, we learn from this passage the comfortable truth, that God's people obtain the victory over their enemies. We are not informed whether any of the Jews perished in this conflict. It is not improbable that some did. Yet, upon the whole, their cause was victorious. Even so, whatever hardships and troubles Christ's people have to endure in the world, and however dark and lowering the cloud may be which sometimes hangs over them, yet, "at evening time it will be light" to them, and death's temporary triumph over them will only lead to their eternal triumph over it and all their foes. Be not discouraged, ye that fear and serve the Lord. Greater is He that is for you, than all that can be against you. Fight the good fight of faith, the crown of life is sure to all who are in Christ.

2. In the second place, Esther's feeling towards the enemies of the Jews, although it is not to be praised, yet suggests a lesson. The people of God cannot look with complacency upon His enemies. Yet they dare not hate them, they cannot wish their destruction, yea, they cannot think without the deepest sorrow of the destiny upon which they are rushing. What a Christian desires is that their enmity to God and to godliness may be destroyed, and that they may be made monuments of saving mercy. Yet the time is coming, and a solemn thing it is to think of it, when God's children shall contemplate with satisfaction the out-pouring of His just vengeance upon His enemies. Mere natural affection will be swallowed up in that supreme love of God, and

reverence for His will, which prevail in Heaven. And when the wicked are condemned, the righteous will add their amen to the fearful sentence: "Depart from me ye cursed." Oh, brethren, strive to save those who are dear to you on earth, that this terrible separation may not be made between you and them when the Lord cometh to the judgment.

3. In conclusion, let me leave with you the lesson before alluded to, that the proclamation of God's purpose of mercy to sinners contains in it a call to His people to be joyful. See to it, that your faith is built upon Christ, the sure foundation. Seek to have your interest in Him cleared up and made sure. Seek to have the witness of His spirit in your hearts; follow Him bearing the cross, and then, whatever difficulties may befall you in your Christian course, you will still be able to rejoice in the Lord, and to joy in the God of your salvation. Amen.

Lecture 15: Chapter 9:20-32 and 10:1-3

In the last lecture, the subject which chiefly occupied our attention was the effect of the edict which was issued in favor of the Jews. As might well be supposed, it caused great joy and gladness among that people, and it also exalted them so highly in the estimation of their heathen neighbors, that many of these publicly professed submission to the law of Moses. And when the day came which had been fixed for their extermination, they obtained the mastery over their enemies, and crushed them with little resistance. Then, after this, we had to look to the conduct of Esther in connection with this work of vengeance. The king having again expressed his willingness to grant her whatever she should ask, she entreated that the dead bodies of Haman's ten sons might be hung upon a gallows, and that the Jews in Shushan might be permitted on the following day to complete the destruction of their adversaries. The request was granted, but we were with reluctance constrained to acknowledge that in proposing it, Esther displayed a spirit of vindictiveness which it is somewhat painful to contemplate. Large allowance must be made for the provocation she had received, and for the rudeness of the age; but with all this, we cannot help feeling that it would have been more seemly if, when the safety of her people was fully provided for, she had exhibited more of the softness and gentleness which befitted a woman so attractive, and a character otherwise so engaging and lovely.

If she had been put upon her defense for this act, she might have urged that love for her countrymen and love for her religion prompted her to deal thus toward the fierce enemies of both. And we shall not question the fact, that it was by these feelings she was chiefly animated, and not by the desire of revenge alone. But it must be remembered, that although this furnishes a sufficiently satisfactory explanation of her conduct, it does not justify it. It has ever been under the pretext of zeal for truth, that the fires of religious persecution have been kindled. Under this plea, for example, Popery has shed the blood of the righteous like water, and even in Protestant countries pains and penalties have been inflicted upon those who refused to adopt the form of religion patronized by the state. Intolerance has always had its arguments in self-defense; but these do not serve for its vindication. And so in the case before us, we believe most assuredly that Esther acted in all good conscience, as also did Mordecai, by whom very probably she was instructed what to do on the occasion. Yet this hinders not our regretting that she was hurried away by the spirit of revenge, rather than moved by what would have become her better—the mild and sweet influence of a forgiving heart. In defense of her religion and her people she suffered herself to act with unbecoming zeal I would take occasion to observe here, that the great principle of toleration in religion is still imperfectly understood, and in many parts of what is called Christendom, as imperfectly practiced.

The principle is utterly to be repudiated, that man is not responsible to God for unbelief. He is responsible, as Christ's words imply, when He says that men "love darkness rather than light, because their deeds are evil." But on the other hand, this other principle is ever to be maintained and urged, that man is not responsible to his fellowman, either for his belief or unbelief, and that pains and penalties to enforce religious conformity are altogether indefensible. That there is a limit to be affixed to the publication of opinions which are blasphemous, revoltingly immoral, or licentious, and subversive of all order and government, is a proposition which very few will call in question. The well-being of society demands that care be taken lest its very foundations be undermined by men whose heart is set in them to do evil. But to punish any one for holding particular views of divine truth, or for refusing to conform to the belief and practice of the majority is manifestly wrong. If no other arguments could be advanced for the assumption and exertion of a power to compel uniformity, these two would be sufficient: that the application of external force in matters of religion implies that those who

Lecture 15: Chapter 9:20-32 and 10:1-3

have recourse to it must deem themselves infallible, which no man, or class of men, can rightly do; and that it evidently supposes that the claims and evidences of true religion are not so powerful of themselves as to be able without external or temporal aid to secure the approval of those to whom they are addressed. Let us hope that the world and the Church also will come to understand better than either has done hitherto, the reverence which is due to the inalienable rights of conscience, when these are pled for.

These remarks are made at present, because the time did not allow them to be offered in the previous discourse. We now proceed to consider the verses which form the subject of the present lecture, and which, although they seem to embrace a wider range than usual, yet do not present many separate topics to be commented on.

Verses 20-32: "And Mordecai wrote these things, and sent letters unto all the Jews that were in all the provinces of the king Ahasuerus, both nigh and far, to establish this among them, that they should keep the fourteenth day of the month Adar, and the fifteenth day of the same, yearly, as the days wherein the Jews rested from their enemies, and the month which was turned unto them from sorrow to joy, and from mourning into a good day: that they should make them days of feasting and joy, and of sending portions one to another, and gifts to the poor. And the Jews undertook to do as they had begun, and as Mordecai had written unto them; because Haman the son of Hammedatha, the Agagite, the enemy of all the Jews, had devised against the Jews to destroy them, and had cast Pur, that is, the lot, to consume them, and to destroy them; but when Esther came before the king, he commanded by letters that his wicked device, which he devised against the Jews, should return upon his own head, and that he and his sons should be hanged on the gallows. Wherefore they called these days, Purim, after the name of Pur. Therefore for all the words of this letter, and of that which they had seen concerning this matter, and which had come unto them, the Jews ordained, and took upon them, and upon their seed, and upon all such as joined themselves unto them, so as it should not fail, that they would keep these two days according to their writing, and according to their appointed time every year; and that these days should be remembered and kept throughout every generation, every family, every province, and every city, and that these days of Purim should not fail from among the Jews, nor the memorial of them perish from their seed. Then Esther the queen, the daughter of Abihail, and Mordecai the Jew, wrote with all authority, to confirm this second letter of Purim. And he sent the letters unto all the Jews, to the hundred and twenty and seven provinces of the kingdom of Ahasuerus, with words of peace and truth, to confirm these days of Purim in their times appointed according as Mordecai the Jew and Esther the queen had enjoined them, and as they had decreed for themselves and for their seed, the matters of their fastings and their cry. And the decree of Esther confirmed these matters of Purim; and it was written in the book."

It followed as a natural consequence of the deliverance which the Jews had experienced, and of the triumph which they had gained over their enemies, that they should celebrate these events with thanksgiving to God who had so graciously interposed in their behalf, and with acts of kindness toward one another. Enlargement of heart is the proper fruit of an escape from peril of any kind. Accordingly, it is mentioned in the preceding verses, that the Jews throughout the provinces, "made the fourteenth day of the month Adar, *i.e.* the day after the conflict, a day of gladness and feasting, and a good day, and of sending portions one to another." And as in Shushan, the royal city, the fourteenth day had been devoted like the thirteenth, to the work of vengeance, the Jews there kept the fifteenth as their festival-day. It was in consequence of this, therefore, that Mordecai sent letters unto all the Jews that were in all the provinces of the empire, to establish this among them, that they should keep the fourteenth and fifteenth days of the month Adar, as a stated festival to commemorate the deliverance which God had given them, when nothing short of utter destruction seemed ready to overtake them. The festival, as

Lecture 15: Chapter 9:20-32 and 10:1-3

instituted by these letters, was called Purim, from the Persian word Pur, the lot, because it was by the casting of lots that Haman fixed upon the thirteenth day of the month, as the propitious day for the extermination of the Jews, although in the providence of God it was made the day of the overthrow of their adversaries.

It is traditionally said that this enactment, binding the Jews to observe the day of their deliverance, was not received by all of them without questioning and serious objection. The excitement of natural feeling led them at first to celebrate their escape from a cruel death; but some of them were not prepared to follow up the requirement that there should be an annual commemoration of the event. It is among the traditions of those times, although of course no firm reliance is to be placed upon it, that out of eighty-five elders, thirty dissented from the requisition that these two days should be regularly observed as a festival. And it may have been on account of some expressed dislike by some of the leading people, that Mordecai and Esther deemed it expedient to issue a second letter, as we see from the twenty-ninth verse they seem to have done, to enjoin the observance of the feast. But whatever may have been the feeling of certain parties with respect to this matter, the festival was established, and has ever since been kept by the Jews. In fact, it is said to be the most joyous festival which they celebrate, being accompanied with an exuberant hilarity, which sometimes unhappily degenerates into intemperance, riot, and licentiousness. The Book of Esther is read from beginning to end on both the feast days. Whenever the name of Haman occurs, there is a loud and vehement expression of hatred in the synagogue. In some places Haman and his sons are hanged in effigy by the children. And—I quote from Kitto's illustrated Bible—"when the reading is finished, the whole congregation exclaim: 'Cursed be Haman! Blessed be Mordecai! Cursed be Zeresh! Blessed be Esther! Cursed be all idolaters! Blessed be all the Israelites! And blessed also be Harbonah (the eunuch), at whose instance Haman was hanged.'" It must not be overlooked, however, that the Jews, if they are chargeable with some extravagances in keeping the feast of Purim, are careful to remember, even at the present day, that it is a season of sending portions one to another. The rich contribute willingly at that time to the relief of their poorer brethren; so that this festival may be regarded as one of the means by which the seed of Abraham, amid their dispersion among the Gentiles, have continued to preserve their national, or, as we might rather call it, their family feeling.

We now come to make some practical application of these verses.

1. In the first place, as it was said in the first lecture, that the establishment and continued observance of the feast of Purim furnish a strong argument for the canonical authority of the Book of Esther—so we may generalize here, and say, that by other public observances of a similar kind, some leading facts of the Christian religion are certified to us, in opposition to the cavils of infidelity. Many of you will remember that this forms a prominent argument in the brief but conclusive treatise entitled, "Leslie's Short Method with the Deists." And even so, go where you will among the dispersed children of Judah, and you will find the feast of Purim annually celebrated, and the history of the events which led to it read in the synagogues as we have it here, bringing the whole series of transactions up to view as freshly as if they had been but of yesterday. And thus it comes to pass, that *time,* which the ancients used to say "destroys all things," serves only to establish the truth of the word of God— bringing down to succeeding generations accumulated proofs of the certainty of those records which reveal the will of God to man.

2. In the second place, the passage before us suggests to us a few remarks with respect to the commemoration of events in the church by appointed festivals. Of these there were many in the Jewish Church; but they were all instituted by divine authority until we come down to this one of Purim. Now, many commentators suppose that Mordecai and Esther were guided by divine inspiration in enjoining the Jews to

Lecture 15: Chapter 9:20-32 and 10:1-3

observe this festival. There is nothing, however, actually to warrant this supposition, except the simple fact that by common consent the Jews did celebrate it, and that the whole train of events recorded in this book indicates the operation of a special providence. At the same time, we would not venture to say that the supposition is to be rejected. On the contrary, it carries probability in it; and we gladly embrace it, because the festival would have been an act of will-worship, if it had not been sanctioned by the authority of Jehovah Himself.

Under the New Testament economy, the observance of holidays or religious festivals is unwarranted on Scriptural grounds, if you except the Sabbath. These were all shadows of better things to come, and the substance is come, which is Christ. The apostle Paul speaks in the language of reproof to those who observed days, and months, and years, and urges the great truth that "the kingdom of God is not meat and drink, but righteousness, and peace, and joy in the Holy Ghost."

Popery, however, which has borrowed much from Judaism as well as from heathenism, has its festivals so numerous that the Lord's own day is almost shut out of view amid the multiplicity of other appointed seasons for worship. And I would take the liberty to say, that there is too much of the same spirit in some sections of the Protestant church. There is a very ingenious defense of the religious festivals of the Church of England by one of her highly gifted ministers, whose holy zeal and sincerity no one will question, I mean Dr. Archer Butler, in which he speaks of these festivals as of vast importance, inasmuch as they afford opportunity to bring before the people a wide range of Scripture reading, and all the leading facts and doctrines of the gospel in succession (*Sermon on Easter Day*, page 49 of his volume).

But surely the Presbyterian form of worship, which sets aside those festivals as human inventions, affords as ample means of bringing the whole system of truth before the people, when it enjoins the regular reading and expounding of the Scriptures in conjunction with preaching every week. We are not chained down to the formality of celebrating the birth and death and resurrection of the Savior, at certain seasons, which it is well known do not correspond to the actual periods when these events took place. But we do not overlook them for all this. We rejoice in these events, and in the opportunity which is given to us of alluding to them from week to week, bringing the one or the other more prominently to view, as expediency may dictate.

Yet, my friends, while we have put away the observance of particular days, as *tending* to superstition, if it does not actually savor of it, let us not forget that there are dealings of God toward us individually which may be suitably made subjects of serious meditation at stated times. A man's birthday, the time of other important events in his history, the visitations of providence, adverse or prosperous, which have left their traces deep in his memory, may well be religiously thought of as the revolution of the year recalls the remembrance of them. And thought of they *ought to be* by us if we would escape the charge brought against those of whom the Psalmist says: "Give them according to their deeds: render to them their desert, because they regard not the works of the Lord, nor the operation of his hands."

3. In the third place, we learn from this passage in what way our seasons of rejoicing should be improved. The feast of Purim was to be "a day of gladness, a good day, and of sending portions one to another:" when in the providence of God any difficulty is removed from our path, when we obtain any advantage which we had not looked for, or when any deliverance is wrought out for us which we could have scarcely anticipated, then our thanksgiving should not be confined to religious services, but should be manifested also in the way of benevolence to the poor and needy. The festival of Purim was and still is a joyous season among the Jews. But the only pleasing thing

Lecture 15: Chapter 9:20-32 and 10:1-3

about it now is that it is a time when the hearts of the rich open for the relief of the poor. Thus far the practice corresponds to the injunction given by the prophet Isaiah (lviii.): "Is not this the fast that I have chosen? To loose the bands of wickedness, to undo the heavy burdens, and to let the oppressed go free, and that ye break every yoke? Is it not to deal thy bread to the hungry, and that thou bring the poor that are cast out, to thy house? When thou seest the naked that thou cover him, and that thou hide not thyself from thine own flesh."

And in what manner can Christians better exhibit their thankfulness to God for mercies received than by combining with their religious services the exercise of charity toward their brethren who are in distress? It is a coldhearted and questionable devotion that is limited to prayers and thanksgivings, while there are so many of Christ's people who need the sympathy and the aid of their brethren on whom providence has smiled more bounteously. Let us not forget that the gospel of Christ calls upon us "to rejoice with them that do rejoice, and to weep with them that weep."

But we now proceed to consider the three verses which form the tenth chapter: "And the king Ahasuerus laid a tribute upon the land, and upon the isles of the sea. And all the acts of his power and of his might, and the declaration of the greatness of Mordecai, whereunto the king advanced him, are they not written in the book of the chronicles of the kings of Media and Persia? For Mordecai the Jew was next unto king Ahasuerus, and great among the Jews, and accepted of the multitude of his brethren, seeking the wealth of his people, and speaking peace to all his seed."

There is not much room for comment upon these verses. But we may notice, first, that they afford us a glimpse of the condition of those who live under an arbitrary government. At the will of the sovereign, and without any opportunity of obtaining redress, except by actual rebellion, the subjects must pay whatever tribute is demanded of them. And this they have to do with the knowledge that what is thus wrung from them will not be applied to promote the interests of the empire, but to gratify the caprices and to minister to the pleasures of the sovereign. In free states, like our own, where no tax can be imposed but with the consent of the community through their representatives, there is the comfort of knowing that what is demanded is necessary for the exigencies of the state; and it should therefore be given most -willingly. "Render to every man his due, tribute to whom tribute is due."

Again, at the conclusion of this book, we see notice taken, as at the beginning of it, of the vastness of the dominions which were under the rule of Artaxerxes. And during his reign there was every indication that this huge empire would long continue unbroken. There was no rival power at the time but that of Egypt: and the two countries were so far separated that they might co-exist and extend their influence far and wide without interfering with each other. But the very extent of the Persian Empire proved its ruin. The great king, as he was called, was brought into collision with the states of Greece, those nurseries of liberty and literature and science in the old world, and from them his kingdom was to receive its death blow. This did not indeed happen until many years after the date of the transactions recorded in this Book. But it had been foretold by the unerring word of prophecy, and accordingly it was brought to pass. Daniel had seen in vision the Babylonian empire falling, and the Medo-Persian arising in its stead.

He had seen this also destroyed by the king of Greece. And so, the event was. Alexander the Great overthrew the Persian power and became for a brief space the monarch of the world. Vast changes there have been on the earth's surface, succeeding ages trampling out the remembrance of what had been before, but the word of the Lord abideth forever. In the last verse of the book we are informed of the continued prosperity of Mordecai. No royal caprice seems to have been exhibited to drive him from the influential place he occupied. And refreshing it is to mark that in his exalted position he did not forget his own people or cease to promote their interests as he had opportunity. There is large room for

Lecture 15: Chapter 9:20-32 and 10:1-3

describing a man of no ordinary character in the words: "Mordecai the Jew was next unto king Ahasuerus, and great among the Jews, and accepted of the multitude of his brethren, seeking the wealth of his people, and speaking peace to all his seed." This is the delineation of the character of a person who, although he was in providence unexpectedly raised to the highest worldly honor, was not dazzled or made giddy by his advancement, who retained the same kindly heart toward his brethren in his elevation which he had shown when he was in humble state, and who used the good gifts which God had conferred upon him not in dainty and luxurious living but in promoting the interests of God's church and people.

There is one point which must not be overlooked here, although it is not adverted to in the history. We had occasion, on reviewing the Book of Nehemiah, to mention that it was during the reign of Artaxerxes, whose queen Esther was, and who had Mordecai as his prime minister, that that remarkable man was sent to Jerusalem to repair the desolations of the city and to build the wall. We do not wonder to find Nehemiah a Jew occupying the important place of the king's cupbearer, when Esther a Jewess was queen, and Mordecai a Jew managed the most important affairs of the kingdom. No doubt it was the high position to which these two were raised, that emboldened Nehemiah to make his request to the king when the queen was sitting beside him, that he should be sent to Jerusalem to help his brethren there, and to put the city in a condition in which it might bid defiance to its enemies. We can trace the influence of Esther and Mordecai in all this, although it is not formally stated, and can perceive that they were instrumental in doing much more to forward the interests of their countrymen, and to advance the cause of true religion, than the record makes known.

The Apocryphal Book of Esther takes up the history at the point where the genuine Book terminates and carries it much farther down; but as no reliance can be placed upon its statements, we do not feel it of consequence to allude to them. It may be mentioned, however, that at

Ecbatana, called in the Book of Ezra, Achmetha, and in modern speech Hamadan, there is a building still in existence, called the tomb of Mordecai and Esther, which is regarded with great veneration by the Jews, and visited by many of them every year. Time and violence have made many changes upon it, but the Jews believe that two ancient coffins, or sarcophagi as they are called, which are kept there, and which bear inscriptions to the memory of Mordecai and Esther respectively, contain the remains of these two benefactors of their race. And whether the fact be so or not, it is very significant. The proud king Artaxerxes, and all the princes of his line have passed into oblivion. No one asks or cares where they were entombed. But the memory of these two servants of God survives. Their supposed resting place is guarded with religious care. They have obtained the only kind of immortality which man can give to man, which ambition and learning often seek for but cannot obtain. And they have the true immortality, having served their generation according to the will of God, and fallen asleep in the faith of His exceeding great and precious promises.

Now in bringing to a close the consideration of their strange and eventful history, there are one or two remarks which the subject naturally suggests.

1. In the first place, in entering on the review of this Book, I adverted to the objection which has often been brought against its divine authority because the name of God does not once occur in it. It is unnecessary to repeat here what was then said in reply to this objection; but I trust it will now be manifest to all, that although the name is not found in it, there is no other part of scripture in which the operation of God's special providence is more clearly revealed. It is indeed from beginning to end an illustration of providential dealing, which it is impossible for any pious mind to contemplate without echoing the sentiment of the Psalmist, "verily the Lord God omnipotent reigneth; the righteous Lord loveth righteousness;" "He

Lecture 15: Chapter 9:20-32 and 10:1-3

delivereth His people from their enemies, yea, He lifteth them up above those that rise up against them; He delivereth them from the violent man."

2. In the second place, I cannot help adverting to a circumstance, which this particular portion of the history of the Jewish people makes it the more necessary to notice, that although the weak and facile mind of Artaxerxes, when practiced upon by the wicked Haman, was turned against the Jews, yet upon the whole there was more favor shown toward them by that monarch and by the other Persian kings, than their descendants experienced from nominally Christian rulers, and than they obtain in some Christian countries at the present day. It is a humbling fact, that the heathen were more friendly to the Jews, and more tolerant of their religion than the followers of Him who according to the flesh was himself of the seed of Abraham. It is true that the Jews are a distinct race. It is true that many of them who come in contact with Christians are mean and who will do anything for worldly gain. But what has reduced them to this condition? Chiefly the oppression and cruelty with which they have been visited, and the suspicion with which they are regarded. We believe that there are among them noble specimens both of intelligence and virtue, and this will be more and more manifested as they are justly and kindly treated. At all events, it is made certain by the word of God that those who attempt to trample on them will not escape unpunished. There are promises exceeding great in store for God's ancient people. Let us pray more fervently than we have done that the veil may be taken from their hearts.

3. In the third place, in the case of Esther and Mordecai, we have a notable example of the power of divine grace to preserve the mind humble and well balanced in the midst of strong temptation to pride and self-will. In no condition are men in greater danger of forgetting themselves and allowing the corrupt tendencies of their nature to obtain the ascendency, than when they have been lifted up suddenly

from obscurity to the possession of wealth and influence. They would fain have their previous history buried. They disclaim the humble friends to whom they owed many kindnesses in former days; and their arrogance and self-consequence are often great in proportion to the meanness of their origin. It is most pleasing then to see a spirit so different exhibited by the two leading personages in the history which we have reviewed. Esther retained all her old affection and respect for Mordecai after she was advanced to the throne; and when he became the chief adviser of the king, and the first subject in the kingdom, he took as deep an interest in the affairs of his brethren the Jews, as he had done when he had to associate with them as his companions and friends. It is instructive to mark this: and it would be well if those among us who have been raised to power and honor would remember that nothing imparts to these gifts greater dignity and gracefulness than a meek and humble spirit.

4. In the fourth place, from the history of Mordecai and Esther, we learn that the special advantages which providence confers on man are most profitably and attractively employed, when they are made conducive to the promotion of the well-being of others, and especially of God's church and people. Esther might have sat in her palace surrounded by her menials, and her luxuries, and forgetting all that was passing in the world without in the midst of her selfish enjoyments. Mordecai might have prided himself upon his dignities and lived to himself without wasting a thought upon the affairs of his people. But would the life of either have been so pleasant, or their death so hopeful, or their memory so embalmed by a grateful posterity! My friends, let us imitate them so far as we have opportunity. Our sphere of influence is limited. Theirs was very wide. They could benefit many thousands; we may scarcely be able to do good to one. But let us not be idle. If we have been led by the grace of God to lay hold of Christ for ourselves, and enabled to commend Him

Lecture 15: Chapter 9:20-32 and 10:1-3

effectually even but to one perishing sinner, verily it may be said of us that we have not lived in vain.

Now, my friends, we have completed our brief examination of the Book of Esther, and in concluding the present discourse there are one or two reflections which we feel it not unsuitable to offer. This is the last of the historical Books of the Old Testament: so that now we have, in the good providence of God, been permitted to survey the whole course of the sacred history from the commencement of the Book of Genesis. Many years have passed, and many changes have we all experienced, since this series of discourses was begun; for the first one was delivered eighteen years ago. Many of those here today were then in infancy and early youth. They have now entered upon busy life and are engaged in contending with its cares and difficulties. Indeed, when I look around me, and mark the changes caused by the removal of so many on the one hand, and the advancement toward maturity of so many upon the other, I feel almost as if I were surrounded by another race. But still I rejoice in the privilege of being able to proclaim among you the word of life.

In the first of this series of lectures, it was stated that among other reasons for undertaking it, there were two more especially by which we were influenced, first to lead our hearers to take a deeper interest in the Old Testament scriptures than many seemed disposed to: and secondly, that we might show the unity of purpose which pervades the whole of God's word, and the doctrinal harmony of the Bible throughout. And now that we have been permitted to traverse this wide field, although we are conscious that the task has been executed most imperfectly, we are not without hope that our chief design has, in some small degree at least, been answered. Were the work to be begun anew, there are many illustrations of the truth which enlarged experience would suggest, many and varied applications of it which we think we might now make, and broader views of many parts which might easily be given. But our scheme of doctrine we would not change.

What we have aimed at has been to draw sinners to Jesus Christ the Savior, and to exhibit His word as a lamp to the feet and a light to the path of His believing people. Interesting, varied, and instructive have been the scenes through which we have had to pass in following the course opened up to us in the Book of God. We first looked into the Garden of Eden, when man, a holy being, was its inhabitant; and we saw him driven thence for his rebellion against his Maker. We watched the history of the race until their wickedness waxed so great and heaven-daring that earth could not bear the burden, and the waters of the deluge were let loose to sweep the transgressors away. Then in the new world we marked how the spirit of apostasy was again developed, and idolatry prevailed, until the call from heaven came to Abraham. We accompanied that patriarch as he sojourned in the land which had been promised to him for an inheritance. We saw his descendants reduced to slavery in Egypt, and delivered by God's outstretched arm. We went with them as they journeyed under the guidance of Moses, and endeavored to descry, in the peculiar institutions of the worship which he was commissioned to establish among them, the shadows of better things to come. We saw them cross the Jordan with Joshua as their leader and take possession of the promised land. We surveyed the troublous times of the Judges, when every man did that which was right in his own eyes; and then we saw the whole nation united under the government of a king. The eventful history of David, and the lights and shadows of Solomon's reign have been before us. We have seen the kingdom torn asunder and have looked at the procedure of the respective sovereigns of Israel and Judah. We have more especially had our attention drawn to the vicissitudes of the kingdom of Judah until Jerusalem was laid waste for her sin, and her children dragged into captivity. We have had to contemplate God's mercy and faithfulness in restoring them from their captivity, a faint foreshadowing of the glory which yet awaits their posterity. And lastly, in this Book of Esther, we have had abundant opportunity to mark how

Lecture 15: Chapter 9:20-32 and 10:1-3

the eye of God is on the seed of Abraham for good amid all their perverseness.

And now I would say, in finishing the review which has been taken of the whole of this wondrous history, that what perhaps most powerfully impresses the mind of a thoughtful reader of it, from its commencement to its close is, the blending together of justice and mercy in God's dispensations, and His displeasure against sin combined with gracious offers of pardon to the sinner. In Paradise, when man transgressed, God spoke in wrath, but yet He gave a promise of deliverance. On Sinai His thunderings and lightnings made the people quake, but even from Sinai He taught Moses how sacrifice was to be offered for the guilty. And when we look to Calvary, we still behold at once the goodness and severity of God; severity in exacting to the full from the Holy Sufferer the penalty due to His people's sin, and goodness and mercy in setting Him forth as the propitiation for sin through faith in His blood.

This mercy would we once more press on your acceptance; oh, refuse it not. To refuse is to put God away from you, and to dishonor His faithful word. This were a terrible sin. Let it not be laid to your charge. "Seek the Lord while He may be found; call upon Him while He is near." Be not driven away by the thought that your sin is very aggravated, for "Christ came not to call the righteous but sinners to repentance," and "He is able to save unto the uttermost." Now, to conclude: many changes, as we have said, have passed over us since this course of lectures on the Old Testament history was begun; sad changes, alas, to many. But there is something permanent. "The voice said, Cry, and he said, What shall I cry? All flesh is grass, and all the glory of man as the flower of grass. The grass withereth and the flower thereof falleth away; but the word of the Lord endureth forever. And this is the word which, by the gospel, is preached unto you." Amen.

Appendix: Historical Context

Medo Persia, the second world empire seen in the prophet Daniel's dream, came into power in the year 539 B.C. It was at that time that Cyrus the Great (who was mentioned no less than 23 times in the Bible) conquered the Babylonian empire.

The Persians didn't start out as an empire. Rather, they were a collection of semi-nomadic tribes raising cattle, sheep, and goats on the Iranian plateau. Cyrus, the leader of one Persian tribe, began expanding his power by defeating the nearby kingdoms of Media, Lydia, and Babylon. Joining the conquered kingdoms under one rule, he founded the first Persian Empire.

Cyrus was known as the "Great" for good reason: he was an excellent general whose strategies and leadership style have been studied and emulated by others in the centuries since his reign. Under Cyrus the Great, Persia soon became a "superpower" of sorts by several of the seats of ancient civilization (including Mesopotamia and the Nile Valley) into an empire that stretched from Europe's Balkan Peninsula (which now includes parts of Bulgaria, Romania, and the Ukraine) in the West to India's Indus Valley in the East. Also known as the "Iron Age" dynasty or the Achaemenid Empire, Persia was a global center of art, religion, culture, science, religion, and technology for more than two centuries, before it fell to the invading Greek armies of Alexander the Great.

The Persians built many new roads. One of the most famous, the Persian Royal Road, ran for more than 1500 miles, from Susa (the ancient capital of Persia) to the Aegean Sea. Royal messengers, through the use of relays, who (according to Herodotus) were stopped by "neither snow, nor rain, nor heat, nor gloom of night," were able to traverse entire road in nine days by using a relay system. Without the relay system, it normally took three months to travel the road. One achievement made possible by the Persian's excellent system of roads was the world's first

Appendix: Historical Context

postal service, which was set-up during the days of Cyrus and which later became a model for the Greeks and Romans to follow. The Persians were also the first civilization to develop regular routes of communication between the continents of Africa, Asia and Europe.

The ancient Persians left behind a rich heritage of art which included architecture, calligraphy, metalworking, painting, pottery, rock art, sculpture, and weaving. As the Persian Empire expanded to encompass other artistic centers of early civilization, the artistic influences of each of those centers found their way into Persian art styles. Some of the most dynamic Persian art featured large, carved rock murals depicting equestrian scenes and battle victories cut into cliffs.

Ancient Persians were also known for their metalwork. The Persian bronze industry, which was greatly influenced by Mesopotamian metalworkers, fashioned many precious objects such as personal jewelry, ceremonial vessels, and objects needed for chariots and horses. Goldsmiths and silversmiths excelled at such techniques as embossing, chasing, casting and inlaying with gemstones. Stem cups, ewers, oval dishes, platters, and bowls are the main forms; animal shapes, hunting and drinking scenes are represented in high relief. In the 1870s, smugglers discovered gold and silver artifacts among ruins near present-day Tajikistan. Many of these precious items were taken to Britain, where they are now housed at the British Museum.

The art of Persian carpet weaving dates back to the nomadic tribes. Persian carpets and rugs were initially woven as articles of necessity to cover the floors of nomadic tribesmen, giving them protection from the cold and damp. Later the ancient Greeks came to price the artistry of these hand-woven rugs, which were for their bright colors and elaborate design.

Although many people would think that Islam would be the historic religion of Persia, the early Persian Empire was shaped by a different religion. Known as Zoroastrianism, that religion, which is still practiced in some parts of Iran and India today, was named for the Persian prophet

Zoroaster. Monotheism, or worshipping only one god, was one of the primary teachings of Zoroaster.

Although the early Persian kings, including Cyrus the Great, were devout Zoroastrians, they didn't impose their religion on conquered people or lands. Cyrus the Great, who is mentioned 23 times in the Bible, was praised in the Hebrew scriptures for freeing the Jewish people from captivity and allowing them to return home to Jerusalem.

Successors of Cyrus the Great, continued his hands-off approach to social and religious norms, which made for a peaceful existence as the various and diverse citizens of Persia were allowed to practice their own ways of life.

The Persian Empire had a tremendous influence not only on the heritage and cultural identity of Asia, Europe, and the Middle East—but on the development and structure of future empires. The best features of the Persian empire were adopted by the Greeks, and later the Romans, in their own quest for dominion.

Considered by historians to be the first "empire in the modern sense," Persia was the forerunner for future imperial realms such as that of Germany or of Napoleon. Although Persia consisted of a number of states, each state retained its own individuality, manners, and laws. In the words of historian Arthur Upham Pope, "the Western world has a vast unpaid debt to the Persian civilization."

Other historians referred to the Persians as sort of a watershed civilization, one which created beauty for thousands of years by pouring its own unique brand of art and religion into the world. At the height of its power, the Persian empire, which was nearly as extensive as the land mass of the United States of America, developed an orderly government, a corridor to facilitate swift communications, a level of administrative competence, and a secure movement of men and goods on imperial roads which was equaled only by Rome at the zenith of its power.

After the costly and failed invasion of Greece by Xerxes 1 in 480 B.C., the Persian Empire began to decline. The costly defense of Persia's

Appendix: Historical Context

lands had taken its toll, depleting the empire's funds. The Persian dynasty finally fell to the invading armies of Alexander the Great in 330 B.C. Although later rulers tried to restore Persia to its heyday, it never again regained the enormous size it had achieved under Cyrus the Great.

www.ingramcontent.com/pod-product-compliance
Lightning Source LLC
Chambersburg PA
CBHW070053080526
44586CB00013B/1036